DIGITAL CREATIVITY: A READER

Innovations in art and design

Series Editor:
Colin Beardon

Digital creativity: a reader

Edited by

Colin Beardon
University of Plymouth, United Kingdom

and

Lone Malmborg
Malmö University, Sweden

Routledge
Taylor & Francis Group

LONDON AND NEW YORK

Library of Congress Cataloging-in-Publication Data

Applied for

First Published by Routledge

2 Park Square, Milton Park, Abingdon, Oxon, OX14 4RN
270 Madison Ave, New York NY 10016

Transferred to Digital Printing 2009

Cover design: Studio Jan De Boer, Amsterdam

Published by: Routledge Publishers
www.Routledge.nl

ISBN10: 90-265-1939-7 (hbk)
ISBN10: 0-415-57968-6 (pbk)

ISBN13: 978-90-265-1939-0 (hbk)
ISBN13: 978-0-415-57968-1 (pbk)
ISSN 1570-7393

Contents

Contents

On digital creativity

Colin Beardon and Lone Malmborg

University of Plymouth, UK and Malmö University, Sweden

1. Origins

The phrase 'digital creativity' is the title of the journal from which the articles in this book have been drawn It was first used as the name of the inaugural Computers in Art and Design Education (CADE) conference, held in Brighton, UK in April 1995. Over the past seven years it has served to focus the work of both CADE and the journal and this book is both a retrospective look at the highlights of the work produced, and an emerging holistic picture that gives insight and meaning into what was, at first, a strange combination of words.

The term was first chosen because, as native English speakers will be aware, one of its terms is ambiguous. The Concise Oxford Dictionary lists two modern uses of the word 'digit':

1. *finger or toe.*
2. *any numeral from 0 to 9, especially when forming part of a number.*

Of course, it is the second of these senses that we immediately think of when we come across the word 'digital' and it is this sense that is commonly used today to refer to anything to do with computers. It is ironic that the digits inside today's machines are the binary 0 and 1, and not the decimal 0...9, but it does not matter because the word 'digital' has come to stand for something broader than number representation systems. It really stands for the 'discrete' nature of representation and processing that occurs within contemporary computers; the idea that every bit is 'on' or 'off' and there is no other possibility (of course there is — failure — but contemporary thinking abhors disorder). The powerful idea that human knowledge and

experience can all be represented within such a strict logic has led to many seeming achievements, but it has also caused some concern particularly among those who are used to dealing with complexity and finely-graded sensitivities. In previous decades, when computers were less powerful and their discrete nature more manifest, there were many people who accepted their efficacy in matters of reasoning but doubted that when it came to matters of the senses.

By 1995, affordable desktop computers were just beginning to handle images, sounds and three-dimensional models. They were crude by today's standards — small screens, black and white images or maybe a 256-colour palette, wireframe models, and so on — but these limitations could already be seen as a temporary phase. The Apple Macintosh, in particular, provided an acceptable operating system and applications were being developed (such as Adobe Photoshop, Quark Xpress and MacroMind Director) that spoke the same language as those in the creative arts. Within academic institutions, in particular, the first questions were being raised about the integration of this technology into traditional practices in the creative arts.

Hence, the second sense of the word 'digital'—referring to our fingers, in particular—was also in our mind when the phrase was first adopted. The association of computers with our human fingers (or, more precisely, with our hands) was thus a deliberate invitation to think of computers in a new way — as something other than machines that abstractly process discrete, symbolic numbers or alphabetic characters. It was an invitation first to think of computers as processors of images, sounds, models, etc., in short the same sorts of objects that people in the creative arts were already familiar with. But it was also an invitation to think more deeply about the relationship of computerised ways of working to more traditional workshop or studio practice.

The creative arts incorporate a range of practice-based subjects that include: fine art, sculpture, printmaking, photography, film and video making, animation, graphic design, illustration, textile and fashion design, furniture design, product design, architecture, landscape design, theatre and performing arts, and many more. These practices are largely studio and workshop based: they involve people using their hands to wield brushes and hammers, to sew garments, to focus cameras, to stretch canvas, and do many other things. While computers were beginning to deal conceptually with the 'raw materials' of these subjects by 1995, the sheer physicality of their day-to-day work seemed to pose a barrier to the full integration of computer technologies.

From the field of computer science there were already critiques of the way that 'design' was conceived and practiced within that discipline and suggestions that a broader concept, that relates it to other forms of design, might be beneficial (Norman 1990). Meanwhile, in the humanities, the advent of new technologies such as hypertext were giving rise to major theoretical debates about the nature of 'texts' (Landow 1992). More practical issues of the relationship of formal digital approaches to the daily experiences of practitioners, and particularly the tacit knowledge that their everyday work and experience embodies, had been the subject of many studies (Cooley 1980, Ehn 1988, Rosenbrock 1989). This concern with the relationship of the formal aspects of computing systems to the everyday life and experience of working people was being furthered by studies of how people behave and make decisions within real work situations

(Suchman), and more recently there have begun to emerge some detailed studies on the changes which computing technology have had upon the creative arts (Laurel 1991, McCullough 1996, Manovich 2001).

Within these developments, CADE has continued its work, organising major 'Digital Creativity' conferences in the UK in 1997 (Derby), 1999 (Teesside) and 2001 (Glasgow) as well as annual events for postgraduate research students. In 1997 the quarterly journal *Digital Creativity* was formed (from an existing journal called *Intelligent Tutoring Media*) and was published first by Intellect Ltd and then, from 1998, by Swets & Zeitlinger publishers.

Thus, within the term 'digital creativity' there was in 1995 a vision—a vision of a transition to a new unified discipline. The starting point was a number of diverse disciplines with interests in, and making contributions to, the field. These included all the creative arts plus computer science (particularly human-computer interaction), participatory design, education and pedagogy, cultural studies and, more generally, contemporary ideas such as may be found in cognitive science, artificial intelligence and elsewhere. The vision was a new discipline which united not only these different fields of knowledge, but also related theory and practice—and, specifically, related formal studies about the nature of computing with the everyday experience of people working in the creative arts.

2. Developments

The twenty-seven articles collected and presented in this book form a statement, from the perspective of 2002, of how far we have come and where we are now with the emerging field of digital creativity. In the following pages we will describe our selection of papers for this book, and introduce them briefly from our current position. Concepts, ideas and projects that were innovative and state-of-the-art at the time the paper was published might seem

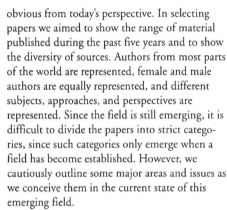

obvious from today's perspective. In selecting papers we aimed to show the range of material published during the past five years and to show the diversity of sources. Authors from most parts of the world are represented, female and male authors are equally represented, and different subjects, approaches, and perspectives are represented. Since the field is still emerging, it is difficult to divide the papers into strict categories, since such categories only emerge when a field has become established. However, we cautiously outline some major areas and issues as we conceive them in the current state of this emerging field.

Many papers address the philosophical issues of human existence and human thinking when working with virtual representations of our bodies and of environments and artefacts. Several papers describe concrete art projects based on virtual reality, while others consider how virtual reality affects our sense of consciousness, and our conception of self.

Theatre and performance based on digital media has evolved as another prominent field of digital creativity. Performance professionals, and researchers coming from a digital media perspective, have been very active in creating new ways of staging performances, in interactive storytelling, in game design, and in using drama as a design approach within other digital applications.

A third group of papers addresses the fact that art and design work is now often based on digital tools. What implications does this have on the way professionals work, on the way we educate students and build curricula, and on the artwork itself?

Pierre Lévy's *Welcome to virtuality* is the opening paper. Since published in the 1997 volume of *Digital Creativity* it become a classic — mandatory reading for anyone who aims at a philosophical understanding of the concept of 'virtuality'. Lévy does not — as in common usage — define 'virtuality' as the opposite of 'reality', but rather of 'actuality'. For him, the 'virtual' contains a rich stored-up potential for realisation.

Pelle Ehn's *Manifesto for a Digital Bauhaus* sets the stage for new school of art and communication in Malmö, Sweden. Ehn discusses the aesthetics of the IT-society, and grounds the idea of a Digital Bauhaus on influences from the early twentieth century German Bauhaus tradition, the Scandinavian tradition for democratic and participatory design ideals, and on the idea of a 'third culture' as the meeting between art and science.

Monika Büscher and her colleagues develop the concept and prototype of the *wunderkammer* in their paper, *The architect's wunderkammer: aesthetic pleasure and engagement in electronic spaces*. Their approach to designing the *wunderkammer* space is grounded in the need for imprecise, fluent forms of categorising inspirational objects as opposed to a view of digital tools as aiming to increase precision and avoid ambiguity. Their work is based on observations of architectural practice in the field.

In *The student's construction of artistic truth in digital images*, Dena Elisabeth Eber raises the important question of what happens to artistic truths when there is no reference to reality, as is often the case with digital images. She suggests that artists have to revisit what a digital image represents. She grounds her arguments in a study of advanced digital art students and how they resolved this conflict by defining their own artistic truths.

In *What is consciousness for?*, Carol Gigliotti's sets up a dialogue between arguments of Daniel Dennett and John Searle in an interesting attempt to understand the meaning of consciousness with relevance to objects created using interactive technologies. In a philosophical discussion about the difference and tension between human consciousness and robotic consciousness, she asks what this means in our daily life and how we should design and understand technological developments.

The desert of passions and the technological soul also addresses our conception of consciousness and memory when experiencing and interacting in virtual worlds. Diana Domingues, a Brazilian artist, demonstrates in her paper (and through her own art work) how interactive art is humanising technologies – it creates a post-biological feeling, which is a symbiosis of artificial and natural life.

In Niranjan Rajah's paper, *Prosthetics for the mind: augmenting the self with microelectronics,* particular focus is put on multi-user environments, telematic communication, immersive environments, and bioelectrical interfaces in relation to human consciousness.

Ryszard W. Kluszczynski discusses artificial creatures, artificial life and intelligence, and their implications for artistic communication. In *Art of virtual bodies,* he examines a number of virtual performance art works, and on the basis of this he claims that body and identity transformations, as well as new concepts of life and intelligence, indicate that we are living through a period of extremely marked and radical change in the whole world we live in.

Whereas Gigliotti, Domingues and Rajah are all concerned about consciousness in relation to digital technology, Johanna Drucker develops another important theme in the area of digital creativity: how digital technology affects our body. In her paper, *The next body and beyond: meta-organisms, psycho-prostheses and aesthetics of hybridity,* she claims that we should consider consciousness, subjectivity, and the body as an interwoven whole as in the Freudian/Lacanian psychoanalytic tradition.

Teresa Wennberg also addresses the question of how we represent bodily senses when acting in virtual environments. In her paper, *Virtual life: self and identity redefined in the new media age,* she claims that we experience conflicts of identity when we are confronted with virtual reality as a total immersion. She suggests that this may lead us to a more ambivalent concept of the self.

Char Davies' paper, *OSMOSE: notes on being in immersive virtual space,* is a major contribution to the area of immersive virtual environment. Also as an artist she discusses her original artistic intentions behind OSMOSE – an immersive virtual environment using an embodying user interface of breath and balance, which has been influenced by her own experience as a diver of deep oceanic space. In OSMOSE, an experiential context is constructed in which culturally learned perceptual/conceptual boundaries are osmotically dissolved, causing conventional assumptions about interior, exterior, mind, body and nature to be questioned by the immersed participant.

Mike Phillips pushes the limitations of contemporary interface design in his paper, *The Sadeian interface: computers and catharsis.* He suggests that interface designers should look to an older heritage of interactive art and see how artists based interaction with their work on a continual negotiation with the real world. He claims that the more simple and 'low resolution' the technology the more immersive, acute and intimate the experience.

In *Art practice augmented by digital agents,* Ernest Edmonds discusses how computers can augment creative processes by playing the role of a catalyst, or a stimulant, to our own creative thinking. Edmonds explores a particular application of intelligent user interfaces in a dialogue with a group of artists as well as in his own work. Edmonds suggests that augmenting the artist by agents does not make life any easier for the artist, but it might make it more interesting.

Emergent constructions: re-embodied intelligence within recombinant poetic networks by Bill Seaman also addresses the question of how computers can augment poetic responses to viewer interactivity via the encoding, mapping, and modelling of operative poetic elements. Seaman proposes that computer-mediated networks present an artistic medium that heightens the potential for an intermingling of the knowledge of the user with the 're-embodied intelligence' of an author.

Artistic communication for A-life and robotics by Naoko Tosa and Ryohei Nakatsu is a further contribution to the question of how computers can be used in interactive generation and experience of poetry. MUSE is a computer-generated poet, conveying short poetic words and emotions in 'Renga' format, which is a combination of ancient Japanese poetic traditions such as 'Waka' and 'Haiku'.

With the paper, *Technological latency: from autoplastic to alloplastic,* from the collective author dECOi Architects we move into a quite different area of digital creativity. Namely, architecture and how digital technologies can bring about a paradigm shift in architecture that reflects the ongoing cultural adaptation of society to an electronic environment. The authors introduce the concepts of trauma and disorientation in explaining their idea of the shift from an autoplastic to an alloplastic mode of operation.

Following the architecture track is Ted Krueger's paper on *Autonomous architecture,* which characterises architecture as the evolution of an independent entity. He proposes that the availability of a wide range of sensing technologies suggests that the kind of awareness developed by architectural entities may be foreign to human experience. The paper addresses the question of what could be the consciousness of an architectural artifact modelled on biological phenomena?

The Polish architect Pawel Szychalski contributes to the same field of architecture through his paper, *Vibrating tectonics: gestural trajectories, energy mappings and self-conditioning design strategies*, which discusses transposition from abstract painting to architecture as the movement from two-dimensional entity to a spatial structure. Szychalski suggests that architects examine the possibilities of abstract expression in the conceptualisation of architectural ideas and strategies.

The field of computer games combines representations of the environment and human action. *Quake® goes the environment: game aesthetics and archaeologies* is a prominent contribution to our understanding of what might determine game aesthetics. Aki Järvinen discusses computer and video games in the context of the cultural history of the moving image. He situates digital games aesthetics at the crossroads of two aesthetic disciplines: aesthetics of the moving image, and aesthetics of the environment.

In *Remediating theatre in a digital proscenium,* Steve Dixon examines and evaluates the transposition of live theatre performance into a digital multimedia environment utilising QuickTime (or equivalent) movie software for use on standard computers. By drawing parallels to Brecht's alienation theory he claims that the flickering, low-resolution picture typical of video playback on CD-ROMs could be a positive virtue for the remediation of theatrical footage.

The young, award-winning performance artist Mika Tuomola focuses on avatar acting in multi-user virtual worlds. His paper, *Drama in the digital domain: Commedia dell'Arte, characterisation, collaboration and computers,* draws parallels to the five-hundred-year-old Italian Commedia dell'Arte tradition, and suggests that this may be used as a design metaphor.

Sita Popat is a choreographer and addresses issues of dance performance in her paper, *Interactive dance-making: online creative collaborations*. It examines the potential for computer technology to enhance the interactive art-making process, enabling participation in choreography via Internet communications. Popat demonstrate her idea of interactive dance composition projects as learning environments through two of her own projects: the *Hands-On Dance Project* and the *TRIAD Project*.

Jools Gilson-Ellis' works explore the connections between voice, writing and performance in relation to new technologies. In *Loa and behold: voice ghosts in the new technoculture,* she traces contemporary thought on femininity, technology and voice. Gilson-Ellis uses her own choreographic/poetic practice as examples in these discussions. She suggests that the voice in relation to writing and new technologies has a radical potential to open up alternative kinds of spaces in digital art practice.

In the final paper, *Playing on a holo-stage: towards the interaction between real and virtual performers,* Kia Ng and colleagues present a number of ongoing projects that will be valuable to the development of technologies for digital theatre and performance. Based on current research on motion tracking, statistical behaviour modelling and simulation, some possible applications, both for visual augmentation and audio generation, are discussed.

We believe that this selection of thought-provoking texts will provide a wider perspective for art and design students and interaction design students and will stimulate further interesting discussions. We also hope to inspire all readers to continue the discussion outside the classroom and studio and to contribute over the next five years to the ongoing development of digital creativity.

Colin Beardon and Lone Malmborg,
Exeter and Malmö, April 2002.

References

Cooley, M. (1980) *Architect or bee?* Hand and Brain, Slough.

Ehn, P. (1988) *Work-oriented design of computer artifacts.* Arbetslivcentrum, Stockholm.

Landow, G. (1992) *Hypertext: the convergence of contemporary critical theory and technology.* The John Hopkins University Press, Baltimore.

Laurel, B. (1991) *Computers as theatre.* Addison-Wesley, Reading, Mass.

McCullough, M. (1996) *Abstracting craft: the practiced digital hand.* MIT Press, Camb, Mass.

Manovich, L. (2001) The language of new media. MIT Press, Camb, Mass.

Norman, D. (1990) Why interfaces don't work. In B. Laurel (ed.) *The art of human-computer interface design.* Addison-Wesley, Reading, Mass. pp. 209-219.

Rosenbrock, H. (ed.) (1989) *Designing human-centred technology.* Springer-Verlag, London.

Suchman, L. (1987) *Plans and situated action.* Cambridge University Press, Cambridge.

Welcome to virtuality

Pierre Lévy

University of Ottawa, Canada

Abstract

The paper contains a philosophical discussion of the concept of 'virtuality'. It primarily argues that 'virtuality' is not the opposite of 'reality' but rather of 'actuality'. Using the concept of 'virtualisation' it describes a number of problem solving scenarios dividing them into specific actualisations on the one hand, and generalised solutions to a general class of problem on the other. This latter group is considered to be a 'virtual problem' with 'virtualisation' providing the general solution. Within this framework, technology is seen as an agent for the materialisation of a solution to such a virtual problem. It is argued that virtuality is the very dynamic of our real world and is what makes the world common and shared. Arguing for a new aesthetics, rather than concern for the mere techniques of making art with computer, the role of art is described in terms of the play of the virtual against the possible.

Far from being a recent trend linked only to digital technology, virtualisation begins with the birth of human race (languages, techniques, religions...) and accelerates nowadays in different fields: virtualisation of bodies, of the economy, of society... Virtuality is the dynamic part of human reality. Therefore, the contemporary choices are not between reality and virtuality but among various kinds of virtualisation processes. Mapping virtualisation had never been so urgent.

Keywords: actuality, philosophy, virtual problems, virtuality

1. Definitions

Before coming to very contemporary remarks, I would like to draw an important philosophical distinction between two dialectic couples: the possible/ real and the virtual/actual. Following a suggestion of Gilles Deleuze, I would say that the possible is a ghost reality: already completely defined, it only lacks existence. The realisation is not a creative process, it is just a selection among determined entities. On the other hand, I would define:

- 'virtuality' as a complex of trends, tendencies, constraints, goals and forces;
- 'actualisation' as a creative problem solving process; and
- 'actuality' as an unforeseen answer to the virtual problem.

Virtuality is not the opposite of reality. Even if we cannot see it out there, the virtual parts of living organisms, human beings or complex situations are probably the most important parts of their identities. A seed is oriented by a virtual tree, but we cannot describe exactly the shape of the future tree. We even cannot be sure that there will actually be a tree. The (virtual) tree is the problem of the seed, and it is at the same time the essence of its identity.

Now, what is virtualisation? It is the creative move that comes from an actual entity, here and now, to a new general problem. The virtualisation implies a shift in the centre of gravity of the entity. The main weight of the being is put on the general problem instead of bearing on some particular solution.

Let us summarise some essential features of these concepts:

Natures
- Potential and virtual are both latent.
- Real and actual are both patent.
- Potential and real are close to substances.
- Virtual and actual are close to events.
- Potential refers to a predetermined set of possibilities.
- Virtual refers to problems, knots of trends, constraints, forces and goals (upstream events).
- Real refers to existing things.
- Actual refers to a particular invented solution, here and now, to a problem (an event).

Moves
- Realisation and potentialisation are close to selection.
- Virtualisation and realisation are close to creation.
- Realisation is an election/elimination, a 'fall of potential'.
- Potentialisation is a supply of resources.
- Actualisation is a creative problem solving process.
- Virtualisation is a shift from a 'particular solution' identity to a 'general problem' identity.

Virtualisation is often associated with an exit from particular space and time coordinates (or deterritorialisation). Let us take the example of the virtualisation of an organisation. The classic organisation is typically defined by some rooms, shops or offices inside a building and special places where people work. It is also defined by agendas and work hours. Virtualising the organisation consists in shifting from the space and time coordinates to the space and time coordination. Particular working moments and places are just transitory solutions of a continuous coordination process. The virtualised organisation identity is not any more linked to actual coordinates but to the special quality of its coordination process.

The emergence of the human race is strongly linked to three virtualisation processes: the developments of languages, of technology and of complex institutions that organise relations between human beings.

2. The birth of languages, or the virtualisation of real time

Languages perform the virtualisation of 'real time' (bound to here and now), open the past, the future and, in general, time as a kingdom in itself with its own consistency. Without languages there would be no possibility to ask questions and to tell tales. The invention of language is one of the greatest virtualisation moves. Here and now, or in real time, becomes a special case of a more general problem in which, from now on, we live: the whole stream of time. Of course, memory and learning already exist in higher animals, even without complex and sophisticated languages. But in an animal's life, memory is mainly an actual behaviour modification related to past events. On the other hand, thanks to language, we have 'random access' to the past. Humans beings can partially detach themselves from present experience and remember, evoke, imagine, play or simulate other places, others times and other worlds. This is not only due to normal spoken language but also to plastic, visual, musical and 'artistic' languages.

Here, we can see another character of virtualisation: in detaching itself from here and now it breeds new spaces and times, new speeds. Linked to the emergence of language, there appears a new speed of learning, a new speed of thinking and a swiftness of cultural evolution that is far quicker than biological evolution. One frequent attribute of virtualisation can be developed from the example of language: the shift from private to public and the mix between inside and outside. Indeed, when you put a feeling, an emotion, a knowledge into words or drawings, it allows you to share much more easily this feeling or this knowledge. What was internal and private become external and public. But it is also true the other way round: when we listen to music, watch a picture or read a poem, we can internalise and personalise a public item. Human languages are tools for the virtualisation of real time, actual things, and ongoing situations. Since the emergence of those languages, complex feelings, knowledge and concepts are externalised, materialised, exchanged and can travel from place to place, time to time and mind to mind.

3. Technology as an agent of virtualisation

Virtualisation is not necessarily a disappearance. On the contrary, it is often a materialisation process. This can easily be shown from the example of technology. The design of a new tool is a virtualisation of many actions. When someone designs a tool, instead of focusing on the action s/he focusses on something much more general, on a type of problem. The tool is not an answer to such or such particular situation but the materialisation of a general function. Of course, one particular tool is an actual thing, but it gives access to an indefinite set of virtual uses. There are few virtualisations of action, but many actualisations of the tools. The hammer was probably invented three or four times during the whole of history. Let us say three or four virtualisations. But how many knocks with a hammer? Billions and billions of actualisations. The tool, the long lasting design of the tool, is a memory of the original virtualisation move. It crystallises the virtual.

One says, sometimes, that tools are some sort of continuation or extension of the body. I do not agree with this theory, because you can give flints to your neighbours, you can produce thousands of flints, but you cannot borrow your

The design of a new tool is a virtualisation of many actions

neighbour's nails or multiply them. My thesis is that a tool is not an extension but a virtualisation of the body. First you identify some functions of the body. Second, you detach the functions from one's private flesh, blood and bones. Third, you combine and materialise the functions. The private become public, shared. The inside is expressed and preserved. But the outside must also be internalised: to use a tool you have to learn gestures, to modify your bodily identity.

Techniques not only virtualise actions and bodies but also things. Before having learnt to knock flints near some tinder, humankind knew fire as simply absent or present. Since the invention of techniques to light fires, fire can also be virtual. Virtually everywhere you can find a match.

4. The virtualisation of violence

Humankind emerges from three virtualisation processes. The first is linked to signs: the virtualisation of real time. The second is undertaken by techniques: virtualisation of actions, of the body and of the physical environment. The third process grows with complex social relationships: it is the virtualisation of violence.

Rituals, law, economic rules, politics, morality, religions are devices for the virtualisation of relations based on violence, impulses, immediate desires and instincts. An agreement or a contract, for example, makes the definition of a relation independent from a particular situation, independent from the emotional variation of the signatories. Inside a certain society, a ritual (let us say a wedding or an initiation ceremony) is independent of a person's identity. The status shift (now you are married, now you are an adult, etc.) is automatic and the same for everybody. You are not obliged to invent and negotiate something new in every new situation. Virtualisation of immediate relations and impulses stabilises rules of behaviour and identity, it fixes precise procedures to transform relations and identities. Coagulated virtual relations are something public and commonly shared inside a society. New procedures, new rules of behaviour are built upon previous ones, and the continuous process of virtualising relationships erects the whole complexity of human cultures: religion, ethics, law, politics, economy.

As for virtual emotions and virtual actions, it is possible to organise travel or the deterritorialisation of virtual relations. By example, you can sell a title deed, shares of a company or a contract of insurance. You can also elect a spokesperson, or teach a prayer, or buy a fetish.

5. Art: the virtualisation of virtualisation

Why is art so fascinating and so difficult to describe? Because art is the height of humanity. No animal species had never practised art. Indeed, art stands itself at the crossroads of the three main virtualisation streams: languages, techniques and ethics. It is fascinating because it is the most virtualising activity. It is hard to define because it is almost always at the frontier of simple language, or technique, or social function.

Art gives an external form to very subjective, impalpable feelings and emotions, making them independent of a particular moment and place. Art helps to share a way of feeling. Virtualisation in general is a war against fragility, pain, mortality; it is a quest for security and control. Art virtualises the virtualisation because it does not simply look for security or for escaping from here and now. Moreover, it plays with those attempts, it deals with knots of emotional problems, with attempts and failures for escaping death.

6. Contemporary virtualisation of body

The virtualisation of bodies, information, communications, knowledge, economy and society that we experience nowadays is a new step in the continuous self-making of the human race.

Now, I would like to explore some of these contemporary trends. In analysing the virtualisation of bodies, we will check and confirm that virtualisation is not a disappearing or dematerialising process. Remember that virtualisation is an identity shift from a particular solution or activity to a more general problem, function or goal. In this case, the virtualisation process detaches some action or effect from one organ or from flesh and blood machinery and identifies a general function. Then, this isolated function can have hundreds of different actualisations and can combine with other actualisations of other functions. So, the body comes out of the body, it acquires new speeds, it pours itself into its outside and its outside into itself, it multiplies itself. All this process is not at all a disembodiment but, on the contrary, a complex re-embodiment, an hetero-genesis of the body.

Let us take some functions and see how it works. The function of perception, for example, is to draw the world here. Telephone, television and telemanipulation systems virtualise the senses. Telecommunication systems organise the sharing of virtualised organs. When people are watching television, they are sharing the same common big eye. Thanks to photographs, cameras and video recorders you can perceive someone else's sensations at another moment in another place. The so called virtual reality system allows you to do the same with, in addition, a dynamic integration of different perceptual modalities.

The opposite function is the projection into the world, a projection of action and projection of image. Projection of action is of course strongly related to machines, networks and weapons. In this case, many people can share the same big, virtual and deterritorialised arms. What we call telepresence is generally related to the projection of the body image but, in fact, it is more. The telephone is already a telepresence device. It does not carry an image or a representation of the voice, it carries the voice itself. Virtual reality systems also carry more than just pictures since clones or visible agents, or virtual puppets can have effects on other virtual puppets and other visible agents.

What makes the body visible? Its surface: the hair, the skin, the sparkling of the eyes. Medical images make the internal body visible, without cutting the actual skin. X-rays, scanners, nuclear cameras, and so on perform the virtualisation of the body surface. Every new visualisation system adds a new skin, a new visible body. And from all these virtual skins you can reconstruct a 3D digital model of the body, and then a hard model. In the virtual kingdom, analysing and rebuilding the body does not imply pain and death any more. Of course, all these virtual skins and bodies have very important actual effects in medical diagnosis and surgery.

As for language, techniques and contracts, the virtualisation of the body allows detachment, travel and exchange. Transplants organise the circulation of organs between human bodies, between living and dead people, but also between species. Implants and prosthesis make permeable the frontier between the organic and the mineral realms (glasses, false teeth, silicon, pacemakers, aural implants, artificial kidneys...). Eyes, sperm, ovules, embryos and, of course, blood are now socialised and preserved in special banks. The blood is a deterritorialised fluid that flows from bodies to bodies through a huge international economic, technical and medical network. Flesh and blood become externalised, public and shared. We can internalise these commodities when we need them (and if we can afford to). Just as we have shared for a long time common languages, a virtual, joint or common body is emerging.

Every individual or personal body is the constituent part of a bigger hyperbody. The individual body itself is constantly modified by drugs and medicines, and the pharmaceutical industry finds every day new active molecules. Finally, thanks to biotechnologies we can envisage actual species (and even the human race) as particular and maybe contingent cases in a much wider and unexplored virtual biological continuum.

Reproduction, immunity from diseases, regulation of the emotions, all these typically private performances are becoming public, exchangeable, and externalised competencies. These functions are every day running through more external, complicated, economic and technological channels.

Now, this virtualisation is not a disembodiment or a disincarnation but, on the contrary, a reimbodiment or a reincarnation, a reinvention of the body. My personal body here and now is a temporary actualisation of a huge social and hybrid hyperbody. The contemporary body is like a flame. Sometimes isolated, small and almost still, sometimes running out of itself, launching some virtual arms far to the sky, into communication or medical networks, becoming public, sharing the blowing wind and the burning wood with other flames, mixing its light and heat with other's light and heat, then quickly returning in its quasi-private sphere, and finally dying.

7. Virtualisation of information and communication

The expression 'virtual reality' sounds like an oxymoron, and this is why it generally provokes fascination. But we know at this point that virtuality, indeed, does not mean imaginary. Strictly speaking, the virtual is not the opposite of the real but the opposite of the actual. In the technological vocabulary, however, virtuality generally refers to the software and digital part of the world.

An image, for example, will be called virtual if its origin is a digital description in a computer memory. Note that, to be perceived, the image has to shine on a screen, to be printed onto paper, to be exposed on a film, and that the binary code has therefore to be translated. If we wanted to maintain the parallel with the philosophical meaning, we should say that the image is virtual on the hard disk and actual on the screen. Virtualisation is digitisation and actualisation is display. The image is even more virtual when its digital description is not a stable deposit in the computer memory, but when it is calculated in real time by a program from a model and a flow of input data.

Video games, hyperdocuments, simulations and computer programs in general are virtual messages. Results, texts, aural, tactile or visual images can be computed according to an initial matrix (program, model), and a current interaction.

For the spectator, a lively cartoon seen on a theatre screen or on the television screen, is the same actual sequence of pictures whether they have been calculated by a computer or been drawn by hand. Maybe some special effects signal the digital origin of the computer-made cartoon, but they do not change the nature of the relation to the picture. Only the team who realised the cartoon was interacting with virtuality.

On the other hand, when playing with a video game, the player is directly confronted with the virtuality of the message. The same cassette contains (virtually!) an infinity of different games, an infinity of different picture sequences. The player will display (or actualise) only some of them. Interactivity is actualisation.

To stress again the difference between actual and virtual information, let us take the example of technical manuals that come with big industrial systems. These manuals are displaying texts, diagrams, captions, indexes, etc., on the surface of their pages. The totality of the information that they contain is already displayed. If the installation is complex enough (military aircraft, space shuttle, nuclear power plant, oil refinery, etc.), it is impossible to draw up the list of all possible breakdowns, because the manual would contain billions and billions of pages and be impossible to print and read. Thereafter, the manual will just give examples of the most frequent cases and will indicate some problem solving principles. In fact, only experienced technicians or engineers will be able to fix the problem.

On the other hand, an expert-system about the same big industrial system will hold explicitly only a few thousand short rules. In each particular situation, the user will feed the system with 'facts' describing the problem that is to be faced. From the rules and the 'facts', the software will compute an adapted reasoning and a precise reply (or a small range of replies) to the user's problem. Thanks to the expert system, even novices or beginners will be able to fix major breakdowns. Of course, the expert system is not as clever as living experts, but the point is that if all the possible arguments had been printed out (actualised) line by line in advance, we would have a document that is impossible to use as well as a destroyer of forests.

The expert system is more useful than a paper manual because of its virtual nature. The replies are not already displayed but actualised in real time in each particular situation. Every special and local situation can be taken into account. Beyond a certain threshold of complexity, this sharp or sheer reaction and adaptation is impossible if you do not make a detour by the virtual.

A virtual world emerges from the coupling of a living user in a dynamic situation and a digital model that can generate a huge quantity of different messages. Interacting with the digital model, users explore and actualise a virtual world. When interactions can enrich or modify the model, the virtual world becomes a vector of collective intelligence and creation.

Networks of computers constitute the fresh infrastructure of the new universe of virtual information. These networks are spreading, their computing power is growing, their memory and transmission capacity is increasing, so digital virtual worlds will probably develop in variety and expand in quantity.

Of course, we find in the virtualisation of information and communication by digital networks the same changes that we have already found in other domains. The more obvious change is perhaps deterritorialisation since, in cyberspace, every piece of information that is on the Net is virtually close to me and actually in my hands when I select or browse it, even if it is really (in physical space) on another continent. This obvious form of exit from the classical geographical space is augmented by a deterritorialisation of the messages themselves. They are no longer some kind of territory with an owner and some boundaries but, thanks to hyperlinks, to sampling, to the plasticity of digital information, they tend to join each other in a constantly dynamic, mixing, public and global flow. Hyperlinks between documents turn the inside out and the outside in. One of the main effects of the virtualisation of messages is that every act of reading has become a potential act of writing. This occurs in a far more effective way than when we use normal interpretation procedures of static structures. If we define a hypertext as a space of possible reading trips, then a text appears as a particular actualisation of a hypertext. The navigator participates in the writing or at least in the editing of the text, because, in reading, he determines its final organisation (the 'disposition' of the ancient rhetoric). The navigator can be made an author in a deeper sense than when choosing between different lines to read. He can create new links. Some systems can even record reading paths and reinforce or weaken links according to the way they are travelled by the navigating community. Finally, readers can not only modify links but also add or modify nodes (texts, images, etc.), connect hyperdocuments to others and thus participate in the global reorganisation of the digital information flow.

As I said earlier about language, technol-ogy and social institutions, collective intelligence begins with culture. But digitisation and virtualisation of information is a new stage in the making of collective intelligence. We can now share in real time not only static records but constantly evolving dynamic memories. We can share, trade and collectively refine simulations, which are externalised and exchangeable dynamic mental models. Expert systems allow a very easy and quick sharing and distribution of empirical knowledge. We can use computer supported cooperative work systems or computer supported cooperative learning networks. We can coordinate actions or competences among thousands of people without a centre, without being obliged to plan or design every step in advance. We can communicate interactively 'many to many' (and not only 'one to many' as in the traditional mass media or 'one to one' as in the traditional communication networks like postal services or telephone). In parallel with the growth of the distributed hyperbody, humankind experiences the fast growth and extension of a global hypercortex.

Indeed, these new forms of collective intelligence can be exploited in very positive ways in the fields of education, arts, organisation and politics. But no positive effect is guaranteed. Every hierarchical and static institution is threatened and will probably resist. The new tools can also be exploited for the increase of power of a few people, organisations or nations.

8. Economy

Contemporary economy is an economy of deterritorialisation or virtualisation. The main sector of activity in the world is tourism: business trips, holidays, conferences, restaurants, hotels. Humanity has never devoted so much resources to eat, sleep and live far from home. If you add to tourism the industries that manufacture vehicles (cars, lorries, trains, subways, boats, aircraft, etc.) and fuel for vehicles, you get probably more than half of the world economic activity. Electronic and digital communication are not a substitute for physical transportation. On the contrary, communication and transport are part of the same virtualisation wave. In addition to telecommunications and transport, you must count data-processing, media, education, training and many other sectors of the rising virtual economy. Among all these virtualising activities, we must devote a particular analysis to finance.

Today, finance constitutes between 5 and 7% of the GDP of industrialised countries. World financial flows are bigger than international trade and, inside the financial sector, the growth of derived products (options, exchanges, futures) is stronger than the growth of traditional products. More generally, the growing domination of the monetary economy and of financial ways of thinking is one of the most vivid manifestations of the virtualisation under way. International finance tends to constitute a sort of distributed collective intelligence in which money and information are gradually converging.

Financial operators make decisions essentially from the supposed arguments of other financial operators, as in a crowd in which every member would practice the psychology of crowds. The 'arguments' of financial reasoning are essentially quantitative economic indicators published by governments and statistics, as well as current prices and rates of the different currencies, actions and financial instruments. Now, these current prices and rates are themselves the 'conclusions' of the collective, distributed, parallel reasoning of the market. Indeed, the financial market takes into account 'external' data (wars, elections, etc.), but it works essentially in a recursive mode, from the output of its own operations.

May I risk a parallel with some aspects of the contemporary world of art? Often, contemporary art makes references to itself and to its own history rather than to something external: quotations, derision, making opposites, plays about the limits or the identity of art, etc. As in

finance, the main operations of contemporary art focus on the judgement of others, the work intervening as a vector, a pointer or a switch device in the recursive dynamics of collective judgement.

Tourism, transport, communications, training and finance are special virtualising sectors of the economy. But all economic sectors depend today, upstream, on very particular economic goods that are information and knowledge. These new major resources are governed by two laws that contradict classical economic concepts and reasoning. When you consume those goods you do not destroy them and when you give them to someone else you do not lose them. On the other hand, as you know very well, if you give a sack of wheat, a car or a work hour, you lose something. If you grind the wheat, drive the car, exploit some work, an irreversible process is performed: wear, expense, transformation, consumption.

The theory and practice of economics is mainly based on the postulate of the scarcity of goods. The scarcity itself is based on the destructive character of consumption as well as on the exclusive nature of transfer and acquisition. Information and knowledge are not ruled by these principles, so they are probably the origin of another form of wealth. We can envisage the emergence of an economy of abundance, whose concepts and practice would be completely different from the conventional economy. In fact, we already live under this new regime, but we continue to use the inadequate tools of the scarcity economy.

Why is the consumption of information non-destructive and its ownership non-exclusive? Because information is virtual. I have already stressed one of the main distinctive characters of virtuality: its detachment from every particular 'here and now'. That is why I can give away a virtual object without losing it: by essence it is deterritorialised. On the other hand, remember that the virtual can be compared to a problem and the actual to a solution. Therefore an actualisation is not a destruction but, on the contrary, a micro invention, a production, an act of creation. When 1 use information, when I interpret it, connect it to other information in order to make sense, when I use it for decision making, I actualise the information. I perform some creative act. The knowledge, again, is the output of a learning process, that is to say the result of a virtualisation of some immediate experiences. In reverse order, knowledge can be applied or, better, actualised in various situations, different from the learning situation. Every effective use of knowledge is an inventive problem solving process, a small creation.

Now, consider sacks of wheat or cars. Their production and consumption cannot be understood as a dialectic of actualisation and virtualisation. In this case, production and consumption are rather the equivalent of potentialisation (manufacturing possibilities) and realisation. Goods whose consumption is destructive and whose appropriation is exclusive are tanks of possibilities, reservoirs of potentials. Their consumption (eating the wheat, driving the car) equals to a 'fall of potential', a realisation. In other words, it is an irreversible and exclusive choice among the possibilities. The realisation gives existence to some possibilities to the detriment of others. The possibles are candidates, they do not sustain a living problematical field. The realisation is an election or a selection rather than inventive problem solving. The virtual object poses a problem, asks a question, opens a field of interpretation, resolution or actualisation while an envelope of possibles must be realised in an exclusive way, with the destruction of potential. The potential is a destructible and completely private object that cannot be both here and there. It cannot be detached from the 'here and now'. It is governed by the exclusive 'either... or... '. Being able to realise itself in two different ways, in two distinct places and moments is, by definition. impossible. Because they are tanks of possibility, those objects whose consumption is a realisation cannot be detached from their physical support.

To avoid misunderstandings, I immediately make clear that I am trying to make here some conceptual distinctions and not an exclusive classification. A work of art, for example, possesses simultaneously aspects of possibility and virtuality. As a source of prestige and aura or as pure commercial object, a picture is a tank of possibles ('the original'). This way, it cannot be realised (by exhibition or by sale) simultaneously here and there. But as a support of a mental model, as an image to be interpreted, as the transmitter of a tradition to be continued or to be contradicted, as an event in cultural history, a picture is a virtual object. In this way original, copies, photographs, reproductions, digitisations, samplings, installations on interactive systems are actualisations. Each cultural or mental effect produced by one of these actualisations is again an actualisation of the picture.

This type of analysis can be applied to the contemporary shift of work. In the conventional vision, workers sell their labour and receive a salary in return. The work is measured per hour. It is a potential since a given hour is irreversibly lost. Usual paid work is a fall of potential, a realisation. On the other hand, new contemporary workers tend to sell, not their labour, but their competence or, even better, a continuously improved capacity to learn and to innovate that could be actualised in an unpredictable manner in whatever particular context. Obviously, competence is not worked out when one uses it, on the contrary. But the actualisation of the competence, the burst of a quality in a living context, is far more difficult to measure than the realisation of the working force. For sure, the hour is no longer a relevant unit of measure for work. What has always been true for artists and intellectuals becomes true for everybody. In summary, with the virtualisation of the economy, we are experiencing the shift from an economy of substances to an economy of events. Events and information: the Moebius ring

An event is an actualisation. On the other hand, the production and the distribution of messages about it constitutes a virtualisation of this event. The message is provided with all the attributes that we have associated until now with the virtualisation: detachment from a particular moment and place, shift to the public and heterogenesis. Indeed, messages that virtualise the event are, at the same time, its prolongation. They participate in its performance, in its determination process. They are part of it. Because of the media and its effects the result of an election, for example, reverberates in some manner in the financial markets of a foreign country and provokes further political or military events here and there. Thanks to the information about the event (thanks to its virtualisation) the event continues to actualise itself in other particular times and places. Very often, this actualisation takes the form of the production of messages and information, that is to say microvirtualisations. Once again, we meet our usual theme of the Moebius ring: the message about the event is at the same time a sequence of the event. The map (the message) is part of the land (the event) and the territory is often mainly built from an addition, a dynamic articulation, an expanding system of maps. In other words, events and information are involved in a dynamic of actualisation (territorialisation, performance here and now, particular solution) and of virtualisation (deterritorialisation, detachment from here and now, sharing, putting in common, move upstream to the problem). Events and information about events exchange their identities and their functions as each step of the dialectic of human meaning processes.

9. Conclusion: toward an aesthetic of hospitality

What about the aesthetic issue, now? May I suggest that it is more interesting to think about 'virtualisation and actualisation art' rather than 'digital art'? What is really important? Using computer tools to draw images? Designing installations with interactive interfaces? Of course it is important, but there are probably higher issues: to recognise the current step in the self-making of the human race, to testify about this mutation. Art can make this jump into deeper virtuality perceptible, accessible for people's senses and emotions. But we can also intervene or interfere in this process. The new fundamental designs are the designs of hyperbody, of hypercortex, of the new economy of events and plenty; it is the architecture of the flowing knowledge space.

Virtuality is not at all what television tells us it is. It is not an imaginary or false world. On the contrary, virtualisation is the very dynamic of our common real world, it is precisely what makes the world common and shared. Virtuality is not the kingdom of lies but the very dimension through which truth and lie can exist. There is no true and false among ants or fishes or wolves: only lures and tracks. Animals have no propositional thinking. Truth and falseness exist only through language. Truth and falseness relate to articulated statements, and every statement assumes (being explicit or not) a question. Interrogation is a strange mental tension, unknown among animals. This active hollow, this seminal vacuum is the very essence of the virtual. I make the hypothesis that each jump in a new mode of virtualisation, each widening of the problem field, opens new spaces to the truth (and, of course, also to lies). I mean the logical truth, which is completely dependent upon language and writing (two great virtualisation instruments), but I mean also other forms of truth, maybe more essential and expressed by poetry, art, religion, philosophy, science, technology and also by people, by each of us in our everyday life. One of the most interesting ways open to contemporary artistic research is probably the discovery and the exploration of the new kinds of truth brought about by the dynamics of virtualisation.

Why may art intervene in the virtualisation dynamics? Because actualisation can sometimes transform into realisation, because heterogenesis can degenerate into alienation, because the invention of a new speed can fall into simple acceleration, because virtualisation often turns to the disqualification of the actual, because putting things in common, which is the virtualisation move par excellence, often falls into confiscation and exclusion.

In this vision, the role of art would be to play the virtual against the possible, the event against the substance. Art would use the universe of things and all its resources for the purpose of a collective and inventive activity: asking new questions and inventing replies.

Art, but also philosophy, politics and (why not?) technology can oppose a re-qualifying, inclusive and hospitable virtualisation to the perverted, disqualifying and excluding virtualisation. The strength and speed of the trend towards contemporary virtualisation is so high that it often banishes or expels people from their own knowledge, identities, jobs, countries... People are forced to become nomads, nomads of the inside, so to speak. In response to this situation, resisting virtualisation would probably be a bad move. We should rather try to accompany it, give it sense, and invent a new art of hospitality. What was the higher ethics of nomads can become a new aesthetic dimension at this moment of great deterritorialisation.

Listen to what could be the sensible message of this art, of this philosophy, of this politics: human beings, people from here and everywhere, you who are caught in this great movement of deterritorialisation, you who are grafted onto the pulsing new hyperbody of humanity, you who think dispersed among the hypercortex of nations, you who live in this immense event of the world that never stops returning to itself and recreating itself again, you who are launched toward the virtual, you who are involved in this enormous jump that our species accomplishes nowadays upstream in the flow of being — yes, in the very heart of this strange whirlwind, you are at home. Welcome to the human race's new house, welcome to virtualisation.

Pierre Lévy is a philosopher. He was born in Tunisia in 1956, has studied in France, and now lives in Canada. He holds a research chair on 'collective intelligence in cyberspace' at the University of Ottawa. Three of his books have appeared in English: *Collective intelligence* (Plenum Press/Perseus, NY); *Becoming virtual* (Plenum Press, NY); *Cyberculture* (Minnesota University Press). The following major works have been published in French (and in twelve other languages); *La machine univers. Création, cognition et culture informatique* (La Découverte, Paris, 1987); *Les technologies de l'intelligence. L'avenir de la pensée à l'ère informatique* (La Découverte, Paris, 1990); *L'idéographie dynamique. Vers une imagination artificielle ?* (La Découverte, Paris, 1991); *De la programmation considérée comme un des beaux-arts* (La Découverte, Paris, 1992); *Les arbres de connaissances* (with Michel Authier) (La Découverte, 1992); *L'intelligence collective. Pour une anthropologie du cyberspace* (La Découverte, Paris, 1994); *Qu'est-ce que le virtuel ?* (La Découverte, Paris, 1995); *Cyberculture* (Odile Jacob, Paris, 1997); *Le feu libérateur* (with Darcia Labrosse) (Arléa, Paris, 1999); *World Philosophie (le marché, le cyberespace, la conscience)* (Odile Jacob, Paris, 2000); *Cyberdémocratie, essai de philosophie politique* (Odile Jacob, Paris, 2002).

This article first appeared in *Digital Creativity* 8(1) 3–10 (1997).

Manifesto for a Digital Bauhaus[1]

Pelle Ehn

Malmö University, Sweden

Abstract

In the history of modern society several grand projects have been launched in an attempt to unite the two sides of the Enlightenment project: the hard (technology and natural sciences) with the soft (values, democracy, art and ethics). One remarkable such project was the Bauhaus. It was a great modern success story, but also a failure. Today, in the digital age we can witness new more post-modern attempts at meetings between 'art' and 'technology'. This emerging 'third culture' of nerds and digerati is promising, but still mostly immature.

With this background, the paper is formed as a general manifesto for a Digital Bauhaus for the twenty-first century, and at the same time an introduction to the attempts to implement this vision of creative and socially useful digital design at the School of Art and Communication at Malmö University in Sweden.

Keywords: Bauhaus, design, Enlightenment, information technology, third culture

1. All that is solid melts into air

All fixed, fast-frozen relations, with their own train of ancient and venerable prejudices and opinions, are swept away, all new-formed ones become antiquated before they can ossify. All that is solid melts into air ...
(Marx and Engels 1848)

All that is solid melts into air. This is how Marx and Engels, more than a century and a half ago, expressed themselves in the best known and most quoted manifesto in our modern time. With this they grasped, maybe more clearly than anyone else, more clearly than they probably could envision themselves, the ironic and dialectical history of modern society, where all development also seems to be pregnant with its opposite[2]. The history of the humanistic Enlightenment project of modern society, to which Marx doubtless was most supportive, expresses this contradiction painfully clearly. The Enlightenment project has more than fulfilled the 'hard' expectations, the natural science-based technological expectations. The latest example is the digital revolution, the exponentially growing information and communication technology. In contrast, however, the more 'soft' expectations of the Enlightenment project concerning values, art, aesthetic ideals, ethics and politics have in no way been met during the last centuries[3].

However, in the history of modern society several grand projects have been launched in attempts to unite the two sides of Enlightenment: the hard (technology and natural sciences) with the soft (values, democracy, art and ethics). One remarkable such

Figure 1.
Cover by
Herbert
Bauer for the
first issue in
1928 of the
Bauhaus
Journal.
The
Bauhaus
Archive).

salvation of modern society, it was at the same time diminished to a program of 'hard' regular geometric white shapes in steel, glass and reinforced concrete under the dictum 'architecture or revolution' with the corollary that a revolution could only be avoided if the modern architects and designers were given the freedom and power to change the world[6]. The social engagement in this version of the Bauhaus had been transformed to anti-democratic professional elitism[7]. Despite the high moral and aesthetic principles, there was no real feeling insight or vivid realisation of ordinary people's everyday life and conditions. Maybe, the 'soft' ideas of participation and democracy never were a cornerstone of the Bauhaus. All that is solid melts into air …

1.2 The nerd generation and the third culture

All that is solid melts into air. This description of modern society can now, by the end of the twentieth century, be given yet another significant meaning. Digital information and communication technology changes our understanding of time and space. A room is no longer only material and solid, but also virtual and fluid. We inhabit the same space, but not at the same time. The walls are there, but somewhere else. Someone is present, but still absent. Neither does time follow a solid pattern. It is not only cyclical as in a tradition-bound society, nor only linear as in modern society, but interactive and fluid as in a narrative where the reader, the observer, the consumer and the user participate in its creation.

Furthermore, in relation to the Enlightenment project, digital technology relates more to the 'soft' side than to the 'hard', since software inherently become codes of values, aesthetic ideals, ethics and politics. At the same time it seems that art has to become 'harder' than ever in an attempt to express fundamental ethical and aesthetic conditions of our life at the end of this millennium[8].

While this happens unbelievable re-

project was the Bauhaus. Today, in the digital age at the turn of the century, we can witness new attempts at creative and socially useful meetings between 'art' and 'technology' — an emerging 'third culture'[4].

1.1 The Bauhaus

The Bauhaus School was founded by the architect Walter Gropius in 1919 in Weimar. Weimar was at that time, just after the war, the centre of the new democratic republic in Germany and Bauhaus was a social and progressive experiment full of belief in the future. A major aim of the project became the unification of art and modern technology to create architecture and design for the modern free man and woman[5]. The school was forced to close as the strength of Nazism grow in Germany and the Bauhaus could only continue in exile. The project survived, especially in the US, and became a success story, but not without ironies and paradoxes. As the Bauhaus became celebrated as 'the international style' for the sources are invested in new mediating technologies around the world, though functionally and aesthetically the results are still poor. The main reason being that the development is technology driven. New facilities are logical follow-ups of earlier technological innovations rather than results of a deeper understanding of user situations and profound human needs. Knowledge from aesthetic areas such as theatre, film, music, literature, architecture, painting, sculpture and graphical and industrial design have been rarely used so far.

A response to this situation, a new meeting between 'the two cultures' of 'art' and 'science', between the 'soft' and the 'hard' sides of the Enlightenment project, is now emerging in what with varying interpretations has been referred to as a 'third culture' [9].

All that is solid melts into air in a digital time where program code is art and architecture, designed by a LEGO generation of nerds, hackers, geeks, techies, digerati and Nintendo kids[10]. Members of this nerd generation, laboriously designing new tools to explore virtual as well as material 'new worlds', may have the potential to transcend the inability of communication that 'the two cultures' of modern society has repeatedly demonstrated throughout history and, through a practical amalgamation of 'art' and 'technology', the soft and the hard, shape the emerging 'third culture'.

This is, however, just as with the Bauhaus, a project full of contradictions and stands the risk of degenerating into an adolescent doctrine of boundless individualism and technophilic hubris[11].

2. The challenge — creating a Digital Bauhaus

In trying to reshape conditions for the hard and the soft side of the Enlightenment project to meet in the design of information and communication technology we are left with a promising but overripe modern Bauhaus tradition in the background and an equally promising but immature postmodern third culture of nerds and digerati in the foreground.

This is a challenge we have accepted at the new School of Art and Communication at Malmö University by trying to create an arena, a meeting place, a school and a research centre for creative and socially useful meetings between 'art' and 'technology' — a Digital Bauhaus for the twenty-first century[12].

In our version of a Digital Bauhaus, nerds and digerati of the emerging third culture will be:

- challenged by established art and the endeavour of expressing fundamental human conditions, not only as aesthetic theory, but even more in practical projects in co-operation with exhibition halls, art museums and theatres[13];
- confronted with the natural science culture and the search for the truth of universe, not only as formulas and proofs, but even more in development projects in co-operation with engineers and natural science professionals in IT and media industry[14];
- forced to take a stance with respect to the Enlightenment project and our humanistic heritage, to ideas and controversies on freedom, democracy and human dignity in the modern civilisation process, not only as the history of ideas and cultural theory, but even more in practical dialogue with people in the surrounding society: in open forums, exhibitions, debates and not least in our own 'third culture cafe'[15].

What is needed in the design and use of the most postmodern of media and technologies — the information and communication technology — is not a modernism caught in a solidified objectivity through the design of modern objects in steel, glass and concrete, but a comprehensive sensuality in the design of meaningful interactive and virtual stories and environments.

What is needed is not the modern praise of new technology, but a critical and creative aesthetic-technical production orientation that unites modern information and communication technology with design, art, culture and society, and at the same time places the development of the new mediating technologies in their real everyday context of changes in lifestyle, work and leisure.

What is needed in the development of the aesthetics of the information and communication technology society is:

- a Scandinavian design that unites a democratic perspective emphasising open dialogue and active user participation;
- the development of edifying cultural experiences and the production of useful, interesting, functional and maybe even beautiful and amusing everyday things and experiences for ordinary people.

What is needed is humanistic and user-oriented education and research that will develop both a critical stance to information and communication technology, and at the same time competence to design, compose, and tell stories using the new mediating technologies.

What is needed are meetings between:

- *constructive knowledge and competence* related to interactive and communicative possibilities and constraints when using the new mediating technologies;
- *aesthetic knowledge and competence* from fields such as television, theatre, film, music, literature, architecture, art and design; and
- *analytical-critical knowledge and competence* from philosophy, social science, and not least cultural and media studies.

The interplay between these kinds of knowledge and competencies will come into play in

a critical and creative aesthetic– technical production orientation that ...

applications in all sectors of society: media, industry, commerce, education, leisure, art and popular culture. Examples could include interactive television, individually adjusted mass communication, simulation and visualisation of industrial processes, virtual workplaces, multimedia for distributed learning, digital interaction tools for the elderly and handicapped, everyday objects with virtual properties, interactive exhibitions, computer games and artistic development in film, theatre, visual art, dance and music.

2.1 The School
2.1.1 The programs
As the first steps towards a practical implementation of this Digital Bauhaus vision the School of Art and Communication has moved in to a new building and we have started the first six educational programs:

- an aesthetic-practical bachelor program in material and virtual design and the design of products with material and virtual components, in physical and digital form;
- a technical-constructive bachelor program in interaction technology with design and construction of software for highly interactive and innovative applications;
- an analytical-critical bachelor program focusing on media and communication studies with a cultural studies perspective on the media society and media production;
- a program in performing arts technology with focus on work with light, sound, and stage technology for different kinds of set design and presentations;
- an interdisciplinary Master's program in interaction design and design of interactive digital systems with special focus on usability and quality in use;

Figure 2. Theatre at the Weimar Bauhaus. 'Triadic Ballet' by Oscar Schlemmer, 1926. (The Bauhaus Archive)

- an interdisciplinary Master's program in technical communication with the purpose to make technical artefacts more comprehensive and usable.

For the next few years we are planning complementary masters and diploma programs directed towards new media producers, curators, and digital artists.

2.1.2 A 'reflective practicum'

The pedagogy at the School is grounded in the type of learning that is required. Each year of students will have its own base, a well-equipped 'home room'. The school puts resources at the students' disposal and staff act as advisors and support the students' learning activity. Practical skills will be supported by studio-based supervision. Needs for analysis and critique will be supported as well as help to guide into unknown knowledge territory. But it is the students that learn, and it is the students themselves that have to take responsibility for their own learning. Staff can only help create the problem-based learning environment — a reflective practicum[16].

Some characteristics of this environment are the premises that understanding and design of digital media and mediating technologies requires teamwork and many different competencies; that knowledge grows in a spiral of action and reflection where learning by doing, coaching rather than teaching and a dialogue of reciprocal reflection-in-action between coach and student is fundamental; and that knowledge matures in open dialogue. This teamwork and

dialogue will also stretch across the programs in common workshops across educational programs, joint projects and interdisciplinary courses.

One example is the introductory half-semester course in cultural history and cultural theory with special focus on design, technology and media that all new students participate in. The purpose is to create a shared platform with tools for analysis of modern cultural products and processes and historic understanding of cultural development during the last centuries.

2.2 The research studios

We are strongly convinced that close interaction with research is a corner stone in an environment for creative studies. Hence, it is most satisfying that the school has been integrated with a network for research into time, space and interactivity. At the *Interactive Institute* we will explore and constructively use new mediating technology to improve people's social interaction capabilities and their interaction with material and virtual environments. This will be supported by critical studies and an integrated artistic program. Research, inspired by the early Bauhaus schools, will be carried out in studios/workshops through close co-operation between researchers, artists and students. Teachers and students will actively participate in research, including research into education[17].

The first two research studios focus on space and virtuality, and narrativity and communication.

2.2.1 The space and virtuality studio

The boundaries between material space and virtual space are growing increasingly harder to define. Virtual reality is perceived nearly as intensely with all senses as material reality. Material space is becoming permeated with virtual information. What happens to ourselves and our conditions for living and working when fact and fiction blend? This will be investigated in our studio for space and virtuality. The overall scope of the studio is to redirect information technology design from its focus on organised task systems and specialised tools towards the both more humble and more demanding challenge of providing people with 'set-pieces' and 'props' for their continuous construction of ever changing lived-in worlds. We take a constructivist stance towards

... places the development of new mediating technologies in their real every-day context of changes in life-style, work and leisure

the notions of space and virtuality. Lived-in space is in our view best conceived as the social construction of shared frameworks in which people orient themselves and act. With this conception the conventional geographical notion of space has no predominance or more assured existence than spatial patterns brought to life through people's otherwise mediated interactions.

With this broader notion of 'action space' the studio will 're-visit' well-known professional environments such as process plants, offices and service shops in order to explore how information and communication technology can 'soften' or dissolve rigorous constructs such as 'the control room', 'the individualised clerical desk' or 'the service technician solitude'.

Outside work many people have ambiguous feelings towards technology. In recent years this image has undergone change and various sub-cultures are defining themselves through relationships to technology. In the larger picture of shaping everyday technology the studio will address the issue of how information and communication technologies can find their shape and place among the other useful and aesthetically pleasing things that make up our everyday environment.

2.2.2 The narrativity and communication studio

Information and communication technology facilitates the development of new and unconventional narrative forms, where narrativity is understood in the broad sense of time-based representation. Contemporary and future narrativity is, however, not to be understood as a product of only new technologies. Several

Figure 3. Design and co-operation. Design exercise during the introductory week at the School of Art & Communication in Malmö.

Figure 4. A scene from Strindberg's 'Dream Play'. Created during a student workshop in digital set design using the Visual Assistant software package.

interacting social and cultural changes are and will be influencing the way we tell stories. These are an increasing cultural pluralism, a changing relationship towards concepts of authority, power and nationality as well as the postmodern sense of 'meaning' as something being continuously related and constructed. As a result of information technology closely interacting with these changes we can observe a new set of æsthetic principles emerge. The boundaries between artists and audiences becomes blurred and the significance of the individual artistic fingerprint grows less important, as in sampling and hybridisation. There is also a stronger emphasis on the narratives' different and changing contexts, of the story commenting upon itself. Narrativity and new media become means of creating syntheses in a constantly changing society. Little is yet known about narrative structures in digital media and their quality: how can they be made challenging, exciting, informative, appropriate and maybe even beautiful? This will be investigated in our studio for narrativity and communication where we will explore interactive storytelling emerging in the blending of information and communication technology with literature, film, television and theatre.

2.2.3 The design studies program
An activity across all studios is design studies of third culture creativity. The design of digital media requires technical and artistic as well as social and political skills. New actors are brought into the design process along with a plethora of social and political issues to consider. How can artistic and technological ideas and traditions be combined in the design process? Which new tools can support these processes? How can work practices and roles in the design process be renewed when all that is solid melts into air?

2.2.4 The artists in residence program
Just as we are convinced that research is a cornerstone for a creative study environment we are equally convinced that the participation of artists is fundamental to a creative research environment. Hence, artistic development is an integral and fundamental part of the knowledge production at the research centre. Art is a perceptive act, forming and expressing questions about conditions, contradictions and uncertainties in modern society. The intention to give people new experiences is an important base for innovation in communication processes. Close co-operation between artists and researchers is necessary for beneficial results in the research studios: researchers get in contact with artistic ways of approaching problems that may result in new solutions, and artists are inspired by new technologies to developing new forms of expression[18]. To achieve this the already initiated five-year Shift program focusing artistic conceptions and expressions of time, change, human experience and technology will be complemented by artist in residence programs. The first is developed in close co-operation with the Swedish international artist in residence program IASPIS[19] and is devoted to artistic development in digital visual media, design and architecture. A similar residence program is planned to address the performing arts.

3. Enlightenment and digital design

A manifesto from the first Bauhaus school
written for the opening of the first Bauhaus
exhibition in Weimar 1923 envisioned how
> an idealism of activity that embraces, penetrates
> and unites art, science, and technology and that
> influences research, study, and work, will
> construct the art-edifice of Man.
> (Schlemmer 1978)

The manifesto ends:
> Today we can do no more than to ponder the
> total plan, lay the foundations, and prepare the
> building stones. But we exist! We have the will!
> We are producing!

In this we can only concur, despite our knowledge of the contradictions inherent in the
Bauhaus, despite the historical tendencies away
from a socially responsible movement towards
technology hostile to man, despite a century of
obstacles and failures in the attempts to establish
the third culture that already the early Bauhaus
tried to create.

In spite of all this, but certainly not
without ironic distance and postmodern lost
innocence, we see no more constructive and
practical way to unite the 'hard' scientific and
technological sides of the Enlightenment project
with the 'soft' ethical and aesthetic sides, than
the grand vision from the Bauhaus manifesto
put in the hands of a young generation of nerds
and digerati. Hence, this is also our vision of an
arena, a meeting place, a school, and a research
centre for creative and socially useful meetings
between 'art' and 'technology'.

However, this vision of a Digital
Bauhaus can never grow strong isolated in a
corner in the far north of Europe. It has to
develop in cross-cultural and international
dialogue. Fortunately similar activities are going
on at several places around the world. What is
needed is an international network for creative
and socially useful Digital Bauhaus design that
embraces, penetrates and unites art, science, and
technology and that influences research, study,
and work — a third culture in the digital age at

the door to the twenty-first century and a new
millennium.
> Digital Bauhaus designers of all countries, unite!

Acknowledgement

During the past year many of my colleagues at
the school of Art and Communication were
strongly involved in the development of the
ideas in this manifesto as a platform for our
work.

Notes

[1] The original version of this manifesto was presented
in Swedish as an inaugural address to the first
students at the opening of the School of Art and
Communication, Malmö University, Malmö,
Sweden, August 30, 1998. I have made a few
revisions in this English version and added
footnotes. As the paper now stands it is intended
both as a general manifesto for creative and socially
useful digital design and an introduction to the
practical implementation of this Digital Bauhaus
vision in our school in Malmö.

[2] For such a contemporary analysis of 'modernity' see
Berman (1982).

[3] In Liedman (1998) this is a main theme in the
analysis of modernity and the Enlightenment
project.

[4] The concept was formulated in 1959 by C.P. Snow
(1959) in an analysis of the division of the two
cultures of the arts and the sciences. Snow pleaded
not without success for the reorganisation of
education and the social system, for a 'third culture'
where the two could meet.

[5] The early Bauhaus project had many socially
'revolutionary' influences and relations. Not only
Walter Gropius but also many other influential
Bauhaus masters, including the sculptor Gerhard
Marcks, were associated with the Working Council
for Art and others masters like the painter Lyonel
Feininger and the architect Mies van der Rohe were
members of the Novembergruppe. Another
example is the painter Wassily Kandinsky who
joined in 1922. He was one of the driving forces
behind RaChN, the Russian interdisciplinary

'academy' for art and research. There was also a strong influence from De Stijl and the attempt was made to create 'collectivist solutions'. The interplay between ideas and ideologies were, however, much more complicated than this. One example is the conflict between on the one hand the strong interest in the Mazdaznan sect and the focus on meditation, ritual and a primitive form of racism as expressed by master Johannes Itten and the focus on understanding with industry and the commercial outside world, including commissions, as prescribed by Walter Gropius. For more background on the early Bauhaus see e.g. Droste (1998) or Naylor (1985).

6   For a critique of the 'international style' and especially how it was presented by Hitchcock and Johnsson (1932) see Berman (1982).

7   For such an ironic critique of the 'white gods' (Gropius, Moholy-Nagy, Mies van der Rohe et al.) and their 'success' in the US see Wolfe (1982).

8   Like in the art works by Charles Ray where human bodies and human relations are expressed as anti-human hard plastic dolls.

9   Since the analysis that Snow made forty years ago there have been interesting changes and different authors have seen new possibilities for a third culture to emerge. The debate was started again in Brockman (1995), where he argued that a number of scientists now had left the ivory tower and engaged themselves and their scientific knowledge in public discourse concerning fundamental questions about the meaning of our lives. Another way of looking at the 'third culture' is represented by Kevin Kelly (www. edge.org/3rd_culture/kelly/index.html), the editor of Wired, the life style magazine par excellence for digerati and the nerd generation. He suggests that "technology now has its own culture, the third culture, the possibility culture, the culture of nerds — a culture that is starting to go global and mainstream simultaneously. The culture of science, so long in the shadow of the culture of art, now has another orientation to contend with, one grown from its own rib. It remains to be seen how the lofty, noble endeavour of science deals with the rogue vernacular of technology, but for the moment, the nerds of the third culture are rising." Other authors discussing the emerging third culture like John Brockman (1995) are more worried that researchers and scientists have replaced the traditional intellectual

author with no room left for the poet, as science is telling the story of our time. And still others like the science journalist Tor Nørretranders have recognised the grand potential if artists and scientists were to collaborate. He thus initiated the seminar *Third Culture Copenhagen* in 1996, creating a platform where the two branches could meet.

10   Lifestyle and values of these nerds, digerati, techies and geeks are well captured in Coupland (1995).

11   Just as the Bauhaus was received as the 'white gods' in the US in the thirties, now digirati — new gods with a job description to design the future — stand the risk of hubris, sacrificing the rigors of democratic deliberation for the pleasures of vitalist enthusiasm. Such a warning is raised by Jedediah S. Purdy (1998). In a critique of the lifestyle bible of the nerd generation he suggests that

the Wired temperament is contemptuous of all limits — of law, community, morality, place, even embodiment. The magazine's ideal is the unbounded individual who, when something looks good to him, will do it, buy it, invent it, or become it without delay. This temperament seeks comradeship only among its perceived equals in self-invention and world making; rather than scorn the less exalted, it is likely to forget their existence altogether. Boundless individualism, in which law, community, and even activity are radically voluntary, is an adolescent doctrine, a fantasy shopping trip without end. In contrast, liberal democracy at its best starts from a recognition of certain limitations that all have in common. None of us is perfectly wise, good, or fit to rule over others. All of us need help sometimes, from neighbours and from institutions. We are bound by moral obligation to our fellow citizens. We share stewardship of an irreplaceable natural world. This eminently adult temperament is alien to the digerati.

12   The resolution to set up a new university college in Malmö was accepted by the Swedish parliament in December 1996. It was part of the policy to expand education at graduate and postgraduate levels in Sweden by setting up new universities, and the idea of a school and research centre for art and communication emphasising interactive media was a central part of the early plans for the new university in Malmö.

13   Such co-operation has already been initiated with the five year Shift program focusing artistic conceptions and expressions of time, change,

human experience and technology. The project initiates and supports collaborations between regional artists from the Sound region (Öresund-Skåne and eastern Sjælland) and students and researchers at the School of Art and Communication. Examples include co-operation with the Music Theatre in Malmö and the Museum for Contemporary Art, Arken, in Copenhagen.

[14] Co-operation with companies within the field of interactive media and information technology will be extensive, not least through agreements with the industrial, research and development park located nearby: Soft Center Malmö. In fact, it is interesting to notice that the first 'Software design manifesto' was written by Mitchell Kapor from Lotus Corporation, a most successful leader from the microcomputer industry. In the manifesto that he delivered in 1990 at a gathering with his fellow leaders in the industry he wrote, "The lack of usability and the poor design of programs are the secret shame of the industry ... By training and inclination, people who develop programs haven't been oriented to design issues. This is not to fault the vital work of programmers. It is simply to say that the perspective and skills that are critical to good design are typically absent from the development process, or, if present, exist only in an underground fashion. We need to take a fresh look at the entire process of creating software — what I call the software design viewpoint. We need to rethink the fundamentals of how software is made." (Kapor 1996)

[15] The 'Third Culture Cafe' is based on the original philosophical cafes emerging in Paris at the end of the eighties, but our focus will be on technical versus philosophical issues: the role of science, technology, the arts and the new media, especially the emergence of cross-fertilisation and hybrids evolving from the encounter between previously separate disciplines.

[16] Strong inspiration for the organisation of studies in a 'reflective practicum' are the experiences discussed and concepts developed for design education in Schön (1987). Another inspiration is the idea of legitimate peripheral participation in 'communities-of-practice', see Lave and Wenger (1991).

[17] The research work is organised in atelier-like studios. Each studio is be led by a studio director (research professor) with scientific or professional-artistic excellence and involves 1–2 post-doctoral

positions and 2–4 PhD students. In the projects they will be assisted by 4–6 master's students. This will be a part of the ordinary masters programs, but the students may also be employed besides the programs paid by project budgets. The studios will also allow undergraduate students to participate in relevant projects. Different kinds of specialists coming from companies could also join the projects in a studio.

The ideas and the structure for the research centre and the studios and their themes were developed in the proposal *Malmö Interactive Media Studios* (Pelle Ehn, , Jonas Löwgren and Peter Ullmark) in April 1997. Now the research centre has become part of the Interactive Institute, a Swedish national research centre focusing on interactive technologies. The plan is to have a network of studios in Sweden. Today the Interactive Institute has four studios. Two in Malmö (in co-operation with the School of Art and Communication), and two in Stockholm (in co-operation with DI (The University College for Film, Theatre, Radio and Television) and CID/ KTH (Centre for user-oriented IT Design/The Royal Institute of Technology).

[18] For an excellent overview of artists as researchers and the importance of the art-technology connection in relation to digital technology see Sommerer and Mignonneau (1998).

[19] International Artists' Studio Program Sweden (IASPIS) enables artists from different countries to stay and work in Sweden and also functions as a forum for dialogue between Swedish and international artists. It has studios in Sweden and abroad.

References

Berman, M. (1982) *All that is solid melts into air — the experience of modernity.* Simon and Schuster, New York.

Brockman. J. (1995) *The Third Culture — beyond the Scientific Revolution.* Simon and Schuster, New York.

Coupland, D. (1995) *Microserfs.* Regan Books, New York.

Droste M. (1998) *Bauhaus 1919–1933.* Benedikt Taschen Verlag, Köln.

Hitchcock, H. and Johnsson, P. (1932) *The International Style.* Museum of Modern Art, New York.

Kapor, M. (1996) A software design manifesto. In Winograd, T. *Bringing design to software*. ACM Press, New York, pp. 3–4.

Kelly, K. (1999) *The third culture*. www.edge.org/3rd_culture/kelly/.

Lave, J. and Wenger, E. (1991) *Situated learning — legitimate peripheral participation*. Cambridge University Press, Cambridge.

Liedman S-E. (1998) *I skuggan av framtiden — modernitetens idé'historia (In the shadow of the future)*. Bonnier Alba, Falkenberg.

Marx, K. and Engels, F. (1848) *The communist manifesto*. Pathfinder, New York, 1987.

Naylor, G. (1985) *The Bauhaus reassessed*. Herbert Press Ltd., London.

Purdy, J. S. (1998) The god of the digirati. *The American Prospect* **37** 12–14.

Schlemmer, O. (1978) The Staatliche Bauhaus in Weimar — manifesto from the first Bauhaus exhibition in Weimar, 1923. In Wingler, H. M. *The Bauhaus*. MIT press, Cambridge, pp. 55–56.

Schön, D. (1987) *Educating the reflective practitioner: towards a new design for teaching and learning in the professions*. Jossey-Bass, San Francisco.

Snow C.P. (1959) *The two cultures and the scientific revolution*. Cambridge University Press, Cambridge.

Sommerer, C. and Mignonneau, L. (eds.) (1998) *Art@Science*. Springer-Verlag, Wien.

Wolfe, T. (1982) *From Bauhaus to our house*. Jonathan Cape, Great Britain.

Pelle Ehn is a professor and the director of research and development at the School of Art and Communication, Malmö University, Sweden. He is also co-ordinator for the Malmö site of the Interactive Institute, the Swedish national centre for research into interactive media and interaction technologies. He has been strongly involved in the Scandinavian participatory design tradition and is the author of many books and articles on information technology and design, including *Work oriented design of computer artifacts*.

This article first appeared in
Digital Creativity **9**(4) 207–217 (1998).

The architect's wunderkammer : aesthetic pleasure and engagement in electronic spaces

Monika Büscher[1], Martin Kompast[2], Rüdiger Lainer[3] and Ina Wagner[2]

[1] University of Lancaster, UK
[2] University of Technology, Vienna, Austria
[3] Academy of Fine Arts, Vienna, Austria

Abstract

This paper reflects on the very first stage of developing the concept of the wunderkammer, a collectively used multimedia archive for inspirational objects (images, sound, video), a collection support, and a view generator. Our approach to designing the wunderkammer space is grounded in the need for imprecise, fluent forms of categorising inspirational objects as observed in our fieldwork of architectural practice. The paper looks at the wunderkammer as both a result and object of architect-users' imaginations, and as an attempt at supporting their practices of collecting, archiving and searching inspirational material and using it for communicating the design concept. It also explores different approaches to the graphical design of the wunderkammer space and their suitability for different situations of use.

Keywords: architectural design, archiving, collecting, 3D collaborative information space, visualisations

1. Introduction

We are currently exploring the design and uses of collaborative computational settings within architectural design and planning. One of our approaches builds on the metaphor of the *wunderkammer*. The *wunderkammer* was imagined (and a first prototype of it is being developed) in talking about architectural practice and the need for ready access to a wide range of inspirational objects in this process (Lainer and Wagner 1997).

In this paper we reflect on the very first stage of developing the concept of *wunderkammer*. We look at it as both a result and object of users' imaginations and as an attempt at supporting work practice. This is grasped by the metaphor *Wunschmaschine und Welterfindung* which alludes to these two aspects of technology — to its visionary potential as an object onto which to project fantasies and desires, and to its power to invent the world:

Technology-based visions are to be seen as mnemotechnical structures that allow to think the un-imaginable, to project an image of the never-before-seen ... Technology as content and medium is in this sense a continuous transgression of boundaries. (Felderer 1997 5)

Our main purpose here is to locate the fantasies and imaginations on which the *wunderkammer* metaphor builds and to investigate some of the conceptual and technical possibilities of implementing these fantasies in a collaborative multimedia environment. This also requires us to envision different scenarios of use of the *wunderkammer*. In doing this we draw on ongoing fieldwork within an architectural office and a studio of landscape architects, which is part of a European Research Project DESARTE[1]. As our current system prototype is still at a rather rudimentary stage, our actual experiences of use are limited.

Figure 1.

The context.

2. Architectural practice: the starting point

Our starting point for talking about the *wunderkammer* were descriptions of work practice (Tellioglu et al. 1998, Lainer and Wagner 1998a). They exemplify what is commonly termed a morphological approach to architectural design which is both procedural and contextual, developing the design from a variety of resources — images, metaphors, analogies, specific project requirements, contextual information, regulations, etc. The art of designing consists in gradually assembling these resources into a whole, tossing them as through a sieve so that their connections remain fluid.

From this perspective, mobilising inspirational resources forms an essential part of an architect's search for an approach to a project and for images that appropriately guide this process and express the basic design ideas.

In the Cinema Project[2] part of this imagination space was formed by the architect's knowledge of place and context, as acquired through being there (Figure 1) and supported by maps of different scale, and some general notion of the requirements. While place, context, and requirements remain fuzzy and in the background, formation of the design idea is influenced by strong images and metaphors. One of these images, for example, is of stacks of compressed paper (Figure 2). It entered the design process on the architect's way back from a first jury meeting late at night, when the train passed a paper factory. The train ride (as a metaphor) stands for a flow of images that pass by, for the unconcentrated look of the (tired) traveller whose gaze is caught by an image. It stands for a flow of random, transient impressions. It resonates the experience that a certain level of vagueness is conducive to ideas taking shape, while at the same time remaining floating.

Images and metaphors provide a rich language for forming ideas and expressing qualities of space (a large volume, "monolithic, hermetic, barely touching" its surroundings (Figure 3), texture (the movie theatres themselves are envisioned as "rocky, stony, craggy" ("*felsig, steinig, gestockt*") with a rough, grey surface, illuminated, and furnished with velvet ("*Plüsch*")). Light is described as flooding through the building, creating a shimmering surface to be projected onto; the combination of light and material as producing an almost imperceptible metamorphosis of the building's

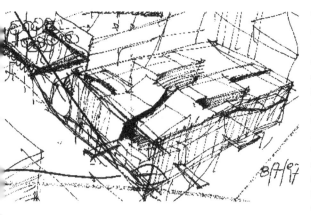

Figure 2.
The first sketch.

brought from home or assembled as a distraction from work (e.g. browsing on the Net, through magazines). When we look at these collections of inspirational objects, each has its own way of mobilising and directing the architect's knowledge and associations. For understanding this we refer to Latour's (1986) observations on the power of inscriptions as mobilisation devices which make it possible to assemble a whole range of resources (from around the world, from different disciplines) for simultaneously constructing the artifact and for staging its performance and understanding by others.

The *wunderkammer* is a response to the problem that not all of the material which could inform the conceptual-creative process is at hand. It is in the very nature of inspirational objects that they are often only peripherally present, in the back of one's mind. Also, putting them into folders and boxes means to archive them in a frozen form rather than a dynamic and fluid one which takes the ambiguous and changing character of the material into account. The central problem is how to keep present and eventually represent memory — the mind's landscape,

> which is often apparently incoherent, and a strange mixture of the sensory and the verbal. It offers us the past in flashes and fragments, and in what seems a hodge-podge of mental 'media'. (MacDougall 1994 261)

This memory, however, should reach beyond the landscape of the individual designer's mind. (Landscape) architectural planning is a collective activity, embedded in a community of practice, shared among people who represent a variety of viewpoints on the design, who move in and out of proximity, are more and less continuously intertwined with one another's work, are harder or easier to reach through different media, are always or alternately recipients or providers of one's work. There is a need for communicating the design concept, to give it presence in project meetings and in the actual process of drawing plans. For a project to

skin, from hermetically shimmering in the morning to communicating the building's contents — projected cinematic images, people's movements — in the evening (Figure 4).

This dynamic interplay of images and metaphors with the 'givens' of context and requirements is not restricted to this first stage of concept formation. Inspirational resources are evoked as the concept is detailed and elaborated (e.g. ideas about construction, materials, colours) when it has to be explained to professional partners and clients in order to mobilise their cooperation.

The nature and sources of association objects are varied and so are the ways of collecting. Individuals as well as the community of practice as a whole collect material for various purposes. One important source is reference material such as visualisations from previous projects. Traces of these projects are visible on the walls of the office which are used as an exhibition space (Lainer and Wagner 1998). Their physical presence acts as an external memory and reminder. The bookshelves are filled with art books, (landscape) architecture journals, maps, catalogues, brochures and CDs. Samples of materials are stored on shelves, tables, and the floor. Designs observed elsewhere are collected and put into boxes, as well as product information, images and samples people like for different reasons and that they have

Figure 3. *Barely touching.*

pass successfully through its various stages it must carry conviction with an evolving set of collaborators. At the heart of the work, therefore, is the need to mobilise and assemble materials, including inspirational objects, for diverse purposes and audiences (Henderson 1995). In face-to-face meetings quality is often communicated in a direct and spontaneous way. An architect may assemble some random objects into a heap to create the impression of dense, get up and fetch an art book for an example of colour or structure and put it beside a sketch. People's immediate environment allows different forms of communication through creating 'innovative combinations' of artefacts. The *wunderkammer* is meant to extend and augment these possibilities.

3. Travel and the world as exhibition

We conceive of the *wunderkammer* as a collectively used multimedia archive (the inspirational objects' home), a collection support, and a view generator. Images and other multimedia documents are placed in a metaphorical space, where they are indexed via their position in this space and some additional attributes. Users will be supported in using the *wunderkammer* for creating their own electronic collection of inspirational objects and in sharing it with others, either locally within the design studio or

over the Internet. The electronic *wunderkammer* will supplement but not replace other, non-digital collections. Its functionalities build on the actual everyday practices of collecting, searching, assembling and displaying inspirational material, as observed in our fieldwork. The long-term development plan is to provide users with the tools for building their own version of the *wunderkammer* world, using different representational techniques.

When we look at the inspirational sources of the *wunderkammer*, it took shape as a modern version of the Rudolf II *Wunderkammer* in Prague. Like many cabinets of curiosities this *Wunderkammer* housed a collection of heterogeneous objects, featuring

hundreds of icons, alluring apparatus, a multitude of mirrors, maps, charts, drawings, instruments. (Stafford 1996 28)

Visitors used it as an inspirational resource for their work in the arts, the sciences, philosophy and politics. The most outstanding feature of a *wunderkammer* was that it presented these objects in a way that did not impose an ordered set of relationships and ways of interpreting on the user. On the contrary, it enticed the discovery of connections among seemingly incongruous objects:

The metaphor of travelling among beautiful strangers is apt, because the compartmentalised organisation makes even the familiar appear unfamiliar. And, in spite of insistent borders, the beholder senses that such extravagantly disparate objects must somehow also be connected. Reminiscent of a vast and perplexing database, the sight of so many conflicting wonders arouses the desire to enter the labyrinth to try to navigate the elegant maze. (Stafford 1996 28)

This alludes to our description of the art of (architectural) design as handling multiple, hard and sometimes overwhelming constraints, without closing down the solution space opened up by imagination. For this it is essential to experiment with new ways of perceiving and interpreting constraints, and as part of this to work with contradictory and seemingly unre-

Figure 4.
**The translu-
cent skin.**

(quoted in Pinney 1994 416)

Said, in his critique of colonial forms of appropriating distant worlds, uses the term 'imaginative geography' for these explorations of cultural and geographical spaces. He points to the fact that space in these (colonial) explorations

> *acquired emotional and even rational sense by a kind of poetic process, whereby the vacant or anonymous reaches of distance are converted into meaning for us here ... not doubt that imaginative geography and history help the mind to intensify its own sense of itself by dramatising the distance and difference between what is close to it and what is far away. (Said 1985 55)*

Objects from a distant world were experienced, collected, judged, represented, and animated within familiar boundaries, one's own terrain.

Participant observation revealed some parallels between the traveller-collector Said characterises and the ways an architect may collect images, metaphors, and material objects while travelling, hiking or walking through a city, watching a movie, browsing in a bookstore, visiting an exhibition. They are stowed away as memories of a distant world and may at some point be re-appropriated as inspirational resources in the context of a design project.

lated images and facts (Lainer and Wagner 1998b). The *wunderkammer* is conceived, in the words of one of our architect-users, as a "mind expanding space". Visitors are invited to and also supported in practising their own combinatorial aesthetics of collage of inspirational objects — to 'relate the unrelatable'.

Another source of the *wunderkammer* concept is the metaphor of travel and, connected with it, 'aesthetic cosmopolitism' as a practice (Lash and Urry 1994). The cosmopolitan moves out of fixed territories, travels through natures, places and cultures, taking in images, collecting (inspirational) objects. Strongly connected to this was a notion of the world as exhibition (Figure 5), to experience it much like walking through a museum. As a one-time Governor of Bombay noted in 1898:

> *When entering on the field of Indian pictur-esqueness I feel like one who looks on some vast collection of beautiful objects, say the National Gallery or Kew Gardens, and knows not where to begin his survey.*

> *We conceive of the wunderkammer as a collectively used multimedia archive*

The old cabinet of miracles and its electronic 3D version differ in the way they connect to the metaphors of travel and imaginative geography. The furnishers of the Rudolph II *Wunderkammer* carried precious objects from far away into one cabinet where they were put into shelves and containers, thereby creating a compressed version of the world of curiosities. Their modern counterparts also collect, but their *wunderkammer* is vast, reaching into far distances, it is a space to be travelled and conquered. The cabinet is turned into an infinitely extended shelf, urban space or landscape which invites to reproduce the journey itself (and infinite variations of it), including the activity of collecting. The still of a cabinet is converted into a film —

> *cinematic landscapes of the mind in which we as spectators walk and talk our bearings.*
> *(MacDougall 1994 266)*

4. Issues of representation

The old cabinet of miracles was a room to be entered, furnished with shelves, tables and containers. While some objects were on display, others were hidden in boxes which (like a file in an archiving system) did not necessarily tell anything about its content, unless labelled. Visitors could enter this cabinet like the "Walking City" (Figure 6), walk around the books or containers, eventually open one of them and examine its contents in detail.

A computational environment offers additional possibilities for designing the *wunderkammer*. Different and quite elaborate iconographies of space can be used. Computer technology is often measured by its ability to seamlessly render the real. Visualisation tools support the kind of realism which is associated with the capacity of pictures to show the truth about things:

> *Truth, certainty, and knowledge are structurally connoted in realistic representations.*
> *(Mitchell 1995 357)*

The world as exhibition can be literally reconstructed, at different levels of detail and concreteness. On the other hand, entirely new notions of space might be necessary to adequately grasp the potential of the technologies. Benford et al. (1996) explicitly question the notion of the virtual world as 'facsimile' or 'literal' interpretation of the real world, arguing for a more symbolic and metaphorical form.

Art work may be a source of inspiration for how to develop this potential. Mitchell discusses an installation by Jonathan Borofsky of the silhouette of a human figure standing and

Figure 5.

The DESARTE Project: 'The world as an exhibition'.

chatting (in a recorded voice) in front of his abstract paintings (Figure 7). "Chattering man" introduces a theatrical element into the painting, it evokes its capacity to dramatise, amaze, deceive, delight, create illusion. Performances can be staged by deliberately using imagery for breaking down the boundary between image (or sensory thought) and language, evoking stories. Surrealist artists collaged images and re-photographed them, they assembled objects into arranged tableaux to present before the camera, they sculptured their objects (such as Man Ray using glass beads of tears), thereby alternating between the representational and the abstract (Grundberg 1990).

Electronic media and their expressive potential offer new and interesting ways of constructing space. Marco Susani argues in discussion of a variety of projects at Domus Academy:

> *The project of spaces we described so far are full of what we called 'inspirational paradoxes': persons and information inhabiting the same space, fishes that live in no place (or in any place actually), digital information 'deposited' over physical spaces of the city but also in our memory, collaborative annotations that live in*

books but don't touch them, infinite fractal audio spaces. (Susani, forthcoming)
These exemplary spaces are no longer geographical and perspectival, and accessible through movement and navigation, but something else which engages our senses in different ways.

5. Imaginative spaces

Our approach to designing the *wunderkammer* space is both symbolic-metaphorical and 'knowable'. It is grounded in the need for imprecise, fluid forms of categorising inspirational objects as observed in our fieldwork. A place should be 'knowable' to support meaningful placings of objects, and sufficiently open to invite different associations. We talk about this placing inspirational objects in fuzzy but culturally connoted places as 'weak indexing'.

The development plans are for a 3D multi-user collaborative virtual environment with a topography and appearance that is derived from categories and characteristics that are of importance to the professions engaged in (landscape) architecture. All landscape designers know what a 'rolling agricultural landscape' is. All architects recognise archetypal images of cities and architectural styles. Although highly complex, heterogeneous and diverse, there are collective cultural experiences of city and landscape to build upon. To put it in a metaphorical way: Strangers, although running the danger of getting lost in a maze of streets without a competent guide or a map, have some chance to orient themselves, following main roads, the tracks of a tramway or a river, heading towards the tower of a church or an agglomeration of sky scrapers. They will have some knowledge of what to find in a natural history museum, department store or park. As will the hiker who, equipped with simple navigation instruments will find her/his way across mountains and through valleys to the sea. Like the experienced cosmopolitan who travels distant worlds, the visitor of a 3D urban space can expect both, discovery and some basic orienta-

Figure 6.   Archigram, 'Walking City', 1994.

tion for finding their way.

We are currently exploring different representations, which to some extent reflect differences between the two design professions, the artefacts they develop, and their inspirational environments. One version is a plug-in world (Figure 8). It is conceived as an open system, rather than a pre-defined world. It will combine different elements of city and landscape into a Collage City (Landscape). The model for this approach is urban planning which today emphasises the necessity to create spaces and connections between them (rather than develop a masterplan), in ways that facilitate diverse appropriations and support adaptation to changing and evolving social uses.

The places in this world are symbolic and schematic (in contrast to realistic — dense and saturated with detail). The places have been selected in their capacity to evoke culturally shared connotations of (historical) time, community, architectural style, etc. There is a great repertoire of forms to be explored for the *wunderkammer* design: from the Roman City to a typical Gründerzeit district, from Le Corbusier's *Plan Voisin* to the urban sprawl and the industrial periphery. While some places may be highly cultivated, others are wild and inaccessible. Places of high density may alternate with voids (placelessness) and spaces of movement (a highway).

The other version of the *wunderkammer* world is rooted in the professional culture of landscape architects, their ways of seeing and representing. It is one that attempts to be both symbolic and detailed at a glance (Figure 9). From a distance it shows broader types like woodland, coast, hills (or city, suburb, infrastructure). Moving closer one is able to see different kinds of woodland — fir trees, plantations, wild woods, newly colonising wood. What this allows is for us to have available at a glance a rich and complex associational space that offers various opportunities to place inspirational objects (and thus equip them with attributes). Each panel in the sea, for example, would have a slightly different set of attributes associated with it. Reaching from things and optical distortions one may find underneath the surface, to activities and the forces of waves, wind and light on the surface, to the panoramic views one might have across the sea, these panels represent different aspects of this landscape type. Simultaneously, from a distance, one has a peripheral awareness of other areas. Seeing the mountains in the distance, a visitor might decide to put an image of a high tree not only in a woodland place, but also into the peak of the mountain, or a panel underneath the sea that shows corals, because it is pointy, spikey, and tall.

A central question here is how much detail, richness and fuzziness is necessary to allow ambiguous placings, evoke emotions, and stimulate contradictory and surprising associations. Connected to this is the question of where the richness is, in the world itself or in the quantity and diversity of the inspirational objects that have been placed there. A schematic, symbolic world may seem lacking stimulating detail when empty. Here it is the material that gives colour and richness to the place. The more continuous and detailed world of a collage of landscape types speaks more for itself. Here inspirational objects would be 'swallowed' as they are placed and retrieved through different modes of engagement with

the archive (outlined below). Both versions are based on different ideas of how to make the way one places things associative, precise and fuzzy at the same time, and the archive and its index exciting. For this we need to experiment with different constructions and representational techniques in different situations of use.

6. The wunderkammer as part of the architect's work environment

Unlike Rudolph II's *Wunderkammer*, this collection not only distracts, entertains or inspires for its own sake. It is also a tool to be used in the everyday accomplishment of the work, with a view to the location and retrieval of material, but also with regard to its assembly, display, combination and use in design documents that communicate the design concept to professional partners and clients.

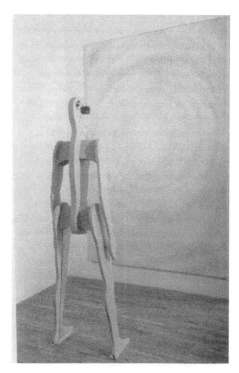

Figure 7.

Jonathan Borofski, 'Chattering man'.

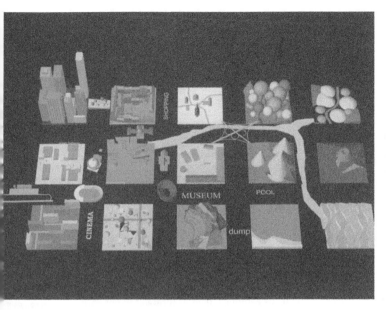

Figure 8.
The DESARTE Project: visualising urban space/ landscape.

them and change their opacity. They also can collect those objects and place them in an exhibition space. Technically, the *wunderkammer* space can be accessed via a conventional 3D viewer with enhanced possibilities for interacting with the pictorial objects which are programmed in Java. It will ultimately be part of a digitally-enhanced workspace which is currently being developed within the DESARTE project.

The starting points for building a first prototype of the *wunderkammer* and for defining its basic functionalities were stories about the difficulties of tapping the hidden and invisible resources (images, metaphors) that might inspire; field work examples from ongoing or previous projects about the multiplicity of these resources and the transient and ephemeral way in which they protrude and inspire (the train ride); observations about the inflexibility of present forms of archiving, project material being stowed away and buried in files and boxes never to be retrieved again, and the need for more intuitive forms of storing and accessing.

These observations were used for developing first scenarios of use which emphasise the need for archiving inspirational objects in a flexible and changeable way, for different modes of movement and exploration, travelling and collecting (flâneur, sightseer, archaeologist, etc.), and for support for assembling and displaying material in surprising, fluid, narrative ways.

At this early stage the *wunderkammer* prototype consists of a rather simple symbolic 3D space (Figure 8). Users can place pictorial objects in this space, scanned images, documents they create as part of ongoing work and also material drawn from, for example, the Internet. They can manipulate objects that attract their attention, turn, enlarge, re-position

6.1 The multimedia archive

The need for imprecise, fluent forms of categorising inspirational objects is one of the main ideas behind the *wunderkammer* as a space for archiving. A second and related concern is to avoid the tedious task of explicitly indexing material. Objects will assume the properties of the place where they have been deposited. As the furnisher might be interested in retrieving the objects s/he has added to the *wunderkammer* collection of inspirational objects, it should be possible to annotate objects and to create links to related information or to other objects.

The problem here is to provide an archiving space which supports the fuzziness and multiplicity of associations, while at the same time allowing retrieval and also more systematic forms of reconstruction. We can discuss these partially contradictory requirements by contrasting two entirely different notions of such an archiving space.

Christian Boltanski's slightly curved archiving or memory space *Menschlich* (Figure 10) consists of a myriad of intriguingly rusty tin boxes, marked with a short label or a small photograph. This is material Boltanski used in earlier works where they were in thematic groups:

Here, they are all presented on an equal footing, in the same format, and mixed up in an

Figure 9.

The DESARTE
Project: a
collage of
landscape
types.

*arbitrary way: the SS officer becomes a neigh-
bour of a member of the Mickey Club, the child
from the Lycee Chases is close to the Spanish
criminal. (Boltanski 1998)*
This object space is neutral. It reflects the idea of
randomness. An infinite variety of documents
can be placed in the nearly indistinguishable
boxes. As the images are very small, none of
them attracts particular attention. The boxes
and the people they represent can be connected
in an infinite variety of ways. In so far
Boltanski's memory space radicalises the idea of
the *wunderkammer* as a place for 'relating the
unrelatable'.

Our *wunderkammer* space, although
meant to invite rich and ambiguous associations, consists of distinct places with which a
number of attributes are associated. These
attributes are transferred to each inspirational
object placed there. So, for example, Medieval
City is a place that has *inter alia* the following
attributes: "cluster, cathedral, church, rooftops,
human scale, narrow, bustle, network, hilltop,
nucleus, smell", arranged under headings such as
"elements, style, scale, enclosure, movement,
texture, colour, stimulus, structure, opposites,
comments". Different types or aspects of
medieval cities could be represented (and reflect
variations in the underlying attributes) through
different panels embedded in the topography of
the *wunderkammer* space or three-dimensional
areas and objects within it. An image placed in a
particular area or in the vicinity of a particular
object would acquire the attributes of this place

and any additional ones its furnisher might want
to add. In a paper prototyping session with
practitioners, they added, for example, "reflection, light effect, city street, shadow, Spanish
corridor" to the image shown (Figure 11). They
also placed the same image under Lake, adding
"ripples"; under Park, adding "leaf"; under
Ruin, adding "light, power, art"; and under
Theatre without any additional attributes. As
anticipated, the prototyping session suggests
that users prefer to be able to define the associations an object provokes through its placing
rather than defining keyword attributes for each
individual object. This, in turn, calls for a
complex and rich, yet intuitively legible space
that brings together a wide variety of meaningful places.

We look at these places not as categories
but more as boundary objects (Star 1989).
While evoking culturally shared connotations, a
place should be sufficiently open to invite
different associations and tell different stories to
different people. It offers the kind of ambiguity
and interpretative flexibility needed for housing
a great variety of objects, some of them straight-
forward and categorisable, others exotic and
open to multiple placings.

6.2 Travelling and discovering
While travelling is a major attraction of such a
multimedia environment, it is, as users familiar
with computer games will know, a quite peculiar
experience. The geometrical properties of non-
immersive electronic spaces build upon a very

Figure 10.
Christian
Boltanski,
'Menschlich'.

In this aspect the space of the modern *wunderkammer* resembles its predecessor, where objects were strongly framed by the spatiality of room, shelves, and containers. While in a physical environment, space and the body are intimately connected and form a choreographic element in space with the body constructing space through movement (Tschumi 1977), movement in the electronic space is limited to navigation. Navigation not only requires particular skills. The very idea of moving has to be re-considered. It concentrates the body in the hand, in an act of distant manipulation. While the body itself stays outside, the spectator's gaze is mediated through selected contact points (keyboard or mouse). This also changes the temporal frame of travel. The traveller not only arrives without even having to set out. Cultural distance loses its temporal aspect.

narrow range of perceptual mechanisms —
a tunnel-like camera vision, ignoring the fluidity of the eye and the intricacies of peripheral vision. (Allen 1995 84)
The spectator is not only kept outside, an onlooker in front of a small screen, a framed world extends in front of his/her eyes. As we know from art, a frame is not innocent, it
emphasises that within its four edges the picture has established an enclosed, coherent and absolutely rigorous system of its own. The frame marks the frontier of composition and the picture's illusionary but all-pervasive three-dimensional space constitutes the rigid laws of order. (Berger, quoted in Pinney 1994 418)
The screen offers an illusionary architecture, comparable to the arrangement of curtain and stage in the theatre, with the difference that it is not possible to enter the backstage.

At the same time such a space offers new and interesting possibilities of moving, from fast, creating a dense flow of information, to slow and concentrated. The 'flâneur' roams through the *wunderkammer* populated with inspirational objects with no particular goal in mind, picking up what s/he likes, disregarding the uninteresting. Another mode of travelling may be guided by some specific interest or by other people's paths that one wishes to follow. An architect may wish to understand the development of a design concept in retrospect, or is interested in the associative material other users place or collect in relation to particular concepts, be it styles, periods, formations, design examples. We envisage that 'sightseeing' can be supported, for example, through structuring the 'hits' of a search according to the degree of compliance with the search criteria (Colebourne et al. 1996, Mariani 1998). The 'best' hits could be placed in the vicinity of landmarks within the *wunderkammer* space (or become landmarks themselves through their size relative to that of less precise hits). Other objects could be arranged as paths leading to a landmark or as clusters (this approach to structuring the *wunderkammer* information space draws on Lynch 1960, see also Benford et al 1996). The 'sightseers' would thus have some information about the importance (as defined by use) of inspirational objects for their current interests. Such a visualisation would have to be flexible so that it is possible to change an object's status within the space, and to add and remove objects. *Wunderkammer* spaces that have been structured in such a way could be saved and made available to other designers to allow them to understand how a design concept was formed.

Also, when free from the constraints normally found in a material environment, the visitor's gaze can suddenly assume new capabilities. It can zoom itself into a pictorial object, transgress its boundaries, enlarge some detail, rotate it with ease. Moving through the door of a tiny house can lead into a vast urban space stuffed with high rising buildings. The objects themselves may be animated. One can let them float, turn, connect, approach the viewer, retreat again. While eliminating the active (simulated) experience of travelling, this comes closer to the familiar experience of watching a movie, being exposed to a (flat) world which moves by.

6.3 Collecting

The richness of the *wunderkammer* world itself, which invites an infinite variety of associations, is a resource for discovery. The richness of the material that is placed in it is another. In the modern *wunderkammer* version, this kind of complex encounter is achieved through the

sheer quantity of the material that can be placed, and the great variety of surprising relations that quantity affords. We may, for example, move from the skyscraper with its associative material to the nearby mountains with their cliffs and glaciers or to a desert area. Multiple users will add to the richness of these environments with the associative objects they place and, through their presence in the space, attract and distract others.

As the *wunderkammer* is populated with images, sounds, video clips, and 3D models, the user can begin to collect and arrange materials in different ways. In the actual process of work collecting often happens in combination with creating representations to a particular audience (Figure 12). One may want to create the impression of a dense, wild garden implanted in an urbanscape of tall, grey Gründerzeit houses. Details of differently coloured flowerbeds, of leaves, grass, stems can be found in the *wunderkammer* as textures for collaging an image of a vegetational wall. These images may be discovered in a variety of places, some of them the familiar places for storing green and flowery objects — in woodland, gardens and mountain areas, others in quite unexpected places, e.g. as textures on the façades of the Skyscraper City. Another occasion for collecting is, for example, the need to find the right combination of material and light for the interior design of a building and to entice the cooperation of technical consultants in working out a solution. Different images, like a scan of a shiny, translucent, woven cloth, onto which light is projected, may help to communicate the notion of light as 'flooding and radiating' and as a 'calm surface', or 'membrane'.

The *wunderkammer* supports collecting

Figure 11.

Defining associations.

Figure 12.

*Hängende
Gärten.*

in two ways. Firstly, objects placed in the *wunderkammer* can be encountered and collected by roaming through the three-dimensional space of the archive itself. However, one of the difficulties we envisage is that the space would very quickly become cluttered. Moreover, a 'pedestrian' movement through a large archive teeming with copious images, sounds, and objects that are ordered in terms of their position in this space might not be conducive to inspiration. Another possibility is to utilise the attributes associated with each object to select some of the material in the archive and generate views that arrange this material in different ways. An example is a recent exhibition, *Rot in der Kunst,* which assembles paintings and other objects of art that express the symbolisms of the colour red in various periods of Russian culture. Used as a keyword, 'red' (in combination with other attributes) would generate an exhibition of quite heterogeneous material the diversity and to some extent also incongruity of which may be a source of inspiration.

'Search', in this context however, is not closely circumscribed by entering keywords or combinations of keywords. The use and assembly of inspirational objects is often guided by an indexical and non-verbal description of what one might be looking for. An architect might express what s/he is seeking through a gesture of a curve or through referring to some edge, rope, or coastline shaped as a curve. A search facility would have to support such an indexical way of looking ("Can I have more like this, please"). Moreover, it is a frequently observed practice to conceive of and describe features of a landscape, cityscape, a design, or an image in couplets of contrasting adjectives, e.g. the surface of the sea can be rough and smooth, the forest can be

comforting and intimidating, light comes with shade, vertical elements contrast with horizontal features, etc. This suggests that it might be interesting to provide for degrees of surprise by allowing people to mix 'opposites' or 'random' images in with their chosen keyword or other guides for the search. From a pre-collection produced in this way, a user could select the objects s/he wants.

6.4 Narrative webs

The (landscape) architects' use of inspirational material is interwoven with stories. These may be rather vague or fuzzy, they can relate to personal experience or taste, a specific project, or even a particular issue that is part of a project. Examples would be the exploration of colours or textures that could be combined in a design, or an interest in flows of people, traffic, or gazes in a landscape/cityscape. Stories may be created around themes that express particular aspects of a design concept. These stories can be spun by an individual or a group of people. 'Sightseeing' as described above already is a form of narrative, but there are other possibilities to display inspirational objects in the *wunderkammer* within a narrative mode of seeing.

Stories can also be a means of making sense of work in progress — relevant design changes and the reasons for them, the evolving design concept. A design concept may have one or several authors. It often has a history — starting with a conversation, a first sketch, it may be re-told, detailed and extended as part of the work process, when it is evoked, has to be explained to significant others, is filled with ideas about construction, materials, colours, etc.

As support for telling these stories we are, for example, considering the provision of 'cinemas', 'whiteboards' and 'museums' within the space of the *wunderkammer*, where images and objects could be presented in a way that suspends them in a narrative web. A two-dimensional collage or hierarchy of images on a whiteboard; a slide presentation or a number of images of the same colour merging into each other on a cinema screen (perhaps accompanied by a piece of music); or a collection of wunderkammer objects in a museum are examples of how narrative links could be produced.

7. Conclusions

The process of inventing a modern *wunderkammer* and struggling with its technical implementation that we are currently going through reveals some fundamental aspects of the relationships between users and their machines. The fantasies and desires are limitless, so it seems. In each prototyping session the image of the *wunderkammer* is turned around, re-examined, re-interpreted, modified, and enriched. On the other hand there are obvious technical limitations some of which have to do with the medium itself, others with the difficulties of developing a technical solution for a complex design problem. Also, there is a constant shifting between perspectives depending on the particular uses that are imagined.

When we look at the contradictions that came to the fore, some of them have to do with aesthetic quality and appearance, others with the functionalities to be developed. One of these tensions results from the obvious difference between the (inspirational) object in its material form which can be touched, carried around, visibly placed, and its representation as an image or 3D object in an electronic world. The architectural office itself, its walls, tables, shelves, are crowded with sketches, printed images, plans, catalogues, art book, samples, models. Although this world of inspirational objects at hand is small in number, their

physical presence in a densely furnished room produces a different kind of sensuality than the urban space environment with its pictorial objects on the computer screen. One particular problem here are the particular aesthetic qualities of computer visualisations, their 'slickness' and sterility, the limitations of representing subtleties of colour, shading, texture, etc. On the other hand, there are specific interesting qualities a computational space may provide and which we are currently exploring: variable colouring and lighting, speed, density, flow, variable scaling, zooming in and out, combinations with sound.

Also expectations as concerns the richness to be built into the world itself vary. The traveller will look for an exciting environment, not necessarily realistic, but saturated with detail which stimulates the eye. The furnisher (and retriever of material) needs an overview of places and clear markers of direction and location. Here a strictly symbolic world with distinct fields seems more appropriate than a subtler and more fluid arrangement of spatial qualities. While finding a place for a great variety of objects, from common to exotic, requires a rich association base, archiving and retrieving presupposes some structure. This structure, however, may reduce the element of surprise and discovery, the chance to find unexpected material in a place, strange combinations of associative objects, 'the unrelatable'.

Some of these tensions also point to potential differences between a *wunderkammer* which is used as a more or less private collection and a multi-user application. The latter will be much richer, but less ordered. It may even contain material that others experience as irrelevant boring, irritating.

This brings us back to the particularities of the user community — architects and landscape designers — and the practice the *wunderkammer* is supposed to support. It should in the first place serve as a space for building the "landscape of one's (or a collective's) mind". As such it should primarily augment the associative base for the design process, through offering access to a wide range of inspirational objects in addition to people's non-digital collections. The *wunderkammer* is also a reservoir from which to draw material for constructing a representation of a project for a particular audience which needs to be convinced of the design concept, particular spatial qualities, choices of material, etc. As we saw in the short example of conceptual design at the beginning, these objects may be of a quite different nature. Some of them are free floating images, transient impressions such as a glimpse of a stack of compressed paper caught while riding a train. Others are more directly associated with a specific design task such as different rock formations for the movie theatres, different kinds of textile structures for the skin of the building. Again others are project specific and maybe created-constructed — sketches, site plans and pictures, a collection of pavement samples.

Wunschmaschine und Welterfindung do not seamlessly map onto each other.

Acknowledgements

Figs. 1, 2, 3, 4, and 12 are visualisations from current projects, Architekturbüro Rüdiger Lainer.
Figs. 5, 8 and 9 are visualizations of the *wunderkammer* created within the DESARTE project.

Notes

[1] Esprit LTR Project 31870 DESARTE, Technische Universität Wien (A), in cooperation with Architekturbüro Rüdiger Lainer (A), Use-It (A), Lancaster University (UK), SGS Environment (UK), Aarhus University (DK), and Mjilner Informatics (DK). We are particularly indebted to Preben Mogensen, Dan Shapiro, Johannes Siglär and Walter Truscott for their contributions to developing the wunderkammer.

[2] This — a cinema centre in the city of Salzburg (Eurocity Salzburg) — is a project-in-development by the architectural office of Rüdiger Lainer.

References

Allen, S. (1995) Terminal velocities: the computer in the design studio. *ARCH+* **128** (September) 58–63.

Benford, S., Ingram, R. and Bowers, J. (1996) Building virtual cities: applying urban planning principles to the design of virtual environments. *Proc. ACM Conference on Virtual Reality Software and Technology (VRST'96)*. Hong Kong, July 1996, ACM Press.

Boltanski, C. (1998) *Derniéres Annees*. Paris, Musee d'Art Moderne de la Ville de Paris.

Colebourne, A., Mariani, J.A. and Rodden, T. (1996) Q-PIT: A populated information terrain. *Visual Data Exploration and Analysis III*, SPIE Proceedings Series, Volume 2656, Grinstein, G.G. and Erbacher, R.F. (eds.), pp. 12–22.

Countryside Commission (1991) Assessment and conservation of landscape character. Countryside Commission, Cheltenham, UK.

Felderer, B. (1996) *Einleitung. Wunschmaschine Welterfindung. Eine Geschichte der Technikvisionen seit dem 18. Jahrhundert*. Springer, Wien, pp. 1–6.

Grundberg, A. (1990) On the dissecting table. The unnatural coupling of surrealism and photography. In Squiers, C. (ed.) *The Critical Image: Essays on Contemporary Photography*. Bay Press, Seattle, pp. 80–87.

Henderson, K. (1995) The visual culture of engineers. In Star, S.L. (ed.) *The Cultures of Computing*. Blackwell, Oxford, pp. 197–218.

Lainer, R. and Wagner, I. (1997) Die Wunderkammer. Zur computerunterstützten Konzeption von Objekten und Räumen. *Architektur & Bauforum* 3 57–62.

Lainer, R. and Wagner, I. (1998a) Vernetzte Arbeitsräume: Orte, Zwischenräume, An-Orte. In Lachmayer, H. and Louis, E. (eds.) *Work & Culture - Büro. Eine Inszenierung von Arbeit*. Ritter Verlag, Klagenfurt, pp. 327–336.

Lainer, R. and Wagner, I. (1998b) Offenes Planen. Erweiterung der Lösungsräume für architektonisches Entwerfen. *Architektur &*

Bauforum.

Lash, S. and Urry, J. (1994) *Economies of Signs & Space.* Sage, London.

Latour, B. (1986) Visualization and Cognition: thinking with eyes and hands. *Knowledge and Society: Studies in the Sociology of Culture Past and Present,* pp. 1–40.

Lynch, K. (1960) *The Image of the City.* MIT Press, Cambridge, MA.

MacDougall, D. (1994) Films of memory. In Taylor, L. (ed.) *Visualizing Theory.* Routledge, New York, pp. 260–270.

Mariani, J. (1998) Chapter Seven: Q-PIT: Evolving an Information Terrain into an e-scape. In *eSCAPE Deliverable 3.1* Lancaster University. This report is available from: http://escape.lancs.ac.uk.

Mitchell, W.J.T. (1994) *Picture Theory. Essays on Verbal and Visual Representation.* The University of Chicago Press, Chicago.

Pinney, C. (1994) Future travel. Anthropology and cultural distance in an age of virtual reality or, a past seen from a possible future. In Taylor, L. (ed.) *Visualizing Theory.* Routledge, New York, pp. 410–428.

Rowe, C. and Koetter, F. (1978) *Collage City.* MIT Press, Cambridge MA.

Said, E. (1985) *Orientalism.* Penguin Books, Harmondsworth.

Schutz, A. (1962) *On Phenomenology and Social Relations.* University of Chicago Press, Chicago.

Stafford, B. (1996) *Good Looking.* MIT Press, Cambridge MA.

Star, S. (1989) *Regions of the Mind. Brain Research and the Quest for Scientific Certainty.* Stanford University Press, Stanford.

Tellioglu, H., Wagner, I. et al. (1998) Open design methodologies. Exploring architectural practice for systems design. *Proceedings of PDC'98.* Seattle.

Tschumi, B. (1977) The pleasure of architecture. *Architectural Design* 47(3) 214–218.

Monika Büscher is interested in the phenomenology of perception in the context of the development of new electronic technologies. She works as a member of interdisciplinary teams concerned with basic research for the design of electronic technologies and has worked on the following projects: Ethnography in Support of Aesthetic Production (ESRC), eSCAPE and DESARTE (EU ESPRIT LTR programme).

Martin Kompast teaches mathematics and physics at a High School in Vienna. He is at the same time engaged in multi-disciplinary research with a focus on spatially distributed work ('teleworking') and on computer-support for art and design.

Rüdiger Lainer is Head of one of the two Master Schools of Architecture at the University of Fine Arts in Vienna. He has his own architectural office with a wide range of projects in architecture and urban planning. Numerous exhibitions and international awards, among them the invitation to the Biennale of Architecture in Venice in 1991 and 1996, and the 1995 Excellence in Design Award of the American Institute of Architects.

Ina Wagner is Professor, Technische Universität Wien, Head of the Institute of Assessment and Design of Technology. Her current interests are ethical and political issues in systems design and computer-support for architectural design and planning. She is currently member of the European Group on Ethics in Science and New Technologies.

This article first appeared in *Digital Creativity* 10(1) 1–17 (1999).

The student's construction of artistic truth in digital images

Dena Elisabeth Eber

Bowling Green State University, USA

Abstract

Images that clearly present a constructed physical truth, like digital images, remind us to question the reality factor of any image. Because many digital images appear to be photographic, or photographic-like, the medium forces artists to revisit what a photograph, and consequently a digital image, represents. In turn, this rethinking influences how students in computer art see reality and truth when they create digital imagery.

Embracing this question, some digital artists have constructed visual narratives that appear photographic, yet lack the physical world referent that their images imply. Since the late 1980s and early 1990s, when this kind of construction became popular, many digital artists have grappled with how to identify the truth in their images. This study describes how some advanced digital art students resolved this conflict by defining their own artistic truths.

Keywords: artistic truth, computer arts, constructed truth, digital images, new media

1. Introduction

The discovery that seeing is no longer believing is not so frightening when you consider that truth itself can only be leased. Show me the truth and I'll ask to see the out-takes.
(Trow 1985)

Images that clearly present a constructed physical truth, like digital images, remind us to question the reality factor of any image. Because many digital images appear to be photographic, or photographic-like, the medium forces artists to revisit what a photograph, and consequently a digital image, represents. In turn, this rethinking influences how students in computer art see reality and truth when they create digital imagery.

Although those that study images understand that the photograph is not a physical truth, digital images make this assertion clearer. Nonetheless, many artists and viewers still assume that photographic representation of physical reality is in essence truth. Digital image-making gives artists the ability to construct a photographic-like image. As artists, viewers and, especially, students see the connection between the notion of photographic and of digital construction, it encourages them to reconsider truth. With the influence of photography and the construction of truth in mind, how do digital art students understand and construct truth in their images?

Embracing this question, some digital artists, like Anna Ullrich, Ken Gonzales-Day, and Pedro Meyer, constructed narratives that appeared photographic, yet lacked the physical world referent that their images implied. For examples of these constructions, see Figures 1, 2 and 3. Since the 1980s and early 1990s, when this kind of construction became popular, many digital artists have grappled with how to define truth in their art; after all, digital art has shifted our traditional notions of representation.

Since the advent of photography in the middle nineteenth century, mainstream Western culture has come to perceive the representation of physical reality in photographs as truth. Since then, philosophers have struggled to challenge this belief. Roland Barthes (1980) explained that photographic images are not physical reality, or even copies of reality, but are representations of past events, of time. Susan Sontag suggested that, although the photograph contains a trace of the physical world, it is also an interpretation, no more or no less than a painting (Sontag 1977). Like Sontag, I believe that a photograph is no closer to physical reality than a painting; further, I believe that the only physical truth an image contains resides in the viewer and the artist. Truth in images, I maintain, is an expression and recognition of lived experiences.

Because two- and three-dimensional digital imaging is a medium that can mimic photography and at the same time give artists control over all aspects of their picture, it compounds the confusion over representation of physical truth. As explained by Druckrey (1994) and Mitchell (1992), digital images are post-photographic: they are photographic-like, yet they no longer have a physical world referent. Digital images exist as pixel information, and many of these pixels are defined entirely on the computer with mathematical algorithms. Because new digital technology is challenging our notions of the truth of an image, I suggest that the post-photographic era is bringing us back full-circle to pre-photography and a constructed truth.

Having grown up with the computer as a natural part of their world, many young digital artists feel it natural to build a true work of art with digital tools. This paper describes how digital art students came to understand, then express truth in their art.

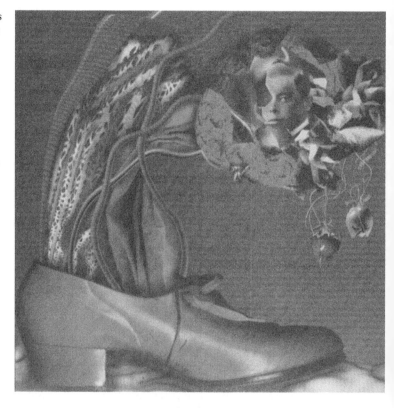

Figure 1.
Anna Ullrich,
'Solecism'.
Ilfochrome
(Digital Lambda Print).

Figure 2. Ken Gonzales-Day,
Untitled #35 *from* **The museum of broken identities (after Goya's Black paintings),** *C-print from digital negative, 30" x 36". 1996.*

2. Purpose

The purpose of this study is to explore how college level digital artists construct truth in their computer art using the new digital system of image-making. As with any imagery, artists construct a truth using symbolic pictures that they derive from lived experiences. In digital construction, the pictures are represented by mathematical models that define a tangling of pixels that may or may not point to anything in the physical world. In more traditional art mediums (photography, painting, drawing) artists often work from a physical object or event from their point of view. In digital art, there is not always a direct physical object or event that artists work from, and even if they do, they use picture elements represented by mathematical models to deconstruct, reconstruct, manipulate and display their image. No matter the source, the image is ultimately digitised into a controllable set of numbers. Many see this kind of digital construction void of the artist's voice, and thus untrue.

Those who see digital image construction as voiceless may do so because digital image creation is a relatively new way of working, and this kind of representation may be foreign or not yet understood by them. Young digital art students have a different reality, one that includes an upbringing with digital technology. For these students, digital tools are a natural way to render art which they consider true: a truth that is not an empty web of pixels, a simulacra, or a simulation, but one that refers back to their body, their lived experiences and their physical world. This study describes how some young digital-savvy artists constructed an artistic truth using the mathematically-based picture elements of digital imaging.

3. What is reality and what is truth?

The definitions of truth and reality I will offer are not the only ones, but they are the ones used throughout this paper and the study. According to Webster's Dictionary (1996), 'true', among other definitions, means 'faithful, loyal, and constant'. In this sense, an artist is true to her work and her viewers if she is faithful to her ideas and the content that she wants to portray, a meaning that comes from within.

Webster also says that the state of being true coincides with fact, and that fact agrees with reality. From this definition, truth equals reality. For this study, truth is often, but not always, the same as reality. Reality is the state of being real, and real is actual, fact, or true in an objective way. Of course, that objectivity is through the eyes of those who define it.

Reality is a collective process that exists both for a group of people and on the individual level and it is socially constructed (Arthur Neal 1998). Reality is also a symbolic construction of the world around us: we construct it through symbol systems such as language, mathematical models and pictures. When humans experience new symbols and facts, we tie this information into our lived and collective experiences and in so doing, we construct our world, our reality. By collective experiences I mean that our realities go far beyond that of our own experiences; they also include those we encounter second-hand or those that we experience through others (Mills 1963). For this reality, we give objective definitions as a form of ratification.

This definition of reality is especially important with respect to constructed truth in digital art. Many, such as Wright (1997), challenge the notion of truth contained in an image that is made of pixel information. They maintain that the pixels are solid fact often with no physical world referent. The pixels and the maths behind them are objective and removed from life experience. At best, the pixels are a simulation of something else.

This point of view does not consider that humans understand facts in the context of their culture and world. According to Mills, "No

[hu]man stands alone directly confronting a world of solid fact". The notion that pixel-based images are simulations of something also relies heavily on defining truth and reality as one thing, that of the 'physically' real. The argument depends on the idea that digital information is no longer a record of the world in the sense that film and painting are. Further, it implies digital art is not a copy of that world or even a copy of a copy; rather it is a simulation, "a mathematical model of the real" (Lovejoy 1977 160). In other words, these models appear 'real' but are actually only pixel or mathematical information. However, I maintain that an artist can use these models in a very real way so they are no longer models but a truth, a pure artistic construction. To embrace this, one only needs to accept the assumption of multiple realities. A beautiful illustration of multiple realities is the story of *Flatland* (Abbott 1884). In it, a two-dimensional square is visited by a three-dimensional sphere who enlightens the square about perspectives from other dimensions. The square encounters a similar experience to that of the sphere when he visits the one-dimensional point land. The tale is a reminder that many realities exist and just because we cannot see or understand them does not mean they are not there.

What some would define as a simulation I maintain is one form of reality, a true work of art that is one manifestation of the mind's eye, an eye that holds ideas of real and true lived experiences. In the case of digital art, the maths and the pixels are tools for artists to construct

> *truth was separate from the software, hardware, mathematical models, and pixels; it was a truth that was an expression from within each artist, an artistic truth*

and faithfully portray their truth and their reality.

In sum, I believe there are multiple truths and multiple realities, and quite often, truth and reality are one in the same. The physical world is one such truth or reality and another is the mind's eye, ideas, and concerns from within. Those ideas and concerns that come from the mind are not isolated in the brain; instead they are inextricably intertwined with the rest of the body and the soul, as well as individual and collective life experiences.

4. Results and discussion

4.1 Truth and reality according to the participants

The artists in this study approached the definitions of truth and reality in a mostly similar way to that I have presented. Almost all of the students equated truth with reality and used the terms interchangeably. Most of the artists defined truth, and therefore reality, as something that comes from within. They acknowledged at least one truth, the physical world, but they admitted to infinitely many others that come from themselves and from others.

One artist refused to accept the concept of truth and instead belittled it as something we need only to cajole our beliefs. He said, "Truth is a word that our culture uses to emphasise perspectives and beliefs held by someone". He went on to explain that we need to believe in a truth so we can live our lives.

A few of the artists felt that to live their lives they had to separate what was true and what was real. For these artists, truth could remain ambiguous; however they needed to

define reality as something more concrete, definitive, and constant. They defined reality as the physical world, something that will always be there, never change, and act as a constant surrounded by a changing truth. One artist explained this difference as follows; "Even though my images are not real, or the real physical world, they are not a lie because the truth is what I am portraying, something from within". Clearly, this artist sees the physical world as real and the truth as something that comes from a person's point of view. She also understands truth by comparing it to a lie.

Rather than a lie, some students made sense of what was true by comparing it to the notion of false. They found that their ideas fell between the two extremes and, further, they saw that things could be both true and false. One artist said, "Everything that we perceive is both true and false; the real and the spiritual world both reside in us". This artist sees truth and falsity in everything because she sees that all her realities start from her perceptions. To this student, the real is as true as the spiritual.

In summary, all the students saw multiple truths, and most equated truth with reality. For those that separated the two, reality was the physical world while truth was their perceptions, something from within. They were all adamant about the truth of their world views but understood that others had different truths. Most of the truths were spiritual or some internal, non-worldly idea. Finally, many of the artists saw true in terms of false; they made sense of their perceptions by understanding that some were not true to their views.

4.2 How the participants related photography and painting to truth

After many readings and discussions about the ideas surrounding photographs, painting and digital images, the artists in this study were asked to consider what kind of truth, if any, a photograph or a painting holds. After that, they were asked to extend that into digital imaging and what truth, if any, a digital image holds. This probing was all in preparation for their ultimate statement on how they construct truth in their digital images.

Surprisingly, most of the students, after some consideration, believed that the photograph was only one view of the physical world, mediated by the artist and her or his camera, a mere trace of events. This view runs contrary to the mainstream gut reaction to a photograph. Academic philosophical ideas aside, the majority of people react to a photograph as if it were fact or reality. After some discussion and working with digital tools, most of the artists in this study believed that a photograph, a painting or any other image was a construction of a reality or truth from the view of the image-maker.

Figure 4. Jack, 'Untitled' from 'The microscope' series. Digital image.

Not all the artists saw the photograph as an interpretation of the world through the filter of an individual; rather, some still saw the photograph as physical reality. These artists also tended towards believing that image manipulation was a non-reality. They ultimately justified the truth in their digital work as something different from reality, thus separating the

Figure 5. Terry, 'She'. Digital image.

definition of truth and reality. These artists were more concrete in deciding what was true and what was not, and their work, as well as their ideas, were quite definitive.

Jack, one artist who initially viewed the photograph as a verification of fact, used the ensuing time between the original question I posed about truth, and his ultimate exposition on truth, to revisit the issue. In that time he came to understand how he, without realising it, manipulated his photographs through lighting and photographic tools. He extended this idea to his digital work and reasoned that there was no difference in the truthfulness of any image; none of it was a single physical truth, and all of it, if created from within, held a truth. In the following excerpt, he explains his sudden insight.

> *Over the past few weeks I have been thinking about the concepts of what is true and what is real. These ideas have come up in both of my computer art classes, and I have put a good deal of thought in the matter. In light of several readings over the course of the semester, I have begun to reshape a few thoughts and opinions of my own concerning my perceptions of the world around me, as well as my definitions of words such as truth and reality.*
>
> *Before any discussion of these matters, I would have been among those who see photography as a truthful depiction of the world or at least an accurate representation of an event. Currently, however, I see photography, as well as the digital arts, as no more truthful than a drawing or a painting. The artist's capacity to manipulate the image is why I believe that I can no longer accept a photo as a single physical truth, but rather a truth .*

(emphasis added)

Although this artist now sees the same kind of non-truth in a photograph, a painting and a digital image, he does not see them as lies; he sees simply a different kind of truth, one that comes from within the artist. For an example of his work, see Figure 4.

4.3 The extension of photography into digital imagery

In considering the realities of a photograph, many of the participants reasoned much in the same way that Jack concluded; that digital imaging is no more or less true than the photograph, or any other medium of art.

We discussed the idea of simulation in which the image on the screen may appear to be something natural when it was only a program. Almost all of the participants believed that the screen information was a truth, not a simulation of anything, simply 'truth' in its pixel representation.

One participant named Jerry took this idea to another level and suggested that the digital image was actually more true for him. He said that through greater control over his tool, he was able to come closer to his intentions. The maths underlying the imagery was pure truth to him. For an example of Jerry's work, see Figure 5.

Another participant named Sam, on the other hand, explained that the digital image was, like the photograph, so far removed from a physical truth that he did not want to attempt a definition in the sense of his physical world. Instead he said, "In a way digital manipulation and modelling can only alter a physical truth that has already been altered through my mind. So in the end, the physical truth is the truth of my mind". Except for the realness of its materials, Sam felt it a moot point to call any image physically real because, in addition to how an image-making tool alters the work, his actions and intentions also skew the result. He went on to explain that he found a greater truth in digital art because he felt he could represent

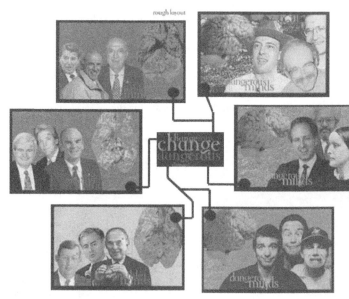

his mind's eye in a more direct way than he could photographically. For an example of Sam's work, see Figure 6.

The reconsideration of the reality in a photographic image and its extension to digital art was something most of the artists in the study experienced. I suggest that this switch in attitude was brought on by the experiences these artists had with digital image-making. These included an ease of image generation, manipulation and acquisition which helped the artists come closer to the truth of their ideas. In fact, I believe that the post-photographic era is helping us to return to pre-photography, to the strength of any image as a truth, one truth of many, constructed through the eyes of the artist.

4.4 The construction of truth

No matter how the participants stated their ideas about truth, reality, and the connection of these ideas to other media, they all believed that their digital art held some sort of truth, one that they constructed. That truth was separate from the software, hardware, mathematical models,

Figure 6. Sam, 'Changerous Assemblage of digital images.

and pixels; it was a truth that was an expression from within each artist, an artistic truth.

Having said that all the participants in this study were able to achieve some kind of artistic truth in their digital art, there were a few students that struggled with finding that truth. The struggle took many forms, but it was mostly related to ethical issues and the need for tactile and haptic feedback. I will present these two struggles followed by how some of the artists in this study explained artistic truth in their digital imagery.

4.4.1 The need for haptic and tactile

As with any art medium, artists must be able to connect with their tools in a way that they can express themselves. If the medium does not provide tools that the artist is comfortable with, then he or she cannot speak with them. In computer art, artists work with ideas that refer back to the reality and truth of the artists: their physical world, their bodies, their minds, their souls and their beliefs. In this sense, the medium is physical.

Despite the embedded physical qualities of the digital medium, there is certainly less haptic and tactile feedback — that is, the sense of force and physical texture. Some people use their body to think and learn more than others and for them the computer medium is more of a challenge. Nevertheless, with some work, the tactually-oriented artists in this study eventually found a means of expression. To do this, we focused on output (print, screen, video and installation) and input (some kind of camera, scanner or objects). Although these things are part of the digital medium, they are often ignored in the teaching and philosophical discussions of it.

The haptic learners in this study ultimately found a way to construct truth in their digital art — that is, to use the tools available to express something. One such participant came to what she ultimately called the essential truth. "When I can focus on the tactile aspects of digital art, my work portrays what I want to express. Further, if the work creates a feeling or reaction in the viewer, then it is essentially true". She overcame the non-tactile part of digital imaging and focused on the print and the presentation of that print to the viewer. In so doing, she found her expression and constructed her truth. For a digital representation of a work she transferred to fabric, see Figure 7.

The artists that had a strong need for haptic and tactile feedback were able to satisfy themselves by focusing on the parts of the digital process that provided this. They were ultimately able to express their definitive truth.

4.4.2 Ethics

When artists make a digital image (whether they generate it on the computer, use digital peripherals, construct it from acquired imagery, or a combi-

Figure 7. Jill, 'Slices of me'. Digital image.

nation thereof), the truth they construct inevitably brushes with ethical considerations. My intention is not to present a treatise on ethics or legal issues connected with digital imaging; rather I wish to mention how ethical considerations affected some students' ability to construct truth in their art. The ethical questions surrounding the construction of truth surfaced on three interrelated levels: the original work of art, the ownership of art and image acquisition.

The notion of an art object in the digital realm is a fuzzy one because a digital image resides on a computer disk as numbers in a file. If that file is opened for display, it lives on the surface of a screen, a screen that will change over time, and one that is different from any other screen. If that file is printed, the digital information is translated to colours and intensities of ink, wax, and toner in various ways. Each time the file is printed, from the same printer, a different one, or any other output device, the resulting object will look distinct from other prints of the same file and quite unlike its display on a screen. To add to the confusion, the actual file can be regenerated to make infinitely many identical copies with no variation in information. When different identical files abound, the original file, let alone the original work of art, is not clear.

What is the art object in such a medium and what is the original? For a number of artists in the study, the lack of a distinct object caused them to wonder if it was at all ethical to think of their digital work as true art. Some reasoned that if they could not define an original or produce a distinct object, they could not invest truth in their work. However, with time, most

of the participants learned to embellish their digital work with truth. They ultimately accepted that the older notions of object representation did not apply in digital art.

Most that struggled with this ethic resolved the conflict in the end. This kind of resolve is best summarised in the following excerpt from a participant.

It used to go against my artistic ethics to make work that really did not result in an object, an original one that is. Therein lies the art. I just thought of it right now: me sitting at a computer trying to make images is kind of like playing music. When I work, it is movement. There is a certain rhythm to my method. Everything is going forward. By this I mean that I take different images and put them together in different ways to see what happens. I think it is kind of like improvising. Maybe that is why I am often not terribly concerned with output because the truth in my art is making it.

This artist has resolved the ethics surrounding the art object by making his process the object. The process holds the truth for him because it is that improvisation that he

Figure 8. Seth, 'Hyperdoll'. Digital image.

Figure 9.
Margaret,
'spirit within.'
still from
animation.

or for the overall content or design of a picture, artists construct digital images from other digital images or code. Whose image, what image, and how to use it are the ethics in question. How these notions are answered by the artist is part of the construction of artistic truth. One artist, representative of many, felt that image acquisition was a natural part of making his digital art, as long as the imagery he used helped him form the ideas he wanted to express. In the following excerpt, this participant connects ethics with image acquisition and the construction of truth in his final project, *Hyperdoll.* One image from this project is displayed in Figure 8.

As far as I have come to understand digital manipulation and image acquisition, I believe ethics are very much involved. However, the area of ethics is just as open as the truth in my digital art. Who is to say what is ethical and not; the artist, the viewer, no one? I feel I can express truth even if I acquire images from the WWW. To best express this truth, I will draw from Hyperdoll, my final art project. I used a lot of Internet images and digital manipulation to create this collage. This piece shows my view of how women are busting out of their feminine closet and are putting masculine power to their use. What I am saying is that the roles of masculinity and femininity are reversing the sexes. What I construct in my piece is the immediate truth I am living through, maybe not to someone else, but to me, even if I find sources for it on the Web.

This artist felt that the truth he constructed was best created with a collage of images that spoke the truth of his experience with women. It was an issue that clearly consumed him as he encountered women who refused to act in the subservient way he was

wants to express. For an example of his art, see Figure 4.

Ownership of art is related to the idea of the original art object. Most of the students reasoned that if the original art work was the idea they held in their minds, then ownership would always reside within them. For others, this was not enough and they needed to overcome the dilemma of who owned their art in order to invest truth in it.

Computer art is a medium in which artists can copy files without degeneration and can acquire images and use them freely both from printed material and the World Wide Web (WWW). Some of the students felt that if people could acquire their images and re-use them, then they may lose claim to their art. For those that had a problem surrounding ownership, some resolved it by accepting that this ethic was part of the new digital aesthetic. This freed them to share their work and feel justified in acquiring images for their own work, thus taking part in image acquisition. Some, still unsatisfied, remained confused over ownership and the boundary of where their work ended where others began.

Digital imaging depends on image acquisition. Whether the acquisition is used for a texture on a model, for a pattern in an image,

Figure 10. Ben, 'Wave'. Digital image.

accustomed to. It was a true expression of growth and realisation through digital collage, manipulation and generation.

The students in this study needed to understand and resolve ethical concerns surrounding the digital art object, digital ownership, and digital image acquisition before they could continue making truthful constructions. Although it was easier for some than others, each artist was able to find closure on these ethical concerns. Most felt that the questions surrounding ethics needed to be answered before they could be truthful to themselves and thus, to their digital constructs.

4.5 Digital truth in the raw

After coming to terms with general truth and reality, the extension of that truth into digital imaging, haptic and tactile concerns, and digital ethics, all the artists in this study were able to construct an essential truth in their digital images. Although there were similarities between their approaches, some of which I have already pointed out, they were all ultimately unique. From here on I will display a sampling of excerpts that define how the artists in this study constructed truth.

One of the most interesting approaches was by a participant who defined the spiritual

and the physical as her truth, both coming from the same internal source. The two forces created a music that she hoped would play in the minds and souls of her viewers. Her construction went as such:

The reality in my digital art is derived from my mind and my soul and it includes both the physical and the spiritual. The real is the emotion, the experiences I have had and am currently involved in… The spiritual and the physical in my art creates a unique music that I play from my images. I mean music in a completely different way than by listening with your ears. I want my viewers to listen with their souls and spirits within.

This artist equated the terms 'real' and 'true' and explained that she constructed her digital art with a music — one that sings from within her, and one she hopes will sound from within her viewers. Her final project was a digital animation that she constructed in whole on the computer. Figure 9 is a still from that animation.

Another artist grappled with how he constructed truth during the process of writing about his digital truth. He started by not knowing how he made that truth, but in so doing, he answered his own questions and resolved truth as follows:

I don't know how I construct truth, if at all, and this is why:
1) The definition of truth is unclear, the word is defined but the idea is not. The idea is entirely different from the word.
2) Truth can be stretched.
3) Nothing is ever consistently true.
4) Thus nothing is true.
But, I guess my truth stems from the idea of truth, not the definition of the word. When I construct my digital images, my truth comes from my ideas and from the conscious thought of my brain… No matter if it is digital or painting, my art work is an expression of my thought.

As many of the artists in this study felt, this participant did not believe in a truth until he defined it for himself. Once he did, he was better able to understand his artistic truth, which in his case was the idea from his mind. See Figure 10 for an example of his art.

One participant flourished in the multitude of tools available to him. In fact, the more tools he had, the more ways he felt he could express himself. The abstract nature of

the underlying numbers were pure truth for him, so long as he was able to use those numbers as a true language, one that expressed him. He explained this in the following excerpt.

Digitally speaking, what I create is true, whether I get images from others or use digital models, it still speaks uniquely of me. It is like speaking through multiple languages. By using different images, software, or hardware, I give myself more tools to express my ideas.

This artist went on to say that the complexities he encountered in his tools drove him to find a way for them to speak his thoughts. He felt he was not always successful, and when he was not, he accepted that the tool was not appropriate. For his final project, this participant made a digital video that was an exploration of his spiritual truth. Figure 11 is a still from that video.

Many of the artists saw truth and nontruth all at once and had no problem weaving that contradiction into their ultimate truth. One excellent example of this notion is in the following excerpt. In it, the artist explains how his work is both true and untrue at once.
As of late, the images I have been putting together are true and at the same time untrue. I think that they are untrue because I have been deconstructing scientific pictures of microscopic organisms, parasites, cells, and the like and rebuilding them into a new environment. I think this can be untrue (maybe even a lie) when I reconstruct them into the new form because the images read as something completely different. However, the new thing they become is true for what it is and the new meaning it holds.

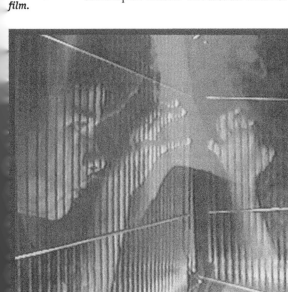

Figure 11. Todd, 'The myth forsaken'. Still from short digital film.

This artist sees his deconstruction of imagery as untrue because he is pulling the image out of context to create something new. The new context and his process of creation is what holds truth for him. This is also an example of how scientific information can also be art. For an example of this work, see Figure 4.

Many of the artists in this study found they could easily make eye-catching work with digital tools. They felt that although this kind of work initially fed the eye with exotic confections, the candy was quickly consumed and they were dissatisfied with the effect. I call the need to make this kind of digital image the 'wow factor', something that, when seen for the first time, elicits a 'wow', but then the interest in the work quickly fades. Unfortunately, digital art is flooded with such imagery, but fortunately, a dedicated artist can overcome this factor on her or his own. Just as a child gets sick from eating too much sugar candy, the novice computer artist gets ill from too much eye candy.

For some, this process is necessary to eventually reach a truth with their digital work. One artist in this study was exceptionally capable of making eye-catching work, art that immediately captured the viewer with colour alone. Her images progressed from eye-catching to include content, and they were often quite intriguing. Despite this progress, she felt this work was untrue because the meanings the images implied were not her concern.

Most recently, this artist focused on work that was a pure exploration of herself. Although she was concerned with composition, form and

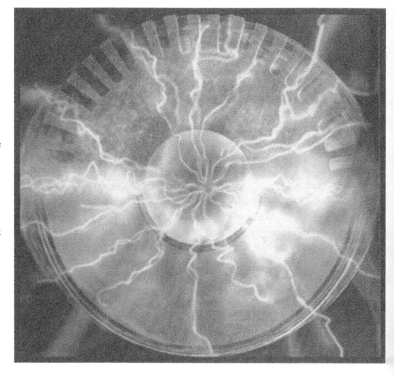

Figure 12. Carol, 'Revolution'. Digital image.

colour, these were secondary to her ideas. The following text explains her transition.

When I use ideas such as those I used in my Revolution series, nothing of me shows through, making it unreal… Sure, it is an issue that may effect others more profoundly, but not me. The work was not from my soul. With Portrait, my most recent work this semester, I have made a real effort to find the truth in me and to try to let go of my inhibitions and reveal my true self. It is an extension of the Cycle of Emotions installation I created at the end of last semester. This was the first time I actually allowed some of my own emotions to come to the fore-screen to make a truthful work of art.

The transition this artist went through is exceptional because her other work was well received. An image from her *Revolution* series was selected for publication in *Computer*

Graphics and is displayed here as Figure 12. Despite the success of her image, she felt it was not a construction of truth for her. Truth, according to this participant, was something from within, something of concern to her.

Although each artist in this study defined his or her own concerns, from formal details and abstract music to inner emotions and spirituality, they constructed truth in their digital images by remaining loyal to their ideas. As I have shown, the artists in this study had some ideas that were similar; however, each had a total approach to constructing a truth that was unique. No matter the approach, all the artists felt that their truth was constructed from within. When they felt their work was successful, it was not a copy or simulation of anything; it was their pure truth.

5. Summary

Using their images and writing as data, I have shown how a few committed digital-imaging students reconciled truth while constructing digital images. With its roots in photography, the digital image has forced artists to reconsider the photograph as a representation of physical reality and, thus, the truth in a digital image. In this process, they came upon the general question of reality in their digital work and how that reality relates to truth. After all, artists in this post-photographic era have more control over the construction of their images, which challenges the reality of them.

In digital art, there is not always a direct physical object or event that the artist works from; rather, she or he works from the constructed reality of those events or objects. Even if the artist uses a digital camera or scans a photograph or an object, the image is digitised into a controllable set of numbers. Because it is a new way of working, this kind of representation may be foreign to or not yet understood by many people, including the artists. The purpose of this study was to explore how digital art

students maintained truth in their art while using the new digital system of image-making.

The concerns that digital imaging is uncovering may not be so new after all. Since the advent of photography, our culture has tended to relate physical truth to photographic images and fabrication to painterly images. Digital imaging is a cross-breed of painting and photography, and it can appear as either medium. Digital artists construct their pictures in a digital form that references photography and painting. They see this construction as a kind of truth from within themselves.

In this paper, I described and displayed some of the unique and varied ways that the artists approached constructing truth in their digital images. The participants shared similarities, but each had a total approach that was his or her own. The approaches ranged from using deception as truth, and using both non-truths and truths at once, to searching their souls for truth and expressing spirituality. Regardless of how they approached their artistic construction, each student created a pure reality and a pure truth in pixel form. There were no copies of copies and no simulations of the natural; these constructions were all real and essentially true.

My intention was not to define the construction of artistic truth or reality in digital images; rather, it was to display how young, digital-savvy artists who were committed to their art resolved truth in their creations. Hopefully, these results will begin a dialogue about truth in digital art, an essential part of the new cyber-aesthetic.

References

Abbott, E. (1884) *Flatland, a romance of many dimensions.* Dover Publications, New York.

Barthes, R. (1980) *Camera lucida: reflections on photography.* Trans. Howard, R.. Hill and Wang, New York.

Druckrey, T. (1994) From dada to digital: montage in the twentieth century. In Haworth-Booth, M. (ed.)

Metamorphosis: photography in the electronic age.
Aperture Foundation Inc., New York, pp. 4–7.

Lovejoy, M. (1977) *Postmodern currents: art and artists
in the age of electronic media.* Prentice Hall, Upper
Saddle River, NJ.

Mills, C. (1963) The cultural apparatus. In Horowitz,
I (ed.) *Power, politics and people.* Oxford University
Press, New York, pp.405–422.

Mitchell, W. J. (1992) *The reconfigured eye: visual
truth in the post-photographic era.* MIT Press,
Cambridge, MA.

Neal, A. (1998) Personal correspondence. September
1998.

Sontag, S. (1977) *On photography.* Anchor Books
Doubleday, New York.

Trow, G. (1985) *Infotainment* (exhibition catalogue).
Berg Press, New York, p.21.

Wright, R. (1997) Visual technology and the poetics
of knowledge. In Mealing, S. (ed.) *Computers and
art.* Intellect Books, Exeter, pp. 23–32.

Dena Elisabeth Eber is an assistant professor of
computer art at Bowling Green State University.
Besides teaching and making art, she researches
creativity and the creative process associated
with new digital media art. Her most recent
research is on the manifestation of artistic ideas
in virtual environment works of art along with
the art and computer science collaboration
necessary to do so. She has presented and
published her research and art both nationally
and internationally. Dr. Eber received her PhD
and MFA from the University of Georgia and
her MS in Computer Science and BS in Mathematics from Colorado State University.

This article first appeared in
Digital Creativity 11(1) 1–16 (2000).

What is consciousness for?

Carol Gigliotti

Emily Carr Institute for Art and Design, Canada

Abstract

The question "What is consciousness for?" is considered with particular relevance to objects created using interactive technologies. It is argued that an understanding of artificial life with it attendant notion of robotic consciousness is not separable from an understanding of human consciousness. The positions of Daniel Dennett and John Searle are compared. Dennett believes that by understanding the process of evolutionary design we can work towards an understanding of consciousness. Searle's view is that in most cases mental attributes such as consciousness are either dispositional or are observer relative. This opposition is taken as the basis for a discussion of the purposes of consciousness in general and how these might be manifest in human and robotic forms of life.

Keywords: artifical life, human consciousness, robotic consciousness, teleology

While working on this paper this spring and early summer I began to consider how different my environments must be to those of some of the philosophers I have been reading. I seldom am able to put aside an entire day towards reading or writing. I do my thinking while driving from West Campus to East Campus, or attempting to simultaneously pay attention in a Committee meeting, while grocery shopping or attempting to unstop a toilet (this scenario always leads to decidedly quirky thought experiments), while cooking dinner, or if I am so lucky as to have a half an hour or so to sit on the back porch, while throwing the ball to my two dogs, who inevitably cannot find it in the overgrown grass that always seems to need cutting. This winter I prepared for and wrote most of an essay written in dialogue with Matthew Lewis, for a panel presentation on *Artificial life research applications in the arts* given at the College Art Association Conference (Gigliotti and Lewis 1997), while driving fairly long distances to sit for two days at a time in the stands at my son's wrestling matches. I am still working on what effect wrestling has had on my thinking in this area.

It is now summer, and school is out. At the moment, there are no teenagers anywhere in the house, on the porch, or even on the phone. This is very unusual. For weeks now, my son and his friends have been here constantly. Eating, sleeping, using the bathroom, talking on the phone, collecting on the front porch to go 'somewhere', and generally, in that way that all youthful beings have, of expanding to fill all available space. They connect with the present in a way that seems to ask only the most necessary of questions. They do not, or so their behaviour leads me to believe, ask themselves the question I have posed as the title of this paper, at least not in the way in which I initially meant to try to answer it. Are they conscious, I ask myself? Truthfully, there are times, if I didn't know better, I might doubt it. But, I know they do ask themselves, occasionally, as I know my son has done, what life is for, why there is so much suffering in the world, and what, if anything, should one do about it.

While I have been reading Daniel Dennett, John Searle, Owen Flanagan, Richard Rorty, Jerry Fodor, and Paul and Patricia Churchland, Richard Dawkins, Mary Midgley, and Evelyn Fox Keller, I have been simultaneously questioning the reasons I might be reading these people. What is it that I hope to find within their writings that might help me answer the question, "What is consciousness for?" Asking such a question seems to me be a worthy, even a necessary, action. Attempting to actually answer that question has an air of brashness about it that makes me cringe. As if I or anyone else could definitively answer that particular question? And yet, it is the question that continues to arise at every turn in my reading and in my thinking about our involvements with contemporary interactive technologies. What purpose do involvements with those technologies serve and how do they affect our conscious perceptions of the world?

The titles of the presentations given by the artists, philosophers and scientists speaking at *Consciousness reframed* referred either directly or indirectly to this question. Each of their conributions answered it in a unique way. The interest we all share in these investigations is the role interactive technologies is playing in our previously accepted perspectives on what consciousness is, how it works, where it might be found and what it is for. We are all looking for meaning in the What , the How, the Where, and the Why of approaches to that interest.

A friend pointed out to me that a preferred interest in any one of these categories

of questions is merely a matter of individual psychology and in some sense I agree. I have always been a why person. "But *why* is it that way?" I whine. "*What* is it for?" Needless to say, I drove my parents and teachers crazy, and at times myself, just as my son drives me crazy at times now.

Daniel Dennett (1991, 1995) is a philosopher who does not shy away from questions about consciousness. He attempts to answer all four approaches in an earlier book, *Consciousness Explained*, and a more recent one, *Darwin's Dangerous Idea*. Dennett insists one of Darwin's most fundamental contributions is showing us a new way to make sense of big *Why* questions, what philosophers call teleological questions. According to Dennett, Darwin's dangerous idea is that evolution is an algorithmic process. The wonders of nature, including us, can be explained by the blind algorithmic process that is evolution, and evolution is the design space in which life exists as opposed to undesigned space, as opposed to disorder, as opposed to non-life, as opposed to nothing. For Dennett, the original source of your being, natural selection, does not preclude your ability to

... transcend your genes, using your experience and in particular the culture you imbibe, to build and almost entirely independent (transcendent) locus of meaning on the base your genes have provided.
(Dennett 1995 426)

I admire this answer to the question "what is consciousness for?" for its sheer elegance. It offers a naturalistic theory of consciousness consistent with our nature as biological beings while at the same time allowing us the gift of human intentionality.

Dennett offers this view in opposition to what he sees as John Searle's and other's view of consciousness as finally unexplainable by either behavioural proof or the workings of the bits and pieces of neurological automata that make up our brain. Dennett believes that by painstakingly understanding the process of evolutionary design and the machine-like bits and parts of that design we can work towards an understanding of consciousness.

Searle, though he accepts that the bits and pieces of the evolutionary process are what make consciousness possible, does not accept Dennett's assertion that understanding all those bits and pieces will explain consciousness.

> *In the brain, intrinsically, there are neurobiological processes and sometimes they cause consciousness. But that is the end of the story. All other mental attributions are either dispositional, as when we ascribe unconscious states to the agent, or they are observer relative, as when we assign a computational interpretation to his brain processes.*
> *(Searle 1992 226)*

Searle, does not think answers to questions about what our consciousness is for are forthcoming from the reverse engineering process on which Dennett places his bets.

What do these philosophical skirmishes have to do with our involvements with interactive technologies? Mostly everyone reading this paper, I would imagine, knows the answer to that one. Will our involvement with computational artificial life and strong AI tell us something about how consciousness works and what it is for? Dennett certainly thinks so and he is a strong proponent for understanding that the possibility of simulating the processes of the brain in a robot would also entail the possibility of that robot over time engendering its own meaning. For Dennett, if you deny this, then you have to deny human beings the capability of creating their own meaning. This is because, if

you accept the original source of your intentionality — evolution — then you must accept the possibility of the original source of your intentionality being automata ... You see how we tend to go in circles here.

I mean no disrespect to Dennett. I can't think of anyone I enjoy reading more right now, even if I don't always agree with him. In fact, I like this argument especially because, like other arguments from functionalism, this one opens up a space for the study of animal consciousness.

The sheer practicality this field of research adds to the discussion of consciousness justifies its inclusion. Those working in cognitive ethology, the study of animal cognition and consciousness, find similarities between human behaviour and the animals they study. Marian Stamp Dawkin explains this best. She says:

> *It is not my own consciousness I yearn for, but that connection with other consciousnesses that tell me beyond a doubt I am here*

> *If consciousness has a definite functional role, it must have effects on behaviour that we might one day hope to understand ... Novelty, unpredictability, and trying to be one jump ahead are the features that seem, in us to provoke conscious events. They are also characteristic of an extremely important part of the lives of animals: their social interactions with each other.*
> *(Dawkin 1993 172)*

But, it is their findings of behaviour unlike ours, but still indicative of consciousness, although in different forms, that is most useful for understanding our own motives in developing artificial consciousness, as well as what our relationship to it may be.

In notes to a critical article on Thomas Nagel's (1979) famous essay, "What is it like to be a bat?" Atkins makes the point that Dennett's idea of method, while attempting to prove that we can scientifically understand the consciousness of other creatures

> ... *is to start with our own experiences and then 'adjust downwards' based on the physiological and behavioural data.*
> (Atkins 1993 155 n.1)

Atkins thinks, as I do, that in this approach lies a major problem with the current method of understanding what it might be like to be something else. We are asking the wrong questions from the wrong point of view. What if the bat has no 'point of view' but still has consciousness?

Somewhere in between Searle's and Dennett's points of view, and really I suppose I could have chosen any number of sociobiologists or cognitive scientists to make this same point instead of Dennett and Searle, and the somewhat cloistered world from which they come, I feel the lack of something just beyond my grasp. It is not my own consciousness I yearn for , but that connection with other consciousnesses that tell me beyond a doubt I am here. Perhaps I have been hanging out with my teenagers and his friends too much, but I want to ask only the most necessary of questions. I want to again feel that incredible expanding to fill all available space, not from the inexperience of youth, since that is not possible for me again, but from the experience of being involved with what is other than me. It seems to me the direction in which we are heading, with our interest in artificial life and strong AI, for the reasons we are doing it, may rush us past possible answers to the question "What is consciousness for?" to the question "What is electronic consciousness for?" Our methodology, at times, only allows us to beg both questions. Why, for instance are we interested in understanding ourselves and our world? Why not just let things go on as they will, in design space? Evolution has done a pretty good job so far. Well, now we've got it, all this consciousness. What do we do with it? What have we done with it so far? We have made more of us.

In fact, we have been doing that for some time now, and although that is a very satisfying activity, I want to continue to ask what consciousness might be for? Why are we placing all our bets on computation? Why are we pushing ourselves further and further from understanding existing consciousness, ours and that of other animals, in which we have played no role in originally creating? If we follow the logic of evolutionary biological process, then the desire to create robotic consciousness stems from evolutionary design and is connected to existing consciousness, ours as well as other's. Why not consider that at least? Could it be fear on our part? The fear that we may find significant purposes and meanings in the development of other's consciousness, particularly that of the other animals, is a fear that has always lurked just beneath the surface of an intellectual acceptance of our shared evolutionary beginnings.

If, as I surmise, one purpose of consciousness is to help us make our way through constant change, then we may need to better understand the limits that fear imposes in us in understanding both our own consciousness and our involvement in the development of artificial life forms with consciousness of their own. We may want to ask ourselves could it be that our consciousness is for making only our meaning in the world, imprinting only ourselves on this vastness, bettering the planet and perhaps space, with only our intelligent creations. But then what is animal consciousness for? And for that matter, what would robotic consciousness be for? For our good? Dennett insists:

> ... *a robot designed as a survival machine for you would, like you, owe its existence to a project of R and D with ulterior ends, but this would not prevent it from being an autonomous creator of meanings, in the fullest sense.*
> (Dennett 1995 427)

If Dennett is right, sooner or later we will need to ask these questions, if the conscious agent hasn't already.

Both Dennett and Searle do not make use of these spaces of other's consciousness that exist within ours, or perhaps, to push the point even further, we exist within theirs. Whether we believe, as Dennett does, that the world is understandable by process, or as Searle does, understandable only to a point, I want to reframe the study of consciousness to include those other spaces. Yes, that may include intelligent agents that we devise, but, how can we hope to understand and develop a positive relationship with beings of our devising if we understand so little of the incredible richness of those beings that already exist and share our conscious and unconscious space here and now.

Carol Gigliotti, an artist, educator, and theorist, teaches Interactive Design at Emily Carr Institute for Art and Design (ECIAD) where she is also Director of the Center for Art and Technology (http:/cat.eciad.bc.ca). She lectures and publishes widely. Her essay. 'The ethical life of the digital aesthetic', is included in *The digital dialectic: new essays on new media* from MIT Press. Her essay on artificial life applications entitled 'Mothering the future' is included in the forthcoming, *Flesh eating technologies* (Banff Center and Semiotexte).

References

Atkins, K. (1993) What is it like to be boring and myopic? In Dahlbom, B. (ed.) *Dennett and his hritics*. Blackwell, Cambridge, Massachusetts.

Dawkins, M. S. (1993) *Through our eyes only?: the search for animal consciousness*. W. H. Freeman, Oxford.

Dennett, D. (1991) *Consciousness explained*. Boston: Little, Brown.

Dennett, D. (1995) *Darwin's dangerous idea*. Simon and Schuster, New York.

Gigliotti, C. and Lewis, M. (1997) Creativity, evolution and ethics: concerning artificial life applications in the art [Abstract]. In R. Ascott (Chair), The artificial life class. *Proceedings of the College Art Association, 87th Annual Conference*.

Nagel, T. (1979) What is it like to be a bat? In *Mortal questions*. Cambridge University Press, Cambridge.

Searle, J. (1992) *The discovery of the mind*. The MIT Press, Cambridge, Massachusetts.

This article first appeared in
Digital Creativity 9(1) 33–37 (1998).

The desert of passions and the technological soul[1]

Diana Domingues

Universidade de Caxias do Sul, Brazil

Abstract

Interacting we experience the emptiness of the real and multiple options of data. We share desires, beliefs and values. I offer interactive installations as 'living' environments where a system of acquisition and transmission of data allows us to intervene in virtual worlds. Interfaces and neural networks recognise patterns and interpret signals from biological systems translating them into computing paradigms. During these dialogues we experience modified states of consciousness which I call 'electronic trans-e'. The post-biological feeling is a symbiosis of artificial and natural life. The real is in this interval, in an elliptical instance of TRANS-E.

Keywords: consciousness, electronic memories, interactive installations, interfaces, neural networks, sensorised environment

Today's scene is a desert of passions and an exciting virtual world of electronic memories. Our consciousness experiences a rupture of excess in a dialectical situation. The full and the emptiness simultaneously. I am taking back the contemporary metaphor of the desert [2] resulting from the death of ideologies in this world where political, public and personal passions do not have a dramatic force. But in the desert, we also have initiation experiences. In the same way, connecting virtual worlds, we live the emptiness of the real and multiple options of data. Interacting, the object of our passion is in displacement. We share desires, beliefs, and values. We cultivate human spirit during ephemeral connections in a fluid context. The post-biological feeling is a symbiosis of artificial and natural life. Interactive technologies are synthetic bodies that feel in our place and we feel differently with them. Through interfaces, blood has the same importance as the electrical current. 'The exhausted man is receiving a technological soul'. Electronic memories offer an exterior existence with repercussions of selfness. Boundaries between exteriority and interiority are shaken. External memories transform us into potential beings able to exist, to recall and to think out of ourselves. However, reading, writing, recording and connecting is not only the expression of our subjectivities. It is a way of losing ourselves. We are in a passage, in a transit from something to another strange and different thing[3]. The real is in this interval, in an elliptical instance. This is an enigmatic experience of TRANS-E.

As an artist, in my recent work, *TRANS-E — The Body and the Technologies* (1994–1997) I offer interactive installations for people to

Figure 1.
Diana
Domingues,
'TRANS-E: My
Body, My
Blood'.
Interactive
Installation,
1997.

experience consciousness propagation in an organic/inorganic life. The interactive installations are 'living' environments that respond to the person participating in a sensitive experience mediated by technologies. Interfaces and electronic circuits receive and transmit data and the body immersed in these sensorised environments has its senses digitalised. Thus the body, as our sensorial apparatus, experiences a sensorial circuit of 'trompe les sens' [4] by the several connections with the system's possibilities. My interactive installations are sensorised environments where electronic interfaces, neural networks or other kinds of acquisition and transmission provide intelligent behaviours, managing signals sent by the body. Neural networks try to simulate the human neurological system. Being still quite simplified, the neural networks can deal with non-linear problems by means of algorithms. The network recognises some patterns and interprets signals from biological systems, translates them into computing paradigms.

My work demands intensive collaboration with scientists and technicians from information technology and industrial automation. In this shared relationship we define the systems' behaviour. It is fascinating to be able to

capture invisible forces and control physical phenomena when we define the 'life' of the work. Following this path, my latest works have sensorised points and the signals are taken back by the sensors which capture and send them to the computer, defining the sequence of images or other mutation to appear in the room. The networks decide when the images change as they interpret the action of the participants and their moving-around in the room. Poetically the installations propose a space where people can get 'virtual hallucinations' mediated by technologies. The system's answers put us in sensorial limits that we cannot experience without technologies. We enhance our field of perception. In this sense we experience modified states of consciousness which I call *electronic trans-e*. Through digital technologies I offer an electronic trance inside a cavern-like dark room with lighted images on the walls. It is believed that in primitive societies wall paintings are works by shamans whose altered states of consciousness would confer them powers to communicate with the beyond and to intervene in the real world because they could dialogue with spirits[5]. In the same way, in my installation *TRANS-E, My Body, My Blood*[6], the body connected with interfaces in a sensorised room

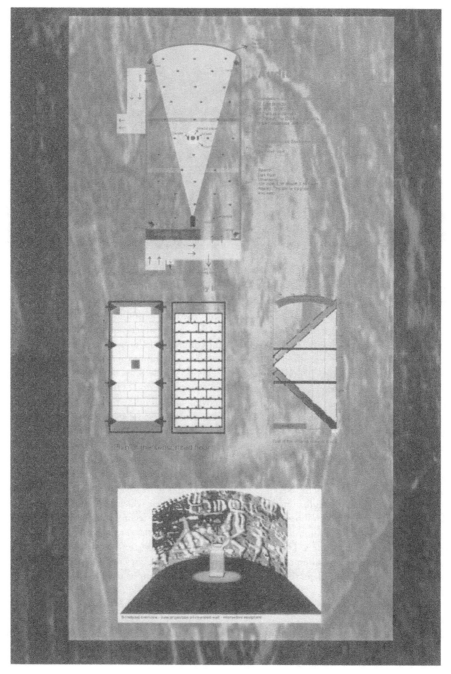

Figure 2. Diana Domingues, 'TRANS-E: My Body, My Blood'. Interactive installation, 1997.

Figure 3.
Diana
Domingues,
'TRANS-E: My
Body, My
Blood'.
Interactive
installation,
1997.

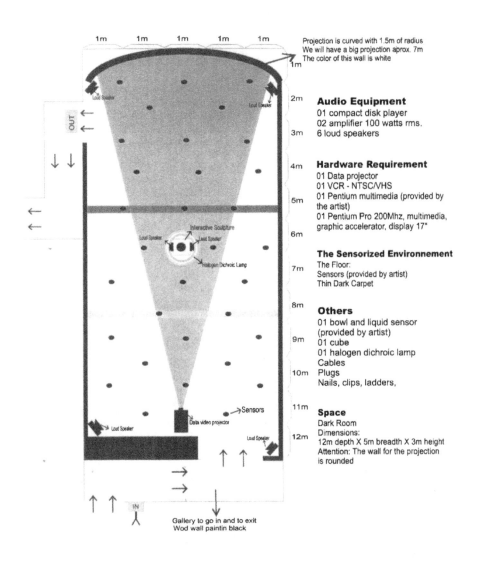

Figure 4. Diana Domingues, 'TRANS-E: My Body, My Blood'. Interactive installation, 1997.

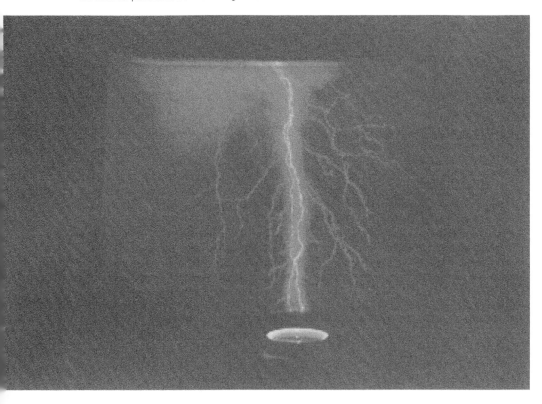

Figure 5.
Diana
Domingues,
TRANS-E: My
Body, My
Blood'.
interactive
installation,
1997.

experiences an immersive environment where the entire body is in dialogue with computer electronic memories that set the life of the environment.

I attempt to simulate electronic trances in sensorised spaces where we acquire shamanic powers by dialoguing with invisible data from computerised memories which in turn give us back answers in real time. I create installations as caverns where people can have 'visions' beyond the real, receiving shamanic powers from interactive technologies that allow them to modify the rock of a virtual wall. In Apud scholars' theories, there are specific places where the shaman experiences trances and one of them is the cavern because it is there where he meets with the spirits. And this is because the shaman believes that rock has a special power. For shamans the cavern walls are alive and act as a veil between the spirits' world and himself or herself. There they experience sequences of visions sprouting from the rock. Their visions are like lighted images that appear on the walls. The shamans, when talking to spirits, intervene in the real world and these visions are materialised through drawings which in turn lead them

to other visions. All the same, the interactive technologies offer to the participant the possibility to intervene physically in the images, generating different ones in real time and giving life to the environment. Interactive technologies 'materialise' the invisible data in ephemeral connections. Participants have visions where the real/virtual is in emergency and they go into unreal and visionary worlds. It is claimed that shamans use their powers to get rid of illnesses, to bring rain, and mainly to establish the harmony of the group. In my installation I stimulate psychic behaviours through digital technologies which allow us to go out of the real world. I offer art spaces for connecting the psychic energy during consciousness propagation in which new identities can emerge.

Three different and simultaneous situations are generated by the action of bodies in real-time. The images change, a red liquid moves within a bowl as an offering to life and the sound of the heartbeats alters. In the back of the room, a big curved lighted wall shows metamorphoses from North Brazil's Inga Stone's pre-historical inscriptions. This installation is divided in three situations simulating three different stages of the shamanic trance. Theoretical approaches concerning these three stages inform us that the shaman can experience three levels during the trance. In the first stage of the shamanic trance only lighted sensations and mutations occur in a neurophysiological way: brilliances, colours, scintillations, flashes of lights, dots, fadings. The mind is stimulated by those images and everybody has the same sensations. The images depend only on the biological apparatus and they have no symbolic cultural weight. In the second stage of shamanic trance, shaman experiences images loaded with religious or emotional significance. In my installation the participant interacts with crosses, chalices, lilies, swords, snakes, and other symbols whose interpretation depends on one's cultural background. The images invoke personal and individual experiences stored along life. The mutations call out to data from religion, geography, ethnic, political and social conditions and change according to habits, emotions and other individual experiences. Many worlds can appear in the participants' minds. In the third stage, the shaman can experience the deepest level of the trance. In this moment the shaman goes into a turmoil. It is then when actual hallucinations take place. The shaman identifies with animals, he or she is attracted by lights, natural phenomena, volcanoes, water, sky, stars and moon appear and immerse the shaman in a kind of whirlwind. In my work these images appear mixed with visceral views and other images from the reverse side of the body and the participant can be taken to distorted ephemeral identities.

Figure 6. Diana Domingues, 'TRANS-E: My Body, My Blood'. Interactive installation, 1997.

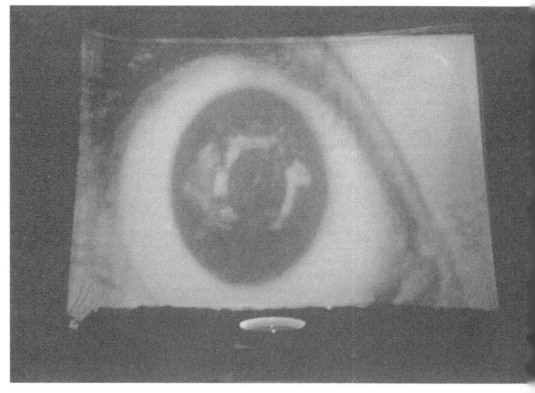

In my installation, these hallucinations are managed by neural networks. Digital images, synthetic images in anamorphic, coloured, bright, scintillating mutations are decided by the network. The mutations of the sequences of images and sounds result from the visitors' behaviour captured by the sensitivity of the sensors' dots installed on the floor and that transmit the body signals to the machines. The variables determining the behaviour of the network are: where you are, for how long and how many people stand on the sensorised carpet. The dots send the signals and each stage of the neural network system learns some patterns of the participants' behaviour, manipulates this data and provokes 'visions' in the room in an enigmatic experience of *TRANS-E*.

In *OUR HEART*[7] I try to create poetic moments of the sensitive perception of the human body scrutinised by the most advanced technologies. I offer echographies in a closed room where the pumping of a heart at full function, recorded during an ultrasound scanning, is shown. These high-performance technologies let us see and listen to the worlds of human bodies in action never known before. The reverse side of the body is put into the scene. We are immersed into the cardiac flow and we can walk between heart membranes. We are in a lighted heart that offers large landscapes projected on the transparent walls. We live in the most secret and intimate territories of the human body. The participant walks into the room with an electronic interface on the body. By using the interface, our bodies send sound signals to the virtual heart on the transparent screens. The interface captures and transmits the body's sounds that are learned by software which gives back metamorphoses of the images on large cardiac landscapes. Internally, a special computer program manages and shows sets of images provoked by the frequence of the visitor's cardiac rhythm and other bodily sounds. The acquisition and communication of data are made by telemetric analysis of the electrical

signals of the body. The signals are received by the computer where they are digitised and processed. Signal analysis extracts parameters like frequency, amplitude and spectral content of the audio signal. These parameters are used to modify the image presented to the participant, changing shapes, brightnesses, intensities and colours of the echocardiogram, according to the image processing algorithm selected. The dialogue between the connected biological and artificial systems provokes the environment life. The echographies, receiving the internal sounds of each participant, show variable mutations caused by their rhythm and determines new landscapes of the heart that will never be the same in a process of communication/discommunication. Each visitor will have a kind of metamorphosis that body is able to produce. All the communication process will be controlled by the internal and invisible signals of bodies. The computer goes out of its logic states and lives the biological signal logic commanded by a body in action. The body lives unfolding out of itself during the connections.

I am not interested in finished things. I prefer accidents, mutations. My installations propose that the interactive technologies are broadening our existential field and changing our self-image. The interfaces are synthetic bodies, and like our sensorial apparatus they receive and give back to us the most wonderful sensations. When we are connected, our body experiences a complex process of mutations, imprevisibilities and dissipations giving back to us new identities. Now technologies embody traces from the biological world translating them into computerised paradigms: plants, human body signals such as gestures, speech, breath, heat, natural noises, water, and so on. Touching, breathing, walking, experiencing algorithm paradigms, infrared sensors provide us with the power to manage invisible forces during many experiences of consciousness propagation. The electronic systems capture the invisible forces, when they learn behaviour and control the physical phenomena. New biological interfaces will be facilitated as permanent prostheses are attached on us and into our bodies and thus we will be reinventing our lives and the ultimate nature of our species.[8]

Each installation proposes a strong behavioural dimension of the Interactive Art. I try to manipulate the technological sublime[9] or the absolutely big, our physical condition and limits enhanced by technologies. Our biological apparatus receiving ultrahuman power. Interactive Art is really humanising technologies. To see, to touch, to experience algorithms, infrared waves, to capture invisible forces, giving them visibility, to check organic laws give us many experiences of consciousness propagation in a symbiosis of organic/inorganic life in this post-biological era.

Notes

[1] This title is related to two theoretical statements:
a) *The desert of passions* by Ligia Cademartori was mentioned at a seminar about the contemporary image (University of Caxias do Sul, Brazil, 1992).
b) *Technological soul* is an expression used by René Berger in his paper 'De la Communication à la Réalité Virtuelle', in ARTMEDIA- Università di Salerno, Italy, 1992.

[2] This text was illustrated with scenes from the following films where the image of the desert is abundantly used: *Thelma and Louise, Baghdad Cafe, Paris Texas, The Sheltering Sky, The Passenger*, by Antonioni, Bertolucci , to introduce the subject, and with images of my interactive installation.

[3] See the Italian philosopher Mario Perniola's aesthetic theories concerning 'cosa' and 'transit'. In: Transiti: Capelli Edit. Italy, 1988 and Enigmi. Edizioni Costa & Nolan, Genova, Italy, 1990.

[4] Pignotti, Lamberto Dal '*trompe l'oeil*' al '*trompe les sens*', ARTMEDIA 92, Salerno.

[5] apud Libération. ' A pintura dos magos das cavernas' In: Folha mais! Folha de São Paulo, 8th December 1996, São Paulo.

[6] Interactive Installation, ISEA 97 Exhibit, Chicago.

[7] Interactive Installation project (work in progress).

[8] See net symposium fleshfactor@aec.at Sherman

Tom moderator

[9] Costa Mario. Il Sublime tecnologico. Salerno, EDISUP, 1990.

Diana Domingues is a Brazilian artist and has a PhD in Communication and Semiotic works from the Universidade de Caxias do Sul where she conducts research in art/technology for CNPq and FAPERGS. As a multimedia artist, she explores the electronic process — Interactive Installation — A web site and Art video. She has contributed several solo and group exhibits to the international Biennales of São Paulo, Taiwan and Cuba and she has had exhibitions in the United States, Spain, Uruguay and Italy. She was the curator of the international *A Arte No Sec XXI: A Humanização das Tecnologias*, São Paulo, Brazil, 1995 and was editor of a book with the same title. She has participated in national and international art/technology events, especially *ARTMEDIA, ISEA*, the 1st CAIIA Conference and *Ars Electronica*. She has published many articles in books and magazines in Brazil and other countries.

This article first appeared in *Digital Creativity* 9(1) 11–18 (1998).

Prosthetics for the mind: augmenting the self with microelectronics

Niranjan Rajah

Universiti Malaysia Sarawak

Abstract

This paper inquires if digital technologies have brought about a shift in human consciousness. Starting from the metaphysical premise of the Philosophia Perennis, and applying contemporary theories of mind, this text attempts to conextualise the ontological consequences of the multi-user environments, the telematic communication, the immersive virtual environments and the bio-electrical interfaces of the 'post-biological era'. This paper attempts to understand these augmentations of mental process and asks whether or not they will bring about a rapprochement with the traditional view and return us to an undifferentiated state of being.

Keywords: aesthetics, metaphysics, mind, ontology, technology

Language is amongst the earliest of human technologies. It has given us the ability to index and isolate individual 'objects' from the continuum of nature. It is this capacity to name things, and to articulate and manipulate them, that has allowed humanity to express its will upon the natural world.

In the universal view of the *Philosophia Perennis*, linguistic differentiation is the very basis of our ordinary reality. It is in the nature of language 'to concrete things'. As Ananda Coomaraswamy (1990 4) explains, "appearances are endowed with reality and a quasi-permanence to the extent that we name them". The names of things give the forms of things their substance. As such, "The world is an epiphany", and as Coomaraswamy (1990 4) exclaims after Anaxagoras, "it is no one's fault but our own if we mistake the 'things that were made' for the reality after which they were made; the phenomenon itself for that of which phenomena are appearances".

In this metaphysical view, the natural world is understood not by its forms or objects but in terms of the 'manner of its operation'. Indeed, as the autonomous, originating and sustaining principle of life, nature was once venerated as the Mother Goddess. Rupert Sheldrake (1990 12) reminds us that even in Genesis, albeit at God's word, the earth and the sea produce their own fauna and flora. Throughout the Middle Ages Christians continued to regard nature as animate and mother-like.

In Quattrocento Florence, however, the personal and the particular began to displace the spiritual unity of the Medieval world view. With what George Holmes (1969 64) describes as a "rather extreme and sudden secularisation of ideas" the Humanist 'avant-garde' initiated a disengagement from the sacred and the natural world. In Coomaraswamy's (1935 3) terms, the Renaissance in Europe gave rise to an 'extroversion of human consciousness'. Indeed the visual technology of this Renaissance has engendered perceptual and cognitive models that index a singular, homogenous human 'self'. The transformation of medieval optics into scientific perspective, and ultimately into photography, has given us our modern ontology.

In the Judeao–Christian–Islamic tradition the expulsion of Adam and Eve from the Garden of Eden marks mankind's separation from God. The tasting of the fruit of the Tree of Knowledge can be read as a symbol for the emergence of human self consciousness or ego and the expulsion, as our separation from nature. In Psychoanalysis, the 'mirror stage' marks the moment of emergence of the human ego. The infant recognises the physical boundaries of its own body and consequently, realises its autonomy and independence from the mother. (Benvenuto et al. 1986 54)

Similarly, Brunelleschi's mirror image of the Florentine Baptistary confirms the notion of a hermetically sealed ego, negotiating its environment via a physical envelope of senses. As Brian Rotman (1987 19) observes, "Each image within the code of perspectival art ... offers the spectator the possibility of objectifying himself, the means of perceiving himself, from the outside, as a unitary seeing subject ...", as the receiver of "... messages whose interpretation requires the active presence of a physically located, corporeal individual who has a 'point of view'".

Modern philosophy is founded on Rene Descartes' *Cogito*, which is itself constituted on the 'concealed presupposition that thinking', unlike bodily action, 'is a self-conscious process'. In the *Cogito*, Descartes infers the fact of his being from the fact of his thinking. As Bertrand Russell (1960 196) puts it, "Descartes concludes that he is a thinking thing, quite independent

from the body". Bernard Kelly notes that in this notion of disembodied being, mind is severed from "a corporeal reality of visible solids", from the world of bodies that is, which nevertheless has the effect of "colouring the concept of being with an externality and a rigid outline not wholly its own".

In traditional philosophy, the body is conceived of as action, and being 'as an act'. (Coomaraswamy 1979 123) In this light Coomarasway (1979 120) views Descartes' positing of being in an individual ego or 'a personality in time' as a form of animism. Descartes severs mind, not just from body, but from other minds or more precisely, from the Mind of minds, giving rise to the cognitive autonomy that is the basis of modern individualism.

With the advent of mass media in the 20th Century, everything that was once directly lived has been mediated by representation and images proliferate beyond the individual's control. Guy Debord has described this 'spectacle' as capital accumulated until it 'becomes an image'. (Marcus 1989 98–99) Paradoxically, this mass communication forges a collective realm of desire while compounding individual alienation. It promises interaction but does not permit it.

Today, however, it is possible that with the networked interactivity of digital media, the alienation of the 'spectacle' has dissolved in an 'ecstasy of communication'. Jean Baudrilliard (1985 130–131) exclaims that there is a loss of 'private space' and simultaneously, a loss of 'public space'. This could mean the dissolution of individualism on a global scale. Alternatively, with microelectronic augmentation, the ego could intensify as human consciousness expands to inhabit virtual realms, beyond the limit of its physical envelope.

As if this ego does indeed represent a fall from grace, humanity has ceaselessly developed 'technologies' that engender a dissolution of self. Prayer, meditation and social ritual all attempt to resolve human alienation and effect a return to an undifferentiated state. In Mahayana Buddhist metaphysics there is an interpenetration of mind and matter. In fact, as Robert Thurman (1991 33–38) notes, the 'strong force' within matter is mind. As absolute reality is voidness, and the objective reality of things is relative, the collective imagination's power to shape things is unlimited. Insight into voidness releases powerful visualisations capable of bringing pure Buddha lands into reality.

The technology deployed in realising these 'Buddha fields' or environments of universal enlightenment is that of the tantric mandala. Two dimensional geometric mandalas in materials like paint and sand are used to trigger inner visualisations of subtle or virtual cosmological environments within which the adept locates himself or herself. These 'heavenscapes' or realms of peace have the power to foster wisdom and compassion in our mundane physical universe, drawing it towards the perfected state. In enlightened comprehension of the void, the distinction between heaven and earth, between mind and matter, are dissolved.

The Hindu practice of visualisation is an imaging technology that 'engineers' just such a return. As Coomaraswamy (1935 5–6) explains, the image of a Hindu *devata*, latent in canonical prescription, must be inwardly visualised by the icon maker in an act of 'non-differentiation'. This finished inner image is the model from which he proceeds to execute in a chosen material. The worshiper, in turn, applies his or her own 'imaginative energy' to the physical

Descartes severs mind, not just from body, but from other minds or more precisely, from the mind of minds, giving rise to the cognitive autonomy that is the basis of modern individualism

icon, 'realising' the *devata* within the 'immanent space in the heart'. Thus, the physical or outer image is instrumental in generating an analogous inner image in whose radiance 'harmony or unity of consciousness' is achieved. (Coomaraswamy 1935 26)

Ananda Coomaraswamy (1956 16) has remarked that *aisthesis,* the Greek origin of the modern term *aesthetic*, refers to 'reaction to external stimuli' or what the biologist calls 'irritability'. Traditional rebuke not withstanding, the moderns have gone on to venerate perception. Rudolph Arnheim (1971 13) contends that "the cognitive operations called thinking are ... the essential ingredients of perception itself". Reductive though this approach may be, it does nevertheless, have the merit of reuniting the mind and the body.

Mike King (1997 40–44) notes that Daniel Dennet emphasises perception in his construction of consciousness. Francis Crick reduces it further to a side effect to neuronal activity. Chaos theorists say consciousness arises from complex phenomena, as a whole that is greater than the sum of its parts. Others like Roger Penrose, David Bohm and Robert Jahn apply the 'indeterminism' and 'wholeness' of quantum theory to infer 'free will', 'a conscious universe' and that 'minds can reach out beyond the bodies that carry them', respectively.

Gregory Bateson (1988 95–137) defines mind as an 'aggregate of interacting parts or components' whose interaction is 'triggered by difference'. As Fitjof Capra (1989 83) explains, in Bateson's view, mind is a necessary and inevitable consequence of a certain complexity which is not dependent on the development of a brain and a higher nervous system.

For Bateson mental characteristics manifest not only in individual organisms but also in social systems and eco systems. Mind is immanent not only in the body but also in the pathways and messages outside the body.

Nevertheless, thought or mental process can be distinguished from the much simpler phenomena of material events. Bateson (1988 95–137) lists some of the characteristics of a mind so conceived as being autonomy, death, purpose, choice, learning ability and memory. He goes on to raise the possibility that such a mind might even be capable of some sort of aesthetic preference. He avoids the question of consciousness altogether.

The size of the human brain can be attributed to the complex relational nature of our communication. Nevertheless, it may be language that is the very origin of our painfully alienated world of objects and subjects. Gregory Bateson (1971, pp.270–277) has theorised that other mammals, cetaceans of course, have developed a direct, emotive, non-linguistic communication akin to music. In their high frequency transmissions, dolphins may be communicating numerous delicate feelings and relationships that cannot be expressed in human language.

Toshiharu Ito (1994 69) longingly speculates that this 'bio-technology' may evidence a culture of pure communication that is superior to our own. He envisages that, with the structures emerging in our new media society, humanity may also be evolving such a culture — a 'culture without objects'. Ito believes that human beings, immersed in an "information environment can be compared with the dolphins or whales in a new kind of sea".

In his exposition on the reconciliation of the transmigration of souls with the theory of evolution, Ananda Coomaraswamy (1979 122) quotes Erwin Schrodinger's statement, made in the context of an explanation of *heredity*, "Consciousness is a singular of which the plural is unknown". This is, in fact, a restatement of the position enunciated in the Upanishads, "That art thou ... there is no other seer, hearer, thinker or agent". Religion addresses 'first causes', while science deals with the 'mediate causes' of the same events.

As we approach the next millennium, bedecked with our imaging and communications technologies — from head-mounts and motion capture vests to ISDN, TCP/IP and MUDs and MOOs — it may seem that we are on the threshold of a shift in human 'consciousness'. In fact, it is as much our understanding of these augmentations of mental process as our wisdom in deploying them that will determine whether or not they bring about a rapprochement with the traditional view and return us to an undifferentiated state of being.

No discussion of new technology, however esoteric, should ignore the question of access. If new modes of perception bring new consciousness or new modes of being, only those who are habituated with neoteric media will witness the new dawn. David Shanken (1997 58)cautions that, "as the information elite becomes increasingly wired technologically, and in turn, psychologically", its relationship to the world "will become increasingly different from those who are not acculturated into advanced technoculture". Shanken states that this is a political issue — a question of power — and he is absolutely right! If race is not as yet an issue in cyberspace, perhaps it is because, to echo Keith Piper (1995 232–235), there ain't many 'niggers' out there yet.

The situation is, however, extremely dynamic. As developing countries capitalise on the investment and technology transfers of a fast globalising world economy, the problem of digital dis-enfranchisement may not, in the future, be racially or geographically determined.

References

Arnheim, R. (1971) *Visual thinking*. University of California Press.

Bateson, G. (1971) *Steps to an ecology of mind*.

Bateson, G. (1988) *Mind and nature; a necessary unity*. Bantam New Age, New York.

Baudrillard, J. (1985)The ecstasy of communication. In Foster, H. (ed.) *Postmodern culture*. Pluto Press, London.

Benvenuto, B. and Kennedy, R. (1986) *The works of Jacques Lacan: an introduction*. Free Association Books, London.

Capra, F. (1989) *Uncommon wisdom*. Bantam Books, New York.

Coomaraswamy, A.K.(1935) *The transformation of nature in art*. Harvard University Press, Massachusetts.

Coomaraswamy, A.K. (1956) Why exhibit works of art? In *Christian and oriental philosophy of art*. Dover Publications Co, New York.

Coomaraswamy, A.K. (1957) The dance of Shiva. In *The dance of Shiva*. The Noonday Press, New York.

Coomaraswamy, A.K. (1979) Gradation, evolution and reincarnation. In *The bugbear of literacy*. Perennial Books, Middlesex.

Coomaraswamy, A.K. (1990) *Time and eternity*. Select Books, Bangalore.

Holmes, G. (1969) *The Florentine enlightenment 1400–1450*. Clarendon Press, Oxford.

King, M. (1997) Artificial consciousness — artificial art. In Mealing, S. (ed.) *Computers and art*. Intellect Books, Exeter.

Marcus, G. (1989) *Lipstick traces*. Secker and Warburg, London.

Piper, K. (1995) The dis-orderly city, a nigger in cyberspace. *Proceedings of the Sixth International Symposium on Electronic Art* (ISEA95). Montreal.

Rotman, B. (1987) *Signifying nothing*. St. Martins Press, New York.

Russell, B. (1960) *Wisdom of the ages*. Macdonald, London.

Shanken, E.A. (1997) Virtual perspective and the artistic vision: a genealogy of technology, perception and power. In *Proceedings of the Seventh International Symposium on Electronic Art*. Rotterdam, ISEA96 Foundation.

Sheldrake, R. (1990) *The rebirth of nature*. Century, London.

Toshiharu, I. (1994) The future form of visual art. *Art and design: art and technology*, Profile No. 39, Academy Editions.

Thurman, R. (1991) Tibet, its Buddhism, and its art. In Rhine, M.M. and Thurman, R. A. F. (eds.) *Wisdom and compassion: the sacred art of Tibet*. Harry N. Abrams, New York.

Niranjan Rajah is a theorist, a curator and an artist. He is associate professor and deputy dean at the Faculty of Applied and Creative Arts, Universiti Malaysia Sarawak. Niranjan has held a visiting appointment at the Department of Design/ Media Arts, UCLA (2001) and was artist-in-residence at the Cyberarts Research Initiative, National University of Singapore (2002). Niranjan sits on the Board of Directors of ISEA and is a doctoral researcher with CAiiA-STAR. Niranjan co-curated Malaysia's '1st Electronic Art Show', (1997) and is co-founder of 'EART ASEAN Online' (1999), an internet portal for electronic art in Southeast Asia.

This article first appeared in
Digital Creativity **9**(1) 48–52 (1998).

Art of virtual bodies

Ryszard W. Kluszczynski

University of Lodz, Poland

Abstract

There is a very interesting movement in multimedia art nowadays, with such artists like Simon Penny, Jane Prophet, Christa Sommerer, Laurent Mignonneau, Stelarc, and many others, working on artificial creatures, artificial life and intelligence. Virtual performances, and first of all, communication with those virtual beings seems to be one of the most fascinating aspects of experimental multimedia art today. In my paper I examine some art works as well as their theoretical context and some artistic attitudes concerning that subject.

Keywords: artificial, body, communication, cyberculture, interaction, multimedia, virtual

Cyberspace is now becoming a place where an expanding number of people spend more and more time. All kinds of human activities belong both to real and virtual worlds. Art is about to reach the end of the road taken at the beginning of this century which means that it is losing its materiality or physicality. A process of communication is replacing an objective work of art.

The broadening of the aesthetic field of the perception of interactive art with real behaviour in real space is paired with broadening of the sphere of symbolical behaviours. When mental activity is the only way of interacting with a work, coherence and aesthetic perception are given *a priori*. When mental activity is complemented with diverse forms of real participation (interaction), coherence of a work's perception may be achieved only by the behavioural saturation with the same qualities which characterise mental and emotional activity. Reflection cannot find its realisation only in a purely intellectual form. It has to be incarnated in gestures and movements. Real interactive behaviours should form a continuation of mental activity. Only then perception of an art work, which is understood in a new way, will acquire inner coherence.

For a long time now we have been living in a post-biologic era, although many of us do not realise this. The increasing number of phenomena constituting our lives is mediated, broadened or transformed by technology. Each person's communication with other individuals, with civilisation, with nature, with the sphere of value, and, last but not least, with herself/himself is carried out through extensive recourse to various interfaces, controls, crutches, amplifiers and magnetic cards. Living in real life we nonetheless spend a lot of time every day in cyberspace. The more frequently we inhabit both worlds, the easier we lose the ability to differentiate between them. They unite to form new realities called simulacra. Here no qualities exist which could enable us to distinguish between virtual and real forms.

Simultaneously its identity changes and it takes an open form of unstable process. New technologies become extensions of the human body and as such influence its identity. The body itself, the way it is defined, its history, its gender and substance also undergo multiple transformations, which has an immeasurable effect on our idea of identity.

Another important consequence of these processes is the appearance of the phenomenon of collective intelligence, which incorporates particular individual intelligences. The collective intelligence is not the resultant of intelligences of individual beings, which constitute its substance but seems to be their source and creative power. As numerous experiments in psychology and physiology of perception indicate, there are cases which influence our contact with the virtual worlds which do not give us the opportunity to control our own activities. Hertha Sturm for instance points out that while watching television we lack time to consciously integrate the assimilated pieces of information, and as a result we become victims to the external power of the audio-visual sequences which are too quick for us.

Individual intelligence, as has already been mentioned, must resist the pressure on the part of the collectivisation process. Apart from this it is confronted with forms of artificial intelligence, appearing in increasing numbers. What follows is abundant phenomena certifying the progress and success of research and experiments on artificial life. They in turn result in the global increase of interest in issues of corporeality. In fact new technologies (especially the virtual ones) change both our perception of the body, of its substance and borders and our attitude towards it. Most of all however, the body itself is transformed - it is operated on, it is transplanted, it is aided with artificial parts and implants, it is re-shaped and cloned. Body art of the cyberculture era, i.e. artistic activities by Orlan or Stelarc provide convincing evidence of the new status of the body.

Body and identity transformations as well as new concepts of life and intelligence indicate with increasing certainty that we are living through a period of extremely marked and radical change in the whole world we live in. The belief by eighteenth century philosophers in the permanence and stability of the human race is with rising frequency perceived as an obstacle in describing the contemporary world, since we are constantly transformed by our own inventions. It doesn't matter whether we like this or not.

The new civilisational situation of human beings and its new, widened environment, where the biosphere has been complemented by the technosphere, strongly influence the shape of contemporary culture. They introduce into it numerous forms, which all together may generally be termed cyberculture.

artists take up various issues related to cyberculture, devote themselves to structural and communicative issues and only in consequence open new perspectives and horizons for the public towards new virtual worlds

81

In this context, art has an important role to play.

On the one hand it prepares us for the approaching world, which differs strongly from the past. This world develops and takes shapes faster than the one we know. And the speed of the transformation, too large considering the stability of a structure undergoing acceleration, may cause its quick mutation or even disintegration (depending on the flexibility of the structure). Neither one nor the other is favourable for psychic health. It is conducive to stress and conflicts in the frame of social structures, where individual groups in different ways define their interests. Facing intensive acceleration of the transformation processes, the communities are divided by conflicts between tradition and innovation into hostile camps leading to disintegration and catastrophe than a complete system overhaul. In the situation where, in Derrick de Kerckhove's opinion, some of us move into the twenty first century with the psychical design of the nineteenth century countryman, an extremely important role for art is to adapt, create and conduct the rites of passage, and to accustom people to the new approaching world. I will come back to this issue later on.

The above mentioned processes do not and do not have to happen with artists' awareness of them and rarely are controlled or purposeful. On the contrary, the most interesting cases of art functioning as an adapting medium indicate that this function is carried out as if on the side, which is to say that artists take up various issues related to cyberculture, devote themselves to structural and communicative issues and only in consequence open new perspectives and horizons for the public towards the new virtual worlds. Artistic works localised on the Internet space accustom us to globalism. They also encourage us to be active as they offer interaction with the system, as well as are showing values of decentralisation and emphasising the need of freedom.

On the other hand, (multi)media art opens the hostile, rejected aspects of the new, technological worlds. By turning its (and so our) attention towards numerous and versatile problems, revealing doubts, questions and fears, it makes us realise that the new world is by no means going to be a Utopia. Nor even a safe shelter against known dangers or social diseases. On the contrary, they perceive new threats and a new collapse in the human dream of perfection. Moreover, it questions the meaning and worth of changes undermining both objectives, methods and results of the action. Only in the confrontation of these two stands and opinions can an acute and deep vision of the present and especially the future appear.

There is a very interesting movement in multimedia art nowadays, with artists such as Simon Penny, Jane Prophet, Christa Sommerer and Laurent Mignonneau, Stelarc, Michael Tolson, among many others, working on artificial creatures, artificial life and intelligence. Virtual performances and, primarily, communication with those virtual beings seem to be one of the most fascinating aspects of experimental multimedia art today.

Let us look at a few examples. Christa Sommerer and Laurent Mignonneau in the interactive computer installation *Phototropy* bring our attention to questions related to artificial life. They enable us to interact with artificial creatures - bionic insects, charging us - like in one of their previous works: *A Volve* - with the responsibility of their fate. It induces also a reflection on the complexity of communication processes. A similar approach is presented by Michael Tolson in his installation *Las Meninas*.

We can also meet works of this kind in the area of Internet art. A particularly interesting example of such a realisation is *TechnoSphere*, a joint work by a group of artists consisting of: Andrew Kind, Jane Prophet, Julian Saunderson, Gordon Selley and Tony Taylor-Moran (www.londinst.ac.uk/technosphere/index.html). This work allows Internet users to build from supplied elements (similar to the case of *A Volve*, or, better, *Genma* - another work by Sommerer and Mignonneau) artificial artefacts - virtual creatures. Once formed they exist in a quasi-independent way in the virtual expanses: they persist, create new generations of similar artefacts, and 'die'. Their creators receive e-mailed information about all the important events in the lives of the beings created and given names by them.

TechnoSphere also creates another level of communication: between various users, those who have created artificial creatures, coming together in mutual relations. In accordance with the character of the medium, the works of net art are developing primarily their communicative aspects.

It is worth also drawing attention to one of the authorial explications of the work described above, i.e. the one which talks about the fulfilling by *TechnoSphere* of the function of a rite of passage. Cyberspace is here understood as an organised mediation, in respect of the problem of the body and identity, between humanism and post-humanism, between an analogue creation and a digital one. As an introduction to a post-biological world.

Those recently made works are rooted in previous activities of such artists like, for instance, Lynn Hershman, or Simon Biggs. In their works (e.g. *Room of One's Own*, *Shadows*) the body appropriated by the look defines a fundamental, almost archetypal situation, when domination is revealed on one side and subjugation on the other. It is a symbol of conquest and bondage. A symbol of enslavement. The rebellion of the body, once it breaks out, is therefore conducted on a total scale; it is aimed both against its internalised controller - the self, the soul or the superego - and against its external guardian - the omnipresent, enthralling look. This struggle sometimes reaches the dimension of a search for rebirth, thus gaining the significance of self-realisation, reconstructing the recently annihilated subjectivity.

I mentioned already that the development of virtual worlds and rising of the cyberculture makes art about to lose its materiality. At the same time there are numerous works of art which present the materiality of the virtual. They reflect one another creating a dynamic, unstable whole.

Kjell Bjorgeengen, for instance, in his video installation *Shift* addresses the relation between the material and virtual worlds. Hanging on the wall, at regular distances from each other, there are 10 monitors in a row. The video image skims across the monitors without wanting to fix itself to any particular place. For a moment, the image only exists in the emptiness, the interval between the monitors. During its passage, the image is sometimes spread across two monitors, which shows that the source of the image is elsewhere than on the electronic surface on which it can be seen now and then. In this installation the image becomes more concrete and material than the monitors which support it.

Similar questions on the status of virtual beings are posed by Croatian artist Dalibor Martinis in his video installations presented at the *OBSERVATORIUM* exhibition in the Museum of Modern Art in Rijeka at the beginning of this year, and later in the Croatian pavilion in Venice. Installations presented within its scope represent various types of relations between the material and the virtual. Put together they create a paradigm of co-existence.

An illustrative example of this form of co-existence of the material and virtual in the structure of a piece is the installation *Eclipse of the Moon*. Here both spheres are combined in a dynamic relationship heading towards the state of equilibrium. Time and again the one or the other aspect gains over and influences decisively the form of the whole, but anyway each of those states is solely a transitional one and in some time it yields to another one, it eventually and inevitably recedes into a flow of incoming transformations.

Searching for and establishing a temporary and unstable equilibrium is now the main area of Martinis' artistic experiments. A game between the material and virtual has been with grandeur and in a virtuoso way realised in the installation *Circles between Surfaces.* The image and the narration here, apparently belonging completely to the virtual sphere, reveals its deep dependence from the material, the physical sphere of the work, but to a careful viewer it discloses its true character, that it is spread between the two spheres. The piece as a whole, in its two-dimensionality (material-virtual), becomes in this case a narration itself, and simultaneously it reveals the materiality of the virtual spheres and the virtuality of matter.

The other example comes from the Polish art scene. The group, *The Central Office of Technical Culture*, with its leader Piotr Wyrzykowski in a provocative and radical way raises issues of the place, function and value of technology in human life. Impersonal, anonymous arrangements of space and objects and techno aesthetics of images are accompanied by similarly anonymous manifestos and declarations in bureaucratic stylistics. The environment prepared by the C.O.T.C. is an ambiguously sanitised, cyberpunk vision of the new world made real.

The interests of Piotr Wyrzykowski concentrate around the body. For some years now he has made performances, single channel videos, and installations dealing with different aspects of corporeality. In one of his recent projects using VR medium viewers are encouraged to interact with his digitised body, to transform its shape, etc. In the environment made in 1994 he rejected completely both the idea of representation and interpersonal communication creating instead an audio-visual space of viewers carnal experience.

All the works referred to in this paper create a new space for artistic communication, in a framework within which virtual creatures assume the attributes of real beings and simultaneously real bodies becoming virtual. In cyberspace all is virtual and all is real. Hypermedia art communication provides all subjects with an ambivalent, real-virtual status undermining both their identity and self-consciousness.

References

Brook, J. and Boal, I. A. (eds.) (1995) *Resisting the virtual life. The culture and politics of information.* City Lights, San Francisco.

Kerckhove de, D. (1995) *The skin of culture.* Somerville House Books Ltd., Toronto, Canada.

Kluszczynski, R.W. (1995) (ed.) *LAB 5. International Exhibition of Film, Video, and Computer Art.* Centre for Contemporary Art, Warsaw.

Kluszczynski, R. W. (1996) (ed.) *Lynn Hershman: captured bodies of resistance.* Centre for Contemporary Art, Warsaw.

Kluszczynski, R. W. (1997) (ed.) *LAB 6. International Exhibition of (Multi)media Art.* Centre for Contemporary Art, Warsaw.

Kluszczynski, R. W. (1997) The material versus the virtual. On dialectics of Dalibor Martinis' Art. In: *Martinis - Observatorium.* Video/audio/interactive installations, La Biennale di Venezia. XLVII Esposizione Internazionale d'Arte, Croatian Pavilion, red. B. Valusek, Museum of Modern Art, Rijeka.

Prophet, J. (1996) Sublime ecologies and artistic endeavours. Artificial life and interactivity in the online project *TechnoSphere. Leonardo* 29(5).

Rucker, R., Sirius, R. U. and Queen, M. (eds.) (1993) *Mondo 2000: user's guide to the new edge.* Thames and Hudson, London.

Sturm, H. (1988) Perception and television: the missing half second. In: *The work of Hertha Sturm.* McGill University Working Papers in Communication, Montreal.

Ryszard W. Kluszczynski. studied literature, aesthetics, philosophy, art, theatre and film at the University of Lodz, and was awarded a PhD in 1987 (avant-garde art and film in Europe 1910-1939) and post-doctoral Degree (habilitation) in 1999 (art of moving image of the electronic age). He currently hoilds professorial posts at the University of Lodz; Academy of Fine Arts, Lodz; and the Academy of Fine Arts, Poznan, Poland. He has been a guest lecturer at numerous universities in Europe and North America and is the curator of national and international exhibitions.

This article first appeared in *Digital Creativity* 9(1) 38–42 (1998).

The next body and beyond: meta-organisms, psycho-prostheses and aesthetics of hybridity

Johanna Drucker

University of Virginia, USA

Abstract

A current trend in contemporary art is to explore the effects of technology upon the body. Exercising a sometimes perverse and sometimes anxious fascination, technological possibilities for the extension, replacement, or enhancement of the perceptual, functional, sexual, and/or psychological aspects of human subjectivity have found expression in a variety of modes of contemporary art making. These explorations touch on the representation of the body as machine, as well as technological metaphors and modes, to produce works which emphasise hybridity, meta-organisms, and prosthetic devices which simulate psychic functions as well as taking on organic, conceptual, and cognitive features of human existence.

Keywords: art, body, genetics, hybridity, technology

Current discussions tend to elide the idea of consciousness with that of subjectivity — as if the 'subject' were a kind of 'who's behind the wheel' driving a fully aware, self-evident person. There is also a tendency to treat 'the body' as some kind of *a priori* whole, a bounded unit, which serves as a giant sensorium, stimulus-and-response-data-gathering 'meat puppet'.

It seems worth reintroducing the psychoanalytic concept of subjectivity and its construal of the body into this discussion — since such a theoretical position contains a fundamental role for representation in the interweaving of consciousness, subjectivity, and the body. It is a basic tenet of psychoanalysis in the Freudian/Lacanian tradition that an infant's fragmentary sense of 'body' can only be constituted as a whole in an illusory manner, through the simulacrum of an image (Lacan 1977). It is this image — classically, the 'mirrored' representation, but in actuality, any symbolically self-representing image — that reassures the 'self' as a somatic illusion. It should be emphasised that this is at a pre-linguistic stage on the cusp of language formation — and that it is imago and not logos which has this primary function[1]. Human subjectivity, self-conscious self-identity, constructs itself in a dialogue between an illusion of authenticity (that the fragmented body is whole, real, and belongs to the 'I' which claims itself through that belief) and simulation (images which serve as self-representation and self-presentation). Thus 'consciousness' is constructed from illusions of the body's authenticity — images which present/represent the one thing you can never actually see as a whole — the somatic site of self-perception. Another implication of this relation between representation and subjectivity is that all bodies are to some degree virtual since they depend upon a representation to be rendered 'real' to their possessor. As sites of experience, sensation, and perception, bodies are utterly integral to mind — they are the source and site of knowledge — but they escape any gestalt of self-perception for conscious subjectivity except when they are available as a representation.

Current representations of anxiety about the body in relation to new technology have surfaced in the work of visual artists who aren't directly using digital or electronic media. These artists are exploring a fantasmatic imaginary realm filled with fearful curiosity about hybridity, mutation, techno-intervention — meta-organisms, psycho-prostheses, machinic interfaces, and tropes of an altered somatic condition. There are three trends I will touch on — without pretending that they provide a definitive map to this field: 1) the machinic analogy; 2) mutant hybridisation of the flesh; 3) abstraction of somatic identity into information as code.

The first of these has a long history. From the Greek myth of Icarus and Daedalus attempting to transcend the limitations of the human form through technological means to the work of contemporary artists with elaborate apparatuses for extending gestural movement or devices for elongating limbs, the desire to maximise the body's potential through some kind of prosthetic addition has been a persistent feature of human innovation and experiment in and out of the realm of art. A focused idea of the body as machine or anthropomorphic apparatus is evident in Eve Andrée Laramée's 1994 work, *Apparatus for the distillation of vague intuitions*. In this piece the machinic image is

> *... all bodies are to some degree virtual since they depend upon a representation to be rendered 'real' to their possessor*

manifest in a form which is both playful and nostalgic. It suggests a laboratory of new sensation, the licensed arena of invention (and I mean the commercial implication of the term 'licensed' to be felt here), unfettered and unchecked — in which the nightmarish lurks, but need not be overt, or even inevitable. Its systematicity is not functional. Rather, it elaborates in fetishistic form the varieties of means for the organisation of sensation, life support, etc. into a traffic of flows, controls, and devices. To quote Marshall McLuhan from *Understanding media* (1964), *Emergent technologies suggest compelling reasons for the flow of goods and services to be directed elsewhere in a continuing series of diversionary tactics.* (McLuhan 1964) And each transaction enters the economic as well as libidinal flow. The continual diversions suggest an excessive administration or bureaucracy for the managing of resources.

In Roxy Paine's 1992 piece, *Lusts*, the fabrication of the body as the machine quotes early 20th century mechano-morphs (such as those designed by Francis Picabia or Marcel Duchamp) in its hybrid intersection of industrialised apparatus and the human form. The machine renders human functions efficient, playing with the sexualised energy of the efficient pistons and parts, interlocking in ineluctable movements of repetition and reproduction. The result is not an eroticisation of the machine, rather, an interpenetration of the technological and erotic into a new synthesis of mutual definition and seductive engagement. The acts of erotic play are shown in tropes which suggest a correspondence between supposedly human operations (emotions such as 'lust') and repetitive actions associated with the mechanical domain.

Figure 1.
Roxy Paine,
usts, 1992.

Photo courtesy
of Exit Art,
New York.

If the body-as-machine is one persistent theme, machines which imply a body are another. The body is transformed by its subjugation/subjection to an already existing technological scenario; a narrative is suggested in a space which so specifically anticipates the body. The body assumes an identity as that which completes the techno-functional apparatus for which it is the servo-mechanism, inverting the humanistic order of things. Daniella Dooling's *Breathing space* (1991) plays on such overtly dystopic anxiety, readily regulated as a set of fears which can be turned into a manageable fantasy — that fantasy which leads to managerial solutions, something administered. In this double dystopia, the body has to be part of the machine to live. The image is of a futuristic somatic flesh-unit support system. The horrific effect is the result of a suggestion of an inefficient and constraining physical solution to a problem of survival combined with the doubtful reliability of an equally inefficient (but more deadly) social order.

Machinic fantasies of techno-extension reach an ad absurdum extreme in Alan Rath's *Hound* (1990). Beyond the evident irony of replacing the sensitive organ of smell with the insensitive monitor, there is another lurking threat made evident in the replacement of organic body parts with electronic equipment and that is the merchandising aspect. Areas of life which were once merely lived now come increasingly to be available for a service fee — looking , listening, sexual activity, and touch are now able to be extended over distance and into the virtual as image, text, sound, and telepresence, paid for as experiences available for consumption. McLuhan, again, wrote that if Archimedes were alive and looking for a fulcrum point of power he would say:

> I will stand on your eyes, your ears, your nerves, and your brain and the world will move in any tempo or pattern I choose.
> (McLuhan 1964 68)

He went on to note that we have leased all of these 'places to stand' to private corporations. A 'nose' is lent by the Turner network, a nervous system is a franchise offered by Rupert Murdoch, and the brain is brought to you by Disney. With every step of increased techno-production comes a corollary dependence on the corporate supply system and sponsorship extortion network which will, inevitably, come to lease us our dependence.

The second category of work images technology without a machine, recording the transformation of the flesh through mutation, as effect. This theme is fraught with anxious and grotesque imagery, such as the sado-masochistic seeming bonding of two young girl mannequins in Jake and Dinos Chapman's *Sad doggie* of 1996 or John Isaac's various sculptures of humans with potato heads or distorted alternatives to the evolutionary continuum, titled *In Advance of the Institution* (1994 to 1996).

Figure 2.
Heather
Schatz and
Eric Chan,
Touchstone,
(varied
materials),
1988.

Photo courtes
of the artist.

Even traditional media lend themselves to such extreme images. Alexis Rockman's hyper-realist paintings of polluted landscapes refer to the long tradition of picturing the natural sublime but here the entire biosphere has been corrupted. Mutation has become a way of life, as it always was, but the new adaptations transgress the old aesthetics.

The work of Orlan extends these activities of techno-transformation into a remaking of the flesh, turning it into something designed entirely as a product for consumption, later to be given a name brand identity. In one plastic surgery operation after another, each recorded as a video performance, Orlan reshapes her body in an image of a canonical ideal form — appropriating a mouth from one icon, her nose from another — to copy in the form of her flesh. McLuhan:

> *Style is the working arm of the aesthetics industry, its applied arts.*

And again,

> *In the electric age we wear all humankind as our skin.*
> (McLuhan 1964 47)

We can now paraphrase this: in the polluted age all human skin is worn as an electric apparatus, or surgically replaced as diversionary entertainment. A communicative surface, sensitised to receive and transmit the broadcast messages of an infinite entertainment network. The fragmented body is a ganglia, a nexus/clump in a global matrix getting its illusion fix.

Another artist who is well-known for his interest in taking the flesh and its transformation and invasion to extremes, blurring the boundaries of self and image, soma and representation, public and private domains of self-identity in presentation is Stelarc. One could say that life with the machine need not mean life as the machine. But setting a humanist-romantic nostalgia for a non-existent past against a techno-futurist vision of a totally electronic future is clearly a false opposition. Stelarc's pieces, such as his early *Third hand* (1981) in which a robotic arm duplicates and then performs the functions of a 'natural' limb to *Hollow body/ host space* in the 1990s, in which a micro-camera enters the body cavity through the digestive system to project the image outward, stretch the limits of such easy binarism. Machines no longer bruise the flesh, they are the flesh. From surrogate extension to technology turned inward — rather than as an outward

Figure 3.
Daniella
Dooling,
Breathing
apparatus:
outerwear,
1991.

Photo courtesy
of Exit Art,
New York.

many discussions which weave through McLuhan's *Understanding media*, the shadow text on which I've drawn repeatedly, a recurring theme is that of technology as extension of the human nervous system. McLuhan perceived that new patterns of mechanised repetition and standardisation colonised the interior life as well as determining social form. But then, at one moment, he suggests that quite possibly human beings are merely "the reproductive organ of the technological world" (McLuhan 1964 116). Terrifying? Maybe. But maybe just a useful insight. DNA makes and uses us. Not the other way around. Code dominates. Code storage in hot media. The flesh is a useful vehicle. Is it necessary or expendable? No moral arbitration takes place at the level of the somatic. Only use. Fears are the fears of an egocentric subjectivity. But this plays out in stress and violence in a societal hierarchy in which control of resources and power are conflictually determined and limited.

Another more elaborate cycle of history, genealogy, and manipulation of information into independent life or body form is being worked in the collaboration of Eric Chan and Heather Schatz. Their *Touchstone* project (begun in 1985 and continuing into the present) has given rise to whole elaborate families, species, and regenerative inbreedings of form in an endlessly mutating combination of elements. Beginning with a single *Touchstone*, they generated a set of glyphic primaries, elemental forms which are incidental and specific. These in turn are combined and recombined, layered in drawings on vellum to make patterns from which new forms are extracted. The governing trope is the genetic lineage of data as form, form as data, in an interchangeable mutuality, a generative bio-chemical imagery of production. And production is an apt term here because it succinctly summarises the intention and the outcome — which is to push the forms back into objects and products, all linked as if by the genetics of an organic relation into a corpus of

extension — this colonisation turns the interior into a new virtuality. Will Stelarc invade the central nervous system so that his next 'ride' will be into the optical nerve fibers so that it can project directly back through various techno-logical media as an image of its own self-observation?

The final category of current artistic activity is concerned with abstraction into information as code. At the micro-level this means an interest in aesthetics as genetics, production, and its lineages — an elaborate genealogy of information as form. Among the work, a body of productivity.

What then is the connection among all these things and what are the cultural implications of such artistic activity. In whose interests is such work produced? To what ends? The simplest of questions. The hardest of answers.

Clearly the technology inspires fantasies — nightmarish and not so nightmarish. Art expresses its anxiety about causes and effects, about the development of new hybrid conditions for experience, sensation, and form (consciousness too, but not in these cited circumstances — by the end of this paper and the work of Chan/Schatz, I've moved far away from subjectivity as well, and into an investigation of an extended metaphor of techno-biological fantasies in art). But there is another anxiety which shadows the fantasy of corporeal transformation, an anxiety about production and consumption. Or maybe it would be more accurate to say, consumerism. Whose body is made of these parts? And what is the source, the brand? What is the role of art? To make a comment? Or to produce an aesthetics of the new techno-body? If aesthetics has a function, is it only to render seductive and consumable the totalising images and texts of the new un-real? It is still only the fact that we are human that allows us to make the distinction between ourselves and the hybrid technology, but no simple binarism applies in age of mutant somatic existence. We are techno-instruments — and technology, like and as capital, has its own will and force. We are used and consumed. Without question. Need it be without limit? In the face of the seductive potential of electronic form we have to decide according to our own disposition and digital orientation, whether to give in to enthralment as consumers of illusion or become sceptics testing that illusory reality in order to 'unconceal' the terms of its production.

The continual need to reconstitute a somatic locus of subjective identity compels our oscillation between belief in the authentic integrity of the soma and the equally seductive desire for an ever renewed techno-produced illusion of mutating simulacra. The extent to which these ideas now intersect with new product lines in the marketplace of new illusions is another essential aspect of the rapidly emerging story.

Note

[1] Advocates of a fixed and determinative relation between knowledge and language perpetually dismiss visual representation as knowledge in all senses of the perceptual, conceptual, or semiotic.

References

Lacan, J. (1977) The mirror stage as formative of the function of the I. In Lacan, J. *Ecrits*, trans. Sheridan, A. W.W. Norton Co., New York, pp. 1–7.

McLuhan, M. (1964) *Understanding media*. McGraw Hill, Toronto/New York/London.

Johanna Drucker has published and lectured extensively on topics related to the history of typography, artists' books and visual art, and digital media. She is currently the Robertson Professor of Media Studies at the University of Virginia where she is Professor in the Department of English, Director of Media Studies, and one of the founding members of the Speculative Computing Lab. Her scholarly books include: *Theorizing modernism* (Columbia University Press 1994), *The visible word: experimental typography and modern art* (University of Chicago Press 1994); *The alphabetic labyrinth* (Thames and Hudson 1995), and *The century of artists' books* (Granary 1995). Her most recent collection, *Figuring the word*, was published in November 1998 (Granary Books).

This article first appeared in *Digital Creativity* 9(1) 19–24 (1998).

Virtual life: self and identity redefined in the new media age

Teresa Wennberg

The Royal Institute of Technology, Sweden

Abstract

In this article, the author discusses her virtual reality installation The Parallel Dimension and goes on to explore the conflicts of identity experienced when a person is confronted with VR as a total immersion. She suggests that the various questions arising through this experience may lead us to a more ambivalent concept of the self.

Keywords: CAVE, identity, immersion, reality, virtual reality

I fell asleep and dreamt that I was a butterfly. Now I no longer know if I am Chuang-Tze dreaming that he is a butterfly or if I am a butterfly dreaming that he is Chuang-Tze. (Chuang-Tze)

In January 1998 I was invited to the Centre for Parallel Computers at the Royal Institute of Technology in Stockholm (KTH) to create a Virtual Reality artwork for a so-called 'CAVE'[1].

The final result, the VR installation *The Parallel Dimension*, was presented to the public during December 1998.

The Centre for Parallel Computers is the Swedish centre for scientific calculations. It has an important supercomputing network, which is among the most powerful in Scandinavia.

The CAVE at KTH — or 'VR Cube' as we call it — is a 'total' VR installation. All sides, including the ceiling and the floor are projection screens. Large video canons project the images from all sides through back projections and with the help of mirrors. This means that the projected images are not disturbed by the shadows of the visitors, permitting a complete immersion in virtual space.

The images are projected in stereo to enhance the impression of depth. Each visitor wears LCD shutter glasses, which allow a view in 3D (each eye sees only one of the two perspectives). Glasses with special tracking sensors, as well as a pointing device or a glove are given to one of the visitors (Figure 1).

In order to navigate in the VR Cube, one person must wear the special glasses which hand over the direct tracking information to a separate computer. This computer's only occupation is to calculate the x-y-z parameters in virtual space, thereby constantly updating the position of this person in real time and of the projected images.

If there are several people at once in the Cube, those carrying 'normal' glasses get a slightly divergent point of view (hardly noticeable).

The construction measures 3 x 3 x 2.5 metres, accommodating up to nine people simultaneously, and thus opening up the possibility for a simultaneous collective experience. In order to allow back projection onto the floor, the floor was raised 2.5 metres to provide space for projectors and mirrors. The floor is made of 40 mm-thick acrylic glass and this glass is covered with the same fabric for projections as the walls and ceiling. One of the Cube's walls serves also as a large door, which is hinged on the outside and swings open to allow access to the room.

The system is run by a special graphic computer: a Silicon Graphics Onyx2 with twelve CPUs and 4 Gb of memory, 100 Gb hard disk and three InfiniteReality2 graphic pipes with two 64 Mb raster managers each. Each pipe manages two of the six surfaces.

The floor and ceiling are currently configured to run with a resolution of 1024 x 1024 pixels at a frequency of 96Hz. The walls run at 1024 x 852 pixels to keep the pixels square and to keep the resolution constant along the edges.

Many steps and phases are involved in creating a VR piece: technological innovation is a costly and complicated activity. Each discovery is preceded by a long process of trial and error. It is also an intellectual challenge to confront this new 'reality'. For me, as an artist, the most exciting aspect is the conceptual confusion with which VR confronts me. The total immersion in a virtually real environment has led to a number of unknown sensations, out of which many questions arise. It has given birth to a stimulating play of thoughts where the identity of self needs to be redefined.

In my VR piece, *The Parallel Dimension*, I concentrated on creating forms which look realistic while challenging our current way of relating to the conventional language of form. For this, I used sophisticated texture maps and unexpected constellations of forms or often perspectives of gigantic space (Figure 2). My artistic intention is always to stretch our concepts of reality. It is a challenge to create situations which, for example, seem to abolish the law of gravity yet look completely natural.

The Parallel Dimension is a metaphor for the human body, where every world represents an imaginary part, filled with strange forms, textures and light effects. I have especially worked with the idea of movement, particularly important in a virtual environment. I want the presentation of this work to be seen as a prolongation of the moving art forms, where the motion itself is an important expression of the artistic intention. Here the movement is three-dimensional and we can change the aspect of the forms and of the worlds at every moment and also go forwards and backwards in time. Thus the work is in constant transformation, which is the first step towards a new form of interaction.

The first and most important thing when we speak about virtual reality is the fact that we are no longer spectators in front of a screen, we *enter* the virtual world as Alice stepped through the looking-glass. We are no longer sitting passively in front of an alienating glass wall, we are standing up or moving and taking part in the action. Image has suddenly become space and we can move around in what we see.

We can approach all the objects as we please, turn around them, even put our head through their seemingly impenetrable surfaces and see what's inside. We can move around freely in this space: go forwards, backwards, change pace, stop, start again. We are moving in a situation which is adapting itself in real time.

We stand in a room which isn't a room but more like a gateway, where the visible

Figure 1.
The author in
the VR Cube
wearing the
'leader glasses'
and holding
a manual
tracking
device.

(Image by
courtesy of
the author)

— visible or hidden — that the visitor must find in order to return to *The Brain Chamber*.

The brain is the centre of our body, where information about the surrounding situation is received, synthesised, and revised. Is the situation safe, or is it dangerous? Can we relax, or should we be on guard? Is it day or night? How is the weather, the temperature?

In a 'normal' situation the brain processes all this information, ignoring some signals, paying attention to others, reaching a conclusion and making decisions about behaviour and actions. In general, the input is processed in a relatively calm and orderly manner. We have learned to behave rather well and to plan our needs in advance.

When we find ourselves in an unexpected situation, however, glands swell, adrenaline floats. We are more alert and concentrated. If the situation really seems out of control, still other aspects take over. We may react violently, sometimes even losing control over our actions, making false moves, wrong decisions. We easily go back to more primitive behaviour with uncontrolled outbursts of fear and anger.

boundaries are illusory. The physical limitation of the walls of the cube are soon forgotten as we are introduced to this other space. The rectangular shapes of the room dissolve into vast cathedrals or faraway horizons. Distance appears as in the real world, with the same relation to perspective: when things are far away they seem smaller. A small point at the far end in a space is thus experienced as actually being very far away — and physically it also takes a certain time to reach that point.

Our visit to *The Parallel Dimension* begins in a big, ochre-coloured oval room. The walls are covered with old-fashioned black-and-white pictures of the brain. This is *The Brain Chamber*, the central location, from which every move is directed. At each cardinal point, an animated screen is seen. If we come too close, it will absorb us and hurl us off to one of the parts of this virtual body. We travel like little particles through thin twisting 'veins' to the different locations: *The Heart & Blood Room, The Thought Cabinet, The Breathing Cathedral, The Flesh Labyrinth*, and through a secret passageway down to *The Dream Cavern*. Every world has an exit

Image has suddenly become space and we can move around in what we see

When we enter the VR Cube and are confronted with a virtual experience, we can establish that, from a physical point of view, we are still attached to earth. Our brain subconsciously registers that our feet are placed on solid ground, the pressure on the skeleton and muscle fibres feels 'normal' and the body weight is distributed like it usually is. If asked how our limbs are placed, we would probably answer, "I am standing up".

At the same time other parts of the body — eyes, ears and subsequently nerves and muscles in the head, neck and back — are bombarded with information about a different situation, for example: "I am flying at high speed, at high altitude, over an unknown territory". This message is stronger than the message telling us that we are standing on the floor. The eyes win out over the extremities. We believe more in the information that our eyes are sending us than in the information from the nerve endings in our feet.

The brain cannot combine these diametrically opposed signals. And so it is confused and our co-ordination falters. We can compare this experience to the feeling generated by a sensory deprivation tank, where the body is afloat in a salt solution, which rapidly makes one lose contact with one's extremities. There are no visual stimuli. The brain becomes a floating, humming centre, an isolated reception unit for the feeble and confused information that comes from our limbs. This is also a 'separate reality' where the brain is fooled.

Apparently the brain is easy to mislead. Is virtual reality more like a waking dream for the brain than a 'true' reality? In fact, we do find ourselves in a state that can be compared to that of a dream: we can fall, but do not hurt ourselves, we can advance with great speed but are nevertheless standing still. Contact with the 'known' world is broken in as much as we accept our presence in this new world. Of course, we can end the experience at any moment, open the door and return to our 'true' reality, but as long as we are in the Cube we accept the information given as valid. And the illusion is perfect: horizontality/verticality, depth/closeness, hardness/softness, transparency/opacity, surfaces, colours, light effects… all exterior attributes of the forms look right according to our customary visual norms.

Through the animated screen for *The Heart & Blood Room* we are sucked into a virtual vein and conducted in high speed to a completely red room. Blood is dripping and running on the walls. In the middle, an amorphous mass is laboriously moving, twitching, moaning. There is a throbbing sound. One is startled, curious, a little disgusted perhaps.

From *The Heart & Blood Room*, we travel back to *The Brain Chamber* by penetrating this metaphor for a pumping heart.

It is an interesting mental exercise to try to define this spatial confusion. Which reality is the true one? (What is 'truth'?) Does it depend on physics, or on what I experience with my senses?

Obviously, nerves don't 'think', they transmit. The eyes relay information about light waves and frequencies that the brain has laboriously learned to analyse and interpret in a special way. Exactly how it transforms these signals into images is a complex procedure that has yet to be explained.

But what is really interesting in the VR Cube is that when we are given two sensory inputs — "I am standing up" versus "I am flying"— the false one seems more real than the true one. The brain is simply not as clever as we like to believe.

In his notebook, *Zettel*, Wittgenstein asks:

How would it be if somebody seriously told me that he (really) doesn't know whether he is dreaming or he is awake?

Can this situation exist: Somebody says "I think I am dreaming now"; in fact he wakes up just after this, remembers this uttering from his dream and says: "So I was right!"

Imagine an unconscious person saying (for example under anaesthetics) "I am conscious" — would we say "he should know that"?

And if somebody in his dream would say "I am sleeping", would we say "He is perfectly right"?

Is a person lying if he says to me: "I am not conscious"? (And is he telling the truth if he says this being unconscious?)
(Wittgenstein 1967 85)

In *The Breathing Cathedral* we fly into an enormous … cathedral? … spaceship? … world?

A star-filled galaxy, with a great number of multicoloured semi-transparent spheres of

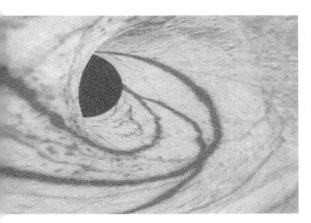

Figure 2. View from the VR installation 'The Parallel Dimension' 1998) by Teresa Wennberg. This image depicts a movement between 'The Brain Chamber' and 'The Thought Cabinet'. We are travelling at high speed inside a virtual nerve.

varying size, gives an overwhelming sensation of infinite space. A sound is heard, difficult to define, but rather pleasant and well-suited to this strong impression of immensity. (Many visitors claimed having a metaphysical or 'near-death' experience when moving softly through this calm and immense world.) We float in space ... or in the womb. A mixed feeling of freedom and apprehension as we advance majestically among the multitude of distant lights and passing transparent planets.

In the far end of this space, an eye-like shape appears. As we approach, the 'retina' turns out to be a narrow cone-like corridor through which we are squeezed into the centre and then swirled back to *The Brain Chamber.*

To go a bit further with this discussion, we can attempt to separate our concept of reality into different layers.

To begin with, there is the 'objective reality', which Kant referred to as *Das Ding an Sich* (the thing itself). This is the reality behind our reality, a realm which we cannot observe, where the objects might live their own life. This reality exists beyond the human capacity to measure in terms of time or space. We can know nothing about this reality, we can only suppose that it exists.

Then we have the 'known reality', the so-called measurable reality. It is the reality we relate to in our everyday life and nevertheless hardly ever define. Here a chair is simply a chair, with no deviations to bring the matter into dispute. A generalised and superficial use of the language is sufficient for referring to the objects.

Our daily life is based on relative assumptions about time, space and the objects in them. In order to live in any community, we need to subscribe to a great number of common expressions which we cannot constantly question, even if they often are based upon vague or even false references. A complex system of relativisation, used by all our fellow humans, creates the symbols we need on a daily basis. Everything has (and must have) a name, even if we question its meaning at times.

And now this new state, this new reality, this magic room where objects, though looking familiar, have yet another character. This room is closed but endless, and time exists far beyond the scanty restriction imposed by a watch. It's like entering a giant brain (Figure 3). VR is a mind expander. It confronts us with an extra dimension, that really exists. And here is the hook. In an instant, reality turns multiple, transcendental, vertical, non linear. We could be approaching a new philosophy of perception and of life: the relation to One could break up and thus a fundamental foundation of Western religion. Back to multiple gods?

In *The Thought Cabinet* we enter what at first seems to be a colourful forest. The trees look as high as the giant seqouias of Northern California. Soon we realise that these trees are in fact gigantic letters forming words and phrases. They are placed in such a way that we can wander between them, beside them, even walk right through them. Again, this sensation of being very small in a gigantic space affects the spectator, who soon discovers that the phrases are fragments from the famous monologue of Hamlet.

A soft voice reads the sentences with a humming sound. The exit is a golden arch at the opposite end of the room.

Time is an important basis of our mode

of perception. Einstein taught us that time is relative, depending on where we are and how we measure. It is also very personal: one minute is a short unit, but a minute can subjectively seem like an eternity. Depending on the amount of sense data we receive during sixty seconds, our experience of this period can be totally transformed.

When we find ourselves in a new environment, information intake is multiplied and our attention is at a high level (especially since we have a tendency to compare everything to our known world and search for our prefabricated definitions). In a situation where the body produces extra adrenaline and our senses are in peak performance, brain activity is much greater than it is when dealing with a familiar situation. We lose our normal apprehension of 'time passing'. This diverts our concept of reality and again time appears to be an elastic variable.

The difficulty in giving a correct analysis of this experience can be seen as a reflection of the difficulties in finding the language to explain what we are apprehending. Having the meaning before our minds is by no means a guarantee for being able to explain anything.

Here is where the conceptual crisis begins: I know that I am standing in a projection room and that the images and forms which are projected in the room are betraying my senses. I know that this is a virtual material and I know that it is created by a computer, thus is not what we can call 'concrete' reality. I know that I can turn off these images and go back to the other existence.

'I' am not fooled. But perhaps my brain is. Is that the same thing? Is my brain playing a game with me? Am I the one who is changing? Who am I?

This is an interesting question to pursue: what is the 'I'?

This question has been treated by most of the great thinkers. Perhaps David Hume comes the closest to an up-to-date interpretation when he claims that the 'I' is a long string of experiences — a great number of different apprehensions following one another with inconceivable speed, constantly changing and constantly in motion. Like a Buddhist, Hume sees consciousness as a kind of theatre, where impressions appear and mix with each other into an endless multitude of positions. We have no underlying 'personality' behind these moods that come and go — we are movement (Hume 1962).

Similar thoughts are also evoked by Flusser:

That what we call 'I' is a knot of relations, which, when unpeeled, reveals itself to have no hook on which these relations may hang...
(Flusser 1994)

In virtual reality, common sense may doubt part of the information, but some of the most important physical means we possess for collecting information from the exterior world are totally fooled. Shall we write off all this information as mental chimeras and sophisticated brain ghosts? Maybe, but 'I' believe them.

In the words of Lucas Manovich:

Throughout human history, representational technologies have served two functions: to deceive the viewer and to enable action, i.e. to allow the viewer to manipulate reality through representations.
(Manovich 1997)

Jean Baudrillard suggests that mass media operate in a manner contrary to the way they present themselves: they do not inform, they impose. They give out information, but people cannot respond. It is a non communication, an ongoing soliloquy which puts us in a state of insecurity concerning our personal choice.

Nevertheless, the contemporary citizen bases most of his visions of the surrounding world and its matters on televised images. Since television entered our homes in the 1950s, we have become visual slaves to its message: seeing is believing. When we turn on the evening news, we see electronic images of something that is

Figure 3. Birds-eye view of the VR Cube at The Royal Institute of Technology, Stockholm. This construction, which uses all four walls plus the ceiling and floor as projection screens, is the first in the world to permit total immersion.

happening far away from home, maybe on the other side of the planet. The truly fascinating thing is that television has created an absolute credibility with the concept of 'live' transmission — that the situation is going on simultaneously in the TV studio or on the war field. But if we really think about it, there is nothing whatsoever proving to us that it is neither 'live' nor 'true'. We just see a lot of images on a screen. What is revolutionary is that so many people are looking at these images simultaneously and talking about them as being part of a collective truth (which could be considered a collective hallucination). It is as easy to manipulate an image as it is to create one. But television has acquired such credibility that we accept the information it offers without questions. Will VR affect us the same way once it becomes an everyday experience?

The Flesh Labyrinth takes us to a construction of pinkish membranes as high as a three-floor building where we move mostly vertically. Virtual pieces of flesh obstruct the passage; the sound when touching them suggests a blow. This is a slightly claustrophobic experience. How do we get out? Find the hidden exit which is encapsulated in a blue ball, coyly avoiding an encounter…

So how come we are aware of the virtuality of these realistic visions and yet react as if they were really part of our external world? We are exposed to an increasing intrusion into all areas of life of the uncertainty and unreliability of the real, with an increasing difficulty to determine where to put the lath. The Swedish philosopher Gunnar Svensson goes even further:

Is there really an external world? The question may seem rather silly at first. The sceptic, however, asks for a justification of something we are all sometimes deceived by, viz. our sense experience. What guarantees that it is not always delusory? Common sense? Logic? God? Clearly, there is no obvious answer. Doubting the existence of an external world does not seem so silly after all. Why, indeed, accept that there is one?
(Svensson 1981)

Or, as G.E. Moore put it:
In order to prove my premises I should need to prove one thing, as Descartes pointed out, that I am not now dreaming. But how can I prove I am not? I have, no doubt, conclusive reasons for asserting that I am not now dreaming; I have conclusive evidence that I am awake; but this is a very different thing from being able to prove it.
(Moore 1953 149)

Perhaps the answer is that there are different levels of consciousness and different forms of the 'I', which all make up a part of what we would call our personality and our reality. Here we have the well-polished surface, the secret thoughts and the repressed instincts, the thief and the sex maniac, the liar and the flatterer, some kept down, some brought forward. But these various qualities all spring from the same brain.

We could think of our brain as a vessel receiving a constant information flow. The 'I'

97

could be seen as the recollection of this information, depending on our individual memory. 'Reality' is the interpretation we give to this information at every moment.

If then the brain decides with a majority of neural votes that we are flying — in spite of the fact that we are not — is it then so? Apparently we can no longer trust our classic brain-body-spirit concept. We are facing a major cognitive shift, where we will have to introduce a new way of conceiving our world, admitting that a double reality — or several simultaneous realities — can exist and be accepted as valid. Our bodily functions will not change, but our consciousness will.

Having tried all four visible doors, we're back again in *The Brain Chamber*.

The final visit is executed through the semi-transparent pillar in the middle of the room. One must discover this oneself; there is no exterior indication of it. But once we get the idea to penetrate the pillar, we are taken by an invisible elevator down to the last world: *The Dream Cavern*.

Dreams are images, sounds and strange sensations that bring us back and forth in our subconscious memory. Here, the images come sailing through the winding cave and the walls are made of more images, images everywhere and voices whispering mysteriously. Written messages float in the air. We read the word 'KEEP', which is almost invisible, then turn around another bend and read 'YOUR ILLUSIONS' ...

At one point in this hallucinatory but fascinating universe we see a burning circle, like the ones felines jump through in the circus. Inside the flames the word 'JUMP' is written. Of course we jump. And we return to *The Brain Chamber*.

Two simultaneous realities? One plus one equals one? Which life, which reality will eventually be referred to as the 'true' one? And — does it matter?

Over the past generation, virtual avatars of ourselves have multiplied ceaselessly. In the financial world there is a constant exchange of virtual money at the same time as film and photographic art portray scenes that never took place between people who never met. MUDs and similar worlds on the Internet are just one aspect of a metaculture which encourages different models, personalities and roles. Hundreds of thousands of people are creating virtual personas, living in groups of virtual societies with multiple identities, undermining the Cartesian idea of the unique subject.

The computer and the television have become machines of reproduction instead of production. Our culture is tainted by the appearance of a new absence of depth, by superficiality in the most literal sense of the word. We are experiencing the dissolution of the individual and a decentralisation of the subject — and the object.

In a very short lapse of time, Scandinavian cyberlife has increased incredibly. Sweden is a forerunner in the use of advanced electronic media, mobile phones, personal computers, and public use of the Net. Surfing is highly encouraged. In fact, Swedish daily life is more and more depending on computerised services. There are very few companies who do not work with computers in one way or another. We can order pizzas and do all sorts of bank errands, pay our bills, study all the way up to a PhD, make legally valid orders and, of course, correspond by e-mail with our friends and colleagues. The art of writing letters by hand is becoming obsolete and the Swedish post office is eliminating more of its customary services every month.

Anders Hector, research scientist at the Institution for Technology and Social Change at the University of Linkoping is working on a thesis about information habits. In a recent article, he mentions an American study which found that the risk of loneliness and depression is increased if one surfs on the Net for even just one hour per day.

Hector says:

Life in cyberspace is after all abstract and reality is concrete. The Net does not offer the same width of interaction with smells, tastes and

feelings. To surf on the Internet does not give the same feeling of social repletion as physical encounters between people.
(Hector 1998 11)

Of course, Hector is referring to a situation which, in nine cases out of ten, means accessing a two-dimensional Internet service on a small home computer. The impenetrable screen mirrors a communication, but is not really communicating. This is why the possibility of interfering with the forms, or affecting a given situation, is perhaps the most important part of a VR experience and where most of the research and development are focusing.

In this new reality, we are not only immersed, but we can interact with it — we are real-time actors and the role we play is that of a decision maker, a secondary creator. Depending on the programming — which will soon include the possibility of travelling within the Net — we can intervene in the scenario and change it to better suit our needs or wishes. We can move existing objects, add new ones, we can meet with and talk to others although they are not in the same room. In fact, we can totally change a given situation in a matter of seconds. This is a major change from passively onlooking at a closed scenario and it is perhaps the most revolutionary shift in computer-based communication. In the VR Cube, there is also the simultaneous collective and physical sharing of an experience (which has nothing to do with looking at the eight o'clock news).

But also here we confront a lot of intricate questions. When I place a secondary 'me' in a virtual board meeting — an alias representing my body and my opinions — who is the person moving in this new room? Is it my

People like to meet physically, to look at each other face to face, to shake real hands and feel, sense and smell each other

usual me? Have I divided myself into two? Is it a 'mental clone'? Is it all of me? To what degree is it responsible for its actions? Are its actions to be considered mine?

If my alias signs a contract — is it valid? Can somebody else direct this avatar of mine? Will we face different degrees of existence, one absolute and others more relative, with various degrees of personal responsibility? Of course, it is nothing new to have a personal representative or substitute. What could be intricate is if and when these aliases become autonomous and start making decisions on their own.

We will certainly have to invent new definitions of legal and moral order.

Virtual space is about to transcend the capacity of the human body to localise itself, to perceptively organise its surrounding and to produce a cognitive map of its position in a recognisable, outer world. We will rely more and more on electronic communication, which also means that we will be more vulnerable in case of a breakdown. If the line is disconnected, we will be lost and retarded. And perhaps without memory. The ultimate amnesia.

But even this may just be a small point. The main criticism of three-dimensional virtual reality could in fact be its lack of physical touch, of flesh and blood or solid matter, so fundamental to us human beings. This lack could indeed contribute to the aforementioned feeling of emptiness in cyberspace. Even with the data glove we cannot really touch the forms, however visually convincing they may be. We can travel, act and inform ourselves, but as long as there is no real physical encounter there will eventually be a feeling of unfulfillment due to the ephemeral quality of the experience.

Touch — is that the final step between the virtual and the physical world? Both Michelangelo's portrayal of God and Adam in the Sistine Chapel and Spielberg's film *ET*, where a divine finger reaches out to the mortal human, offers us a metaphor for the importance of physical touch. Most encounters, chats and business deals on the Net either end up with a personal rendezvous at some point — or whither. People like to meet physically, to look at each other face to face, to shake real hands and feel, sense and smell each other. It is a fundamental need for us to be with other people, it is part of our genetic heritage.

So, how do we solve this problem? Either we invent a new definition of the idea of 'touching' or we manage to create virtual substitutes that are as impressive as the visual and auditory information is now. The most interesting thing now is to see what kind of avatars we can come up with.

Can we manage to create virtual substitutes as impressive as a human being? Like in Gibson's *Idoru*, where the hero falls in love with a virtual girl, who only exists inside the computer (Gibson 1996).

My tip is that we will become so alienated from this harsh reality that we will eventually prefer the ephemeral company of virtual creatures and the timeless pleasure of virtual lives. Touch is a sensual experience, on a par with seeing but communicating with other centres in our brain. So far the computer experience is mainly a visual one. Will seeing overtake touching? Can we become so dependent on our eyes that other senses are reduced to a secondary position?

Time will show.

Notes

1 'CAVE Automatic Virtual Environment', a technique for projecting three-dimensional pictures on several walls of a room, originally developed by Carolina Cruz-Neira and Tom DeFanti at the University of Illinois in Chicago.

References

Baudrillard, J. (1995) *The Gulf War did not take place*. Trans. Patton, P. Power Publications, Sydney.

Flusser, V. (1994) On memory (electronic or otherwise). *Art/Cognition*. Cyprès/Ecole d'Art d'Aix-en-Provence.

Gibson, W. (1996) *Idoru*. Norstedts Förlag, Stockholm.

Hector, A. (1998) *Svenska Dagbladet* 19.9.1998, p. 11.

Hume, D. (1962) *A treatise of human nature. Book one*. William Collins, Glasgow.

Manovich, L. (1997) To lie and to act: Potemkin's villages, cinema and telepresence. *ISEA 97*.

Moore, G.E. (1953) Proof of an external world. In Moore, G.E. *Philosophical papers*. George Allen and Unwin, London.

Svensson, G. (1981) *On doubting the reality of reality*. Almquist & Wiksell International, Stockholm.

Wittgenstein, L. (1967) *Zettel*. Trans. Anscombe, G. and von Wright, G. Blackwell, Oxford.

Teresa Wennberg is known as a pioneer videomaker and for her complex multi media installations using computer-generated 3D animations. Since 1998, she has been attached to The Royal Institute of Technology (KTH). In 1998, the VR-cube was inaugurated with her VR-piece *The Parallel Dimension*. Invited by the InterCommunication Center in Tokyo, she created a new VR-piece—*Brain Songs (Welcome to my Brain)*— during autumn 2001.

Web site: http://www.nada.kth.se/~teresa

This article first appeared in
Digital Creativity 11(2) 65–74 (2000).

OSMOSE: notes on being in immersive virtual space

Char Davies

Immersence Inc., USA

Abstract

This paper discusses the original artistic intentions behind the immersive virtual environment OSMOSE (1995). The strategies employed to manifest them include the use of an embodying user interface of breath and balance and a visual aesthetic based on transparency and spatial ambiguity. The paper examines the medium of immersive virtual space as a spatio-temporal arena in which mental constructs of the world can be given three-dimensional form and be kinaesthetically explored through full-body immersion and interaction. Throughout, comparisons are made between OSMOSE and conventional design approaches to virtual reality. The tendency of such approaches to reinforce the West's historic devaluation of nature and the body is also discussed. It is suggested that this medium can potentially be used to counteract such tendencies. In the case of OSMOSE, an experiential context is constructed in which culturally learned perceptual/conceptual boundaries are osmotically dissolved, causing conventional assumptions about interior, exterior, mind, body and nature to be questioned by the immersed participant.

Keywords: immersive virtual space, nature embodiment, virtual reality

By changing space, by leaving the space of one's usual sensibilities, one enters into communication with a space that is psychically innovating … For we do not change place, we change our Nature.

Gaston Bachelard. *The poetics of space.*

1. Introduction

These notes were developed during the process of conceptualising and realising the immersive virtual environment, OSMOSE (1994–1995). As theory and practice, OSMOSE addresses a number of aspects related to the medium of 'virtual reality' that are often overlooked: these involve the very essence of the medium, in terms of immersive spatiality and the role of the physical body within its domain. In OSMOSE, I set out to create a work which not only communicates my own particular vision of the world, but which demonstrates the medium's potential to enable us to experience our place in the world afresh, or to paraphrase Bachelard, to change space in order to change our Nature.

2. As installation

OSMOSE is an immersive virtual environment, utilising stereoscopic 3D computer graphics and spatialised sound through real-time interaction. The central experience is that of the *immersant*, enabled through the wearing of a stereoscopic head-mounted display and a motion capture vest with breathing and balance sensor. During public exhibitions, this rather intimate experience takes place in the company of an attendant in a small private chamber facing on to a larger audience space of relative darkness with two luminous screens. This public space is filled with sound, as it is generated in real-time by the immersant's behaviour in the virtual space. One of the screens is a stereoscopic video projection of the three-dimensional world as it is experienced by the immersant, enabling museum visitors to vicariously witness each immersive journey as it takes place in real-time. The other screen bears the projected shadow of the immersant's body silhouette as he/she moves and gestures in response to the work. The use of this shadow-silhouette alongside the real-time video projection serves to poeticise the relationship between the immersant's body and the work, drawing attention to the body's role as ground and medium for the experience.

3. As a medium of expression

The desire to express a particular content or vision preceded all else in OSMOSE. The themes in OSMOSE, i.e. archetypal aspects of Nature, and the desire to dissolve boundaries between interior and exterior within the context of enveloping luminous space, have been the focus of my artistic practice — through the media of painting and 3D software — for more than fifteen years. My background as a painter, i.e. thinking in terms of simultaneous relationships rather than linear narrative, of ambiguous figure/ground gestalts rather than literal illustration, has profoundly influenced OSMOSE's visual aesthetic. Although I began in the mid-seventies as a representational painter and mastered the conventions of photo-realism (inspired to some extent by Aldous Huxley's call in *Doors of Perception* to recognise the "dharma-body in the hedge at the bottom of the garden"), subsequent exploration into my own extreme myopic (near-sighted) vision led me to abandon the photo-realist world of hard edges and solid surfaces for a world of enveloping space filled with ambiguous volumes of luminosity. This 'loosening' of a habitual reliance on external

appearances eventually led to OSMOSE.

While painting, however, the two-dimensionality of the painterly picture plane however became an insurmountable limitation to representing enveloping space and, by the mid-80s, I abandoned the medium of painting for that of 3D computer graphics — because this new medium offered the potential of creating in a virtual three-dimensional space on the other side of the picture plane. In 1988, I became a founding director of the software company Softimage and began to work with the company's technology for my own artistic purposes. Between 1990 and 1993, I produced a series of 3D computer graphic images titled *The Interior Body* series, all of which dealt with metaphorical themes which recur in OSMOSE. However, although these images were created in virtual 3D working space, they were output through photographic media as two-dimensional stills, thus defeating my original intent. And so, seeking a more effective means with which to communicate a sense of enveloping spatiality, I began to work with VR, or what I prefer to call 'immersive virtual space'.

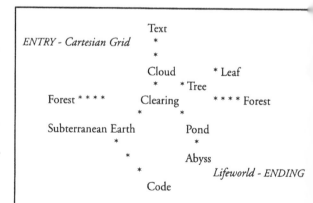

Figure 1: A simplified schematic of OSMOSE

4. As content

Simply stated, OSMOSE is about being-in-the-world in its most profound sense, i.e. our subjective experience as sentient, embodied, incarnate, living beings embedded in enveloping flowing space. Osmosis: a biological process involving passage from one side of a membrane to another. Osmosis as metaphor: transcendence of difference through mutual absorption, dissolution of boundaries between inner and outer, intermingling of self and world. OSMOSE as an artwork is motivated by the desire to heal the Cartesian split between mind/body, subject/object, which has shaped our cultural values and contributed to the West's dominating stance towards (and estrangement from) life. In this context, OSMOSE seeks to re-sensitise — reconnecting mind, body and world.

There are a dozen virtual world-spaces within OSMOSE. Most of these, with the exception of an introductory Cartesian Grid, are based on archetypal elements of Nature: they include a Forest, Leaf, Clearing, Pond, Abyss, Subterranean Earth and Cloud. Two other worlds, Code (containing lines of custom software used to create the work) and Text (my own writings and excerpts of relevant philosophical and poetic texts on Nature and technology), function as a conceptual substratum and superstratum parenthesising the work. All of these worlds connect to one another in various ways. There is also a Lifeworld, symbolising Life/Earth/Nature itself, which appears when it is time to bring the immersive session to a close. (see Figure 1).

> *OSMOSE as an artwork is motivated by the desire to heal the Cartesian split between mind/body, subject/object ...*

5. As visual and aural aesthetic

The visual aesthetic of OSMOSE relies on transparency and ambiguity. I have developed this aesthetic over many years of my own art practice, first through painting and then through making 3D computer graphic still images. Most of the various world-spaces of OSMOSE are represented poetically, in terms of their implicit, interior qualities rather than phenomenal outward appearances. Representation hovers midway between figuration and abstraction and figure/ground relationships are ambiguous to allow for open-ended emotionally-associative interpretations, rather than superficial illustration. Temporal transitions between world-spaces are slow and subtle, creating fluid, spatially complex, non-Cartesian relationships between worlds and, under certain circumstances, allowing multiple world-spaces to be experienced simultaneously. These various elements work together to loosen the mind's rational hold, dissolving the subject/object dichotomy and, in a dream-like way, shifting the immersant's mode of experience away from the everyday bias of eyesight to one that resonates deeper within the physical body.

The sound in OSMOSE is spatialised and interactive in real-time, responding to changes in the immersant's location, direction and speed. My goal was to have sound that was neither literal nor illustrational, musical nor sound effect-like, but which was, in equivalence to the visual aesthetic, aurally ambiguous. I also wanted the sound to be hauntingly emotional rather than abstract or chaotic. The composer and designer thus were faced with the challenge of spatially and temporally shaping a composition that would change in real-time according to the immersant's interaction. All the sounds in OSMOSE are derived from samplings of a single male and female voice, a compositional decision which subliminally re-affirms the presence of the human body within the work. The significance of sound in the design and experience of virtual spaces is often underestimated: in OSMOSE, sound and imagery have become one, amplifying each other.

6. As interactive sensibility

The interaction or user interface of OSMOSE has been designed to be body-centred, based on the intuitive, instinctual, visceral processes of breathing and balance. Through breath, the immersant is able to rise and fall in space with ease and precision. By subtly altering the body's centre of balance, the immersant is able to change direction. The use of these methods has been largely inspired by my own experiences of scuba diving and has many implications for the work as a whole, both on an instrumental level and in terms of metaphor. The methods are intended to reaffirm the role of the living physical body in immersive virtual space as subjective experiential ground. They are also intended to act as channels of communion rather than tools of control, encouraging the immersant to effectively 'let go'. As in meditation, the practice of following one's breath and being centred in balance opens up a profound way of relating to the world:

> Breath is a potent tool of overcoming dualism. *Physiologically, respiration stands at the very threshold of the ecstatic and visceral, the voluntary and the involuntary ... inside and outside, self and Other are relativized, porous, each time one takes a breath.* The air is constantly transgressing boundaries, sustaining life through inter-connection. One may have spent years studying the mystics on the unreality of dualism and this remains an abstract idea. But in following breath, one begins to embody this truth.
> (Leder 1990 178, emphasis mine.)

> *Balance is a question of centering. When we are properly centered, our experience of Being is in equilibrium. Being well-centered, we can encounter other beings in a more open, receptive way. Finding our center is a necessary step in the development of our ontological capacity to open ourselves to the larger measure of being and to encounter other beings with a presence that is deeply responsive. Coming home to our true center of being, we can begin to relax our egological defences, and begin to experience things outside the subject/object polarization. Being well-centered in Being is therefore at the very root of Gelassenheil, that 'way of being' in virtue of which according to Heidegger, we are going to be most favoured with a deeper experience of beings, and the presencing of Being as such.*
> (Leder 1990 274, emphasis mine.)

The chiasmatic interrelation between embodied being and world has long been a focus of western philosophical inquiry by Heidegger, Merleau-Ponty and others. The Buddhist and Neo-Confucian traditions of 'forming one body with all things', otherwise known as expansive awareness, also explore this interrelationship (Leder 1990, Callicott 1989). Such expansiveness of self towards other must be tempered by discretion however, if aggressive trampling across another's borders is to be avoided. This can best be accomplished through the recognition of 'difference' in addition to continuity, i.e. approaching the world with 'tact'. The implications of this *tactful* attitude, as well as its more usual absence, have been explored by various feminist and environmental writers, and is alluded to by Heidegger in his notion of 'releasement toward' the world (Conley 1993, Scheibler 1993, Plumwood 1993).

7. As space

The medium of immersive virtual space is not merely a conceptual space but, paradoxically, a physical space in the sense of being extended, three-dimensional and enveloping. As such it is

Figure 1.
Tree.
Digital image
captured
during a live
fly-through
of the
immersive
virtual
environment
OSMOSE.

an entirely new kind of space that is without precedent. I think of immersive virtual space as a spatial-temporal arena, wherein mental models or abstract constructs of the world can be given virtual embodiment in three dimensions and then kinaesthetically, synaesthetically explored through full-body immersion and interaction. No other space allows this, no other medium of human expression. At present, bodily access to immersive virtual space is most effectively achieved through use of a stereoscopic head-mounted display. Such an encumbered ap-

proach is disparaged by many because of its inconvenience and health risks. However, as a diver who dons a tank of air, mask, fins, weights and buoyancy-control vest to access oceanic space, I consider wearing a head mount a small inconvenience because it offers access (or at least the illusion of it) to this unique space.

As humans, we have bodily access to very few kinds of space: most people are in fact limited to the terrestrial, i.e. life as it is experienced on the surface of the Earth. Others, through recreational diving, have access to what

I call oceanic space. Most designers of virtual environments rely on everyday experience of terrestrial space to define the appearance of their virtual worlds and modes of interaction within. As a result, their virtual worlds are filled with hard-edged solid objects, horizontal floors and walls. Similarly, interface/navigational methods are biased towards walking on treadmills and driving with joysticks. Not only do these approaches to immersive virtual space limit its potential to recreating our everyday experience, but they tend to uphold the status quo and the conventions of a Western world view.

OSMOSE, on the other hand, has been influenced by my experience as a diver of deep oceanic space. Oceanic space is not empty but enveloping and sensuous, not horizontal but vertical, often beyond measuring. At depths of 100–200 feet of water over a 6000 foot abyss, the ocean takes on the quality of pure limitless space: fluid, enveloping, interior, embryonic. Distinctions between near/far and inside/out become blurred: a luminous speck can be a distant shark or rod misfiring in the retina of one's own eye. Divers do not walk or drive or fly or manipulate joysticks, but float, free from gravity, using subtleties of breath and balance to ascend and descend. Buoyancy control is an essential skill that enables divers to hover motionlessly in 'mid-air' and move subtly and sensitively, literally approaching the world with tact. In this way, diving can become a very calming, centring experience. Two years ago, I was diving above a blue hole in the Bahamas, floating between cold layers of lacy white cobweb-like algae and warm layers of ochre gas-clouds. I lost all sense of where I was, whether I was inside a dream or having a hallucination: there was nothing familiar, the experience was completely outside my earthly references, and filled me with exhilaration and awe. In this way, diving offers a means of changing space, as referred to by Bachelard.

There is another physical space which bears relevance to immersive virtual space. This is the subjectively-felt interior space of the self, i.e. where our minds and visceral organs project the immaterial imagery of dreams. Joseph Campbell has written that all human imagery arises from a single psycho-physiological source, namely the human imagination grounded in the material body (Campbell 1986). Although our culture has drastically separated exterior from interior, valuing the objective over the subjective, and mind over body, poets such as Rainer Maria Rilke and the philosopher Gaston Bachelard spent much of their lives reaffirming the interrelationship, the interplay, between exterior physical world-space and the interior spiritual space of self. The Buddhist and Neo-Confucian traditions also explore this relationship (Leder 1990, Callicott 1989).

8. As body

Both interior and exterior space merge osmotically through the body. It is impossible to speak of immersive virtual space or of enveloping physical space without speaking of the body, for the very experience of being spatially enveloped depends on having a centre of being. And for us, as incarnate beings, this centre is the body. It is only through the living organic body that we can access the world. And paradoxically, it seems that it is only through the body that we can transcend the body. My concerns with the body in immersive virtual space are not with its objective representation, i.e. how it is perceived by others, but rather how the immersant's mind and body are subjectively felt, how the immersant senses his or her own interior body as a centre-of-being within immersive space. By its very nature, immersive virtual space invites full-body kinaesthetic exploration, leading to deeper engagement than that involving just the mind.

I believe that it is only through the body, through body-centred interfaces (rather than devices manipulated at arm's length) that we can truly access this space and explore its potential. Such emphasis on the body's essential role in immersive virtual space may be inherently female. The whole notion of space as enveloping a body at its centre is probably feminine rather than masculine, as may be the desire to use this technology to re-integrate, re-sensitise, and re-affirm life itself.

OSMOSE has been deliberately designed as a solitary immersive experience. Use of a head-mounted display to evoke a sense of full body envelopment, a separate immersion chamber, and the overall hush and darkness of the public area tend to heighten this sense of solitude. My intent was to construct a site whereby participants could enter a state of calm and contemplation rather than hyperactivity, of self-reflection rather than linking up with other people. According to Bachelard, "… through their 'immensity' these two kinds of space — the space of intimacy and world space — blend. When human solitude deepens, then the two immensities touch and become identical."

The paradox of immersive virtual space is that the immersant feels embodied and disembodied at the same time. In OSMOSE this paradox is amplified. After a certain period of immersion (usually about ten minutes), various conditions related to the imagery, luminosity, semi-transparency, spatial ambiguity, slow subtle transitions between worlds, evocative resonant sounds, along with solitude, deep breathing and maintaining one's centre of balance within the space all combine to create a suspended dreamlike state in the immersant's mind, which is experienced as a distinct shift of awareness as he or she lets go of the rational urge to control, and boundaries between inner, outer, mind, body, space and time begin to dissolve.

9. As immateriality and temporality

Another key aspect of immersive virtual space is its immateriality, i.e. its capacity for containing three-dimensional representations of ideas or metaphors which cannot exist physically in the real world. This quality differentiates immersive virtual space from two-dimensional media such as painting, photography, film and video and also from three-dimensional media such as sculpture and theatre, in that its virtually embodied forms have no solidity. In OSMOSE, such immateriality is heightened through the use of transparency and translucency and by enabling immersants to float through things, so that material barriers between self and world disappear.

OSMOSE also attempts to encompass a temporal dimension, by the use of particle flows, streaming through the various world-spaces to represent the flows of rivers, root nutrients, and so on. In addition to the immersant's more obvious experience of real-time interaction and movement within the space, there is a more subtle, visual transformation. This is achieved through the use of multiple semi-transparent objects and textures, which pass by one another, in front or behind, in relation to the immersant's changing point of view as he/she moves through the space. The ensuing perceptual ambiguities allow the experience to become very personal, actively engaging the participatory imagination of the immersant.

10. As nature

It is important to address here the relationship in OSMOSE between Nature and technology. In this context, by *Nature* I mean that which is born, not-man-made, i.e. the living flowing world around us, not the cement and pavement and plastic and steel that surround us in cities but rather earth and rivers and forests and fields. These elements have a deeply life-affirming power, because they are not-us, and are the source from which we came and to which we will return. As technology, OSMOSE does not seek to replace Nature. Immersion within OSMOSE is not a replacement for walking in the woods. OSMOSE is a filtering of Nature through an artist's vision, using technology to distil or amplify certain interpretive aspects, so that those who enter OSMOSE can see freshly, can become re-sensitised, and can remember what it's like to feel wonder. In reminding people of the extraordinariness of simply being alive in the world, OSMOSE acts as a spatial-temporal arena where we can perhaps re-learn how to 'be'.

11. In context

The context in which OSMOSE is situated is of prime importance. Our culture's privileging of mind over matter has led to devaluation of the body, as well as of women and various 'others'. Historically, this world-view has contributed to the plundering of non-human beings and their habitats as objects for human use: the negative implications of this stance are becoming ever more apparent as evidence of worldwide environmental degradation increases. As 'unspoiled' unmediated Nature recedes from our lives through urbanisation of exploding human populations and habitat destruction, there is evidence that while the biological consequences for many species (including ourselves) are devastating, the effects may be psychologically damaging as well. This premise, known as the Biophilia Hypothesis, suggests that the increasing loss of access to Nature — as a source of our human spirituality — may prove to be at the root of our collective psyche's deepest wounds (Wilson 1993).

As a culture, we are on the cusp of a new technological paradigm: the emergence of cyberspace. As a means of global communication it will alter our world significantly. We must however be wary: as a realm ruled by mind, cyberspace is the epitome of Cartesian desire, in that it enables us to create worlds where we have total control, where the presence of aging mortal flesh and animal-others is absent, where there is, to paraphrase Laurie Anderson, no "dirt". Popular and media-hyped expectations of 'virtual reality' seem to reflect a longing to transcend the limitations of our physical surroundings and, indeed, its long-term

effect may be to seduce us to turn away en masse from our bodies and Nature, enchanted and distracted while we continue wasting the resources that sustain us and erasing the futures of countless other-beings on the Earth. Given the cultural context, I believe that this desire to escape the confines of the body is symptomatic of an almost pathological denial of our materiality and mortality. For me, it is even tempting to suggest that belief in artificial intelligence and silicon as a means of delivery into immortal omnipotence on some other Eden is but a testosterone-induced dream.

Many forms of digital media offer evidence of dominant Western values. In its most prevalent form, virtual reality can be considered to be "a literal re-enactment of Cartesian ontology" (Coyne 1994, Gigliotti 1993) representing the human subject as an omnipotent and isolated viewpoint, "an island of consciousness in a sea of insensate matter" (Leder 1990) manoeuvring in empty space and probing objects with an acquisitive and most often masculine hand (Tikka 1994). Most 3D graphic techniques are laden with conventions such as Cartesian space which have been inherited from the Western scientific and military paradigm. The conventional 3D computer graphic aesthetic relies on polygonal textured-mapped models — or what I call hard-edged solid objects in empty space — a combination of low-level mimetic realism with emphasis on surface appearance, Cartesian space and Renaissance perspective, all of which reinforce a dualist way of seeing the world in terms of mastery and control (Jones 1989, Wright 1989). Commercial computer games approach interactivity as a means of empowering the human subject through violence and aggression (Cornwall 1993). These conventional approaches to digital media reflect our culture's Cartesian world-view, with its tendency to reduce the world and its myriad of inhabitants to 'standing-reserve' for human consumption (Heidegger 1977).

12. Conclusion

OSMOSE approaches these issues by seeking to use immersive virtual space and the technology associated with it as a means of resisting the trajectory described above, as a way of acting artistically against the biological, ecological, and spiritual impoverishment of our age. OSMOSE approaches computer technology as an expressive instrument (not value-free but one whose conventions can potentially be subverted) to access another kind of space, a paradoxically virtual/physical space — that, yes, is entirely of human making, but which, because of its various unique properties, has the potential to act as a site, as a place, where artists can project their visions of the world — so that people might experience another kind of 'being', relatively unbound by everyday cultural assumptions. Instrumentally, my goal has involved developing the visual, aural and interactive aesthetic capable of creating the context for such experience — and in so doing, demonstrate the potential of immersive virtual space as a medium for paradoxically reminding us of our place in the world.

In some ways, OSMOSE is an expression of longing. The desire to reaffirm our essential physical and spiritual inter-connectedness, to heal the estrangement between ourselves and Nature, between ourselves and 'being', is a germinal force behind OSMOSE. If those who enter OSMOSE can experience, however fleetingly or ephemerally, a sense of self, of being, of being alive within an enveloping world, of surrendering the desire for control in exchange for experiencing wonder — returning afterwards to the real world with greater serenity — then OSMOSE will have achieved its most fundamental goal. Speaking in terms of initial public response to the work, in certain ways OSMOSE has succeeded: immersion within its space is often experienced as exhilarating yet grounded, disembodied yet physical. For many the experience is deeply personal. In the words of one immersant:

OSMOSE heightened an awareness of my body as a site of consciousness and of the experience and sensation of consciousness occupying space. It's the most evocative exploration of the perception of consciousness that I have experienced since I can't remember when.
(Karim 1995)

OSMOSE Credits: John Harrison, custom VR software; Georges Mauro, computer graphics; Dorota Blazsczak, sonic architecture/programming; Rick Bidlack, sound composition/programming. Produced by Softimage Inc. 1994–1995.

Postscript

This is a revised version of a paper originally presented at the Sixth International Symposium on Electronic Arts (Montreal) in 1995, when OSMOSE was first shown to the public. Since then I have written two other papers on OSMOSE, one on the technical aspects of its construction and one on the paradoxical effects of immersion on participants. (See References)

References

Bachelard, G. (1969) *The poetics of space*. Beacon Press.

Bishop, P. (1990) *Greening of psychology: vegetable world in myth, dream and healing*. Spring Publications.

Callicott, J.B. and Ames, R.T. (eds.) (1989) *Nature in Asian traditions of thought*. SUNY Press, Albany, New York.

Campbell, J. (1986) *The inner reaches of outer space: metaphor as myth and as religion*. Harper and Row, New York.

Conley, V. (1993) Preface / Eco-subjects. In Conley, V. (ed.) *Re-thinking technologies*. University of Minnesota, Minneapolis.

Cornwall, R. (1993) From the analytical engine to Lady Ada's art. In Druckrey, T. (ed.) *Iterations: the new image*. MIT Press, Boston.

Coyne, R. (1994) Heidegger and virtual reality. *Leonardo* 27(1).

Davies, C. (1998) Changing space: VR as an arena of being. In Beckman, J. (ed.) *The virtual dimension: architecture, representation and crash culture.* Princeton Architectural Press, Boston. Also published (as a paper-in-progress) in Ascott, R. (ed.) *Consciousness reframed: art and consciousness in the post-biological era.* Proceedings of the First International CAiiA Research Conference, University of Wales College Newport.

Davies, C. and Harrison, J. (1996) Osmose: towards broadening the aesthetics of virtual reality. *ACM Computer Graphics: Virtual Reality* 30(4).

Evernden, N. (1985) *The natural alien: humankind and environment.* University of Toronto Press, Toronto.

Gaudin, C. (1987) *On poetic imagination and reverie: selections from Gaston Bachelard.* Spring Publications.

Gigliotti, C. (1993) *Aesthetics of a virtual world: ethical issues in interactive technological design.* Doctoral dissertation, Ohio State University.

Harrison, R.P. (1992) *Forests: the shadow of civilization.* University of Chicago, Chicago.

Heidegger, M. (1971) What are poets for? In *Poetry, language and thought.* Harper and Row, New York.

Heidegger, M. (1997) *The question concerning technology.* Harper and Row, New York.

Huxley, A. (1954) *Doors of oerception.* Harper and Row, New York.

Izutzu, T. (1975) *The interior and the exterior in Zen Buddhism.* Spring Publications.

Jones, B. (1989) Computer imagery: imitation and representation of realities. *SIGGRAPH'89 Art Show Proceedings.* ACM SIGGRAPH.

Karim, Y. (1996). Letter to the author.

Leder, D. (1990) *The absent body.* University of Chicago Press, Chicago.

Plumwood, V. (1993) *Feminism and the mastery of nature.* Routledge, New York.

Rilke, R. M. (1992) *The Duino elegies.* Norton.

Scheibler, I. (1993) Heidegger and the rhetoric of submission: technology and passivity. In Conley, V. (ed.) *Re-thinking technologies.* University of Minnesota, Minneapolis.

Tikka, H. (1994) Vision and dominance: a critical look at interactive systems. *ISEA'94 Proceedings.*

Wilson, E.O. and Kellert, S. (eds.) (1993) *The biophilia hypothesis.* Island Press.

Wright, R. (1989) The image in art and computer art. *SIGGRAPH'89 Art Show Proceedings.* ACM SIGGRAPH.

Char Davies has achieved international recognition for her work in virtual reality. Integrating real-time stereoscopic 3-D computer graphics, 3-D localised sound and user interaction based on breath & balance, the immersive environments Osmose (1995) and Ephémère (1998) are world-renown for their artistic sensibility, technical innovation, and powerful effect on participants.

Recent honours include an Honorary Doctorate of Fine Arts from the University of Victoria, British Columbia (to be presented in June 2002) and a Regent's Lectureship from UCLA (February 2002). Davies is currently a Visiting Scholar at the University of California – Berkeley (Center for Design Visualization), and an Artist in Residence at the Emily Carr Institute of Art and Design in Vancouver.

She is based in Montreal and San Francisco: in addition to her artistic and technological research in virtual environments, Davies cares for 400 acres of land in rural Quebec, the 'real' environment that is the source of inspiration for much of her work. More information can be found at http://://www.immersence.com

This article first appeared in
Digital Creativity 9(2) 65–74 (1998).

The Sadeian interface: computers and catharsis

Mike Phillips

University of Plymouth, UK

Abstract

This paper explores the limitations of contemporary interface design and offers the potential of more profound forms of interaction by drawing on the rich and much older heritage of interactive art. Whilst HCI design is preoccupied with making the computer more simple to use, installation work, kinetic sculpture, and interactive multimedia art forms have generally been more concerned with the predicament of human/technological negotiation, whilst remaining a salient form of human communication. HCI activity sets out to make the complex systems of computing easy to understand and use, whilst interactive art often uses simple technology to make complex, inspiring and esoteric statements and experiences. In many ways the more simple and 'low resolution' the technology the more immersive, acute and intimate the experience. 'Low resolution' examples such as telephone-sex-lines are explored alongside more immersive systems, such as bio-feedback interfaces, and other interactive experiments drawn from the 'technic' strand of art history.

Keywords: design, interactive, interface, metaphor, pain

1. A hammerphor a fossilised metaphor

Metaphor is often used as the key to achieving greater accessibility by providing users with a 'familiar' way of negotiating through the computer's complexity. In nearly all cases the application of metaphor within interface design has severe limitations, given the suspension of disbelief can only be stretched so far. However, one of the often ignored problems with the use of metaphor is that, as well as reducing the potential of a computer to fit known human experience, it reduces the 'real' object or process to a simplistic level in order that its characteristics can be transferred to the computer. By reducing the 'real' world to simple icons and actions designers ignore a fundamental element of human activity, namely the continual negotiation with the real world. By refining human experience of the real world and siphoning off these complex interactions, the resulting interface will inevitably be sterile and uninteresting. It is the difficulty with which humans negotiate the real world that makes life interesting and engaging. The more difficult the activity the more rewarding the gains. The 'no pain, no gain' approach to interface design discussed within this paper offers the potential of enabling deep, profound and cathartic experiences through human computer interaction.

Person A: *Pass me the hammerphor.*
Person B: *What's a 'hammerphor'?*
Person A: *Knocking in nails!"* [1]

Person C: *Pass me that metaphor.*
Person D: *What's a 'metaphor'?*
Person C: *A metaphor is:*

n. a figure of speech in which a word or phrase is applied to an object or action that it does not literally denote in order to imply a resemblance... [2]

In practice the Graphical User Interface (GUI) hardly deserves the label of 'metaphor'. Likewise the term 'icon' is a crass simplification, stripped of its rich spiritual and artistic heritage. The technological determinants that require us to look at pretty pictures in order to understand, not only reduce the richness of the world to two dimensions, but also reduce meaning to a level of simplicity that ignores the rich discourse of literature and philosophy. I am as guilty as the next designer, in that I have sweated blood for hours trying to invent a new 32x32 pixel icon for that obscure screen interaction, but in the end what I and most designers have come up with is catachresis, not metaphor. They may signify something, although most fail to do that beyond marking a space on the screen that marks the spot where the interaction takes place, but as metaphor they are dead and fossilised.

The screen is a 'window' on the internal workings of the computer or a 'mirror' which reflects our intentions and ambitions. We see on the surface our aspirations and failures, a point of contact, an intimacy between the computer and the user. If this intimacy is framed by dead and fossilized metaphors how clear will the visions revealed or reflected be? A better model might be the successor to the *Phantasmagoria* magic lantern show, the theatrical optical illusion employing virtual images in an angled sheet of glass and variable illumination, the *Pepper's Ghost*. In its day (circa 1860) the illusion was so convincing that even the scientist Michael Faraday found it incomprehensible, until he actually touched the glass. Here we have an illusion that is both mirror and window. By varying the illumination in the spaces behind and in front of the angled glass sheet composite images can merge and fade. When looking at the computer screen the user sees, through varying degrees of mental illumination, the

reflection, the human computer composite, and the computer. The 'virtual' image in this scenario applies to the user rather than the computer, the screen is the sheet of glass and the digital content is the true image. Like the window and mirror metaphor above, our reliance on the interface between vision and language lies at the heart of the GUI design problem. If metaphor is

a figure of speech in which a word or phrase is applied to an object or action that it does not literally denote in order to imply a resemblance,
a rich process that breathes through interpretation, then the reverse process of trying to represent literally an action through an 'icon' must surely produce stagnant and ultimately meaningless metaphor.

2. Three in the bed and the little one said...

Human computer interaction is a complicated area of study and practice, which combines two rather uneasy bedfellows, psychology and computer science, and often ignores a third partner, 'creative' design. Even when employing troilistic design, the focus of most interface design is the screen and the fairly immediate layers in front (interaction initiated by the user) and behind (impact of user activity on internal processes). Multimedia communication technologies do not simply present technical challenges, they create a range of new, conceptual, linguistic and philosophical problems requiring solutions that feed upon the expertise and experience of a multidisciplinary mind. Traditionally the 'graphic' designer has been the poor relation in the HCI designer threesome, reduced to making things look 'nice', an activity that can be seen by the other two disciplines as being trivial. If the role of the creative designer is just to make visual catachresis then the accusation is justified.

Part of the reason why interface design is seen as trivial decoration is the inability of creative designers to articulate the creative process. Creative design process generally falls outside the protocol of the scientific method, into 'black box' territory. It cannot be described, adequately measured or proved through experiment. The knowledge and understanding of media form is manifest through the making of media, so that unlike scientifically-based disciplines little effort is generally made to articulate the processes employed in media creation. The output is often as undefined as the input, neither top-down or bottom-up design. Discourse surrounds its consumption and informs its production, but this is not objective, empirical or experimental. Indeed the intent with many media forms is to bypass the viewer's objectivity and generate a new experience.

The images have no narrative meaning, they are rather a series of visual stimuli intended to create a psychological drama within the viewer, 'rousing the mind by osmosis without verbal transposition'.
(Curtis 1972)

The interactive montage of information, text, sound, image, animation, digital video, infused with seductive qualities promises to revolutionise the way people use and work with computers. Conventional media production, computing and traditional communication forms will wither in the bright light of these emerging technologies, unable to compete with this rich new wave of audio-visual consumption. New media engenders new affordances. The elements that are used to construct new media forms have an established vocabulary, and a discourse exists that may adequately describe the integration of these elements. Media theory

The legacy of the media elements that construct new media provide a safety net (to be kind) or a safety blanket (to be truthful) for digital designers

offers a provocative and juicy language to articulate and understand the non-objective complexities of static and time-based imagery. One of the reasons traditional (i.e. old) HCI is such a moribund subject is that it has failed to acknowledge that it is dealing with systems of human emotional system and meaning, and not just a system of measurable cause and effect. New media is concerned more with sounds and visions than with bits and bytes.

An enduring criticism of new media products is their lack of emotional engagement, and the fact that people generally find a greater sense of immersion in a book than they ever do in info/edu-tainment products. It is of course possible to account for this by recognising the fact that verbal/written communication has been an integral part of human evolution, whereas integrated and interactive media has only been possible for two decades. Any audience must be forgiven for not understanding the complexity of new media forms, the failure of new media to touch must surely be the fault of the audience? It couldn't possibly be that 'writers' are considerably better at 'writing' than 'New Media' designers/makers are better at making 'New Media'?

3. 'Simile, you're on candid camera...'

Digital media forms have a 'heritage', the integration and saturation of media forms in the cultural environment ensures that casual consumers take the complexity of audio visual language, and the distributing technology, for granted as a continuum of this heritage. Screen design can trace a clear lineage through print, graphic design, typography, photography, and other 2D forms of representation. The evolution of aesthetic forms is based on a symbiosis of technological and cultural determinants: painting provided an aesthetic for photography, print-making (etching) inspired the process; illuminated texts inspired metal type, and the mechanical press informed the structure of page layout; theatres impact on cinema and cinemas impact on TV, and TV's impact on video… Complex languages of editing, camera angles and effects have evolved to the point where we may even think in film forms. As yet we have no obvious 'interactive' heritage, apart from the short history of data navigation. We can look to the theatre for inspiration, we can look to architecture for spatial models, psychology for theoretical underpinning, in fact we can see models and metaphors in everyday human interaction and the structures that contain them. It is the convergence of these design practices that should be forcing a paradigm shift to a holistic media experience rather than a fragmented mish-mash of muddled aesthetics.

Our fine arts were developed, their types and uses were established, in times very different from the present, by men whose power of action upon things was insignificant in comparison with ours. But the amazing growth of our techniques, the adaptability and precision they have attained, the ideas and habits they are creating, make it a certainty that profound changes are impending in the ancient craft of the Beautiful. In all the arts there is a physical component that can no longer be considered or treated as it used to be, which cannot remain unaffected by our modern knowledge and power. For the last twenty years neither matter nor space nor time has been what it was from time immemorial. We must expect great innovations to transform the entire technique of the arts, thereby affecting artistic invention itself and perhaps even bring about an amazing change in our very notion of art.
(Valéry 1964)

We have a gleaming new technological pen with hyper-linked ink, and yet we insist on reproducing our monosyllabic utterances, a Cyclops with binoculars, cave painting with lasers, we lack the language and thought process to manipulate and articulate. By viewing the computer as a digital 'paintbrush' we are denying the development of the technology's quintessential aesthetic, suppressing emergent form. The legacy of the media elements that construct new media provide a safety net (to be kind) or a safety blanket (to be truthful) for digital designers. Typographers have been thinking in metal type and strips of lead for too long, photographers are too 'fixed' by their developer, and writers too typecast by their own scripts. The most significant factor in the demise of new media publishing in the 90s (apart from bad management) was the dominance of graphic designers in defining the look and feel of products. Two-dimensional minds shovelled two-dimensional 'book' content into the screen dimension and generated endless supplies of pseudo-metaphors held together by lashings of decorative interface. Unable to make the dimensional leap through to the 3rd dimension, towards the 4th (temporal), and finally the 5th dimension of interaction, the new media industry all but imploded under gravitational pressures of its two-dimensional reality. In general art and design education continues to produce one-dimensional, single discipline practitioners who continually fail to think and act on a multidimensional level.

So, we are left with an interface that consists of an optical illusion that reflects back to us our inability to deal with new media other than in cheap metaphor: 'its a bit like film', 'its a bit like text', 'its a bit like photography'. 'Oops', those are simile. Well that's a bit like a metaphor, you can use it to knock more nails into the new media coffin. In this version of the digital *Pepper's Ghost* we see neither our true selves nor the true computer.

4. Enjoying human computer interaction

*The more pain I train myself to stand, the more
I learn. You are afraid of the pain now, Unk,
but you won't learn anything if you don't invite
the pain. And the more you learn, the gladder
you will be to stand the pain.*
(Vonnegut 1959)

    I once read a prescription for 'good'
interface design, which stated that an interface
should be 'polite', 'friendly' and 'enjoyable'.
Having been raised a good Catholic I could
easily relate to this suggestion, but also recognised that lurking underneath there must be
something far more sinister. Wherever there is
pleasure there must also be pain in that the two
are intrinsically linked. In practice the gratification obtained from using a computer reaches
outside the grey box and into the psychic and
social life of the user. Thimbleby (1990), in his
outline of the benefits of employing a user
interface, highlights 'enjoyment', among others,
as being a primary benefit for the user:

*Enjoyment: The user may wish to enjoy himself
through using the interactive system. Obvious
examples are playing games, hacking programs,
exploring interesting problems and using the
computer as a medium to communicate with
others. Less obvious examples are creative systems
for musical and artistic design, or word processors for easy verbal expression. Users may obtain
enjoyment from using an acquired skill with a
complex interactive system. Paradoxically, the
'worse' the system design, the more it may be
enjoyed after getting used to it: users may find
satisfaction by being repositories of detailed
information about a system! However, such users
would not have had status if the system had been
so easy to use that there was no need for experts.
Enjoyment may be quite subtle; for instance, if
some users have certain special skills, they may
prefer to be in a position where an organisation
relies on goodwill.*
(Thimbleby 1990)

    To achieve the level of expert the novice
user must perform Herculean tasks, involving
great discomfort. Once achieved this position
wields power over others. The problem with
most interface design is that it considers only
the most immediate layers of human computer
interaction — the user, the screen and the
computer's actions — and not intimate interaction with others. The computer is isolated, an
object to be acted upon and that responds
accordingly. There is little emphasis on the
'dialogue' that builds up as a result of this cause
and effect, especially as the computer is increasingly found at the centre of human social
networks.

*...human beings rarely appear as psychological
individuals. They are usually in symbiosis with
others, each supplementing the various psychological defects of the other.*
(Harré et al 1985)

    The 'psychological defects' of the
computer 'expert' within a social environment,
as outlined by Thimbleby, are often vital for the
wellbeing of the workplace, and the self-
satisfaction gained by maintaining network
servers late into the night can reach almost
heroic proportions. The enjoyment of using a
good looking GUI is nothing compared to the
pleasure of controlling a network, knowing all
the user ids (and egos) and allocating/restricting
file space. It is interesting that the personal
computer wrestled control from the mainframe
manager and the IT service department and
placed it firmly in the hands of the user, a
process of empowerment. As our reliance on
networks increases we are slowly devolving
control back to the service providers and the
network administrators. To evolve HCI needs to
consider not only the media design of the screen
but also the complex social interactions that take
place beyond the screen, into the social environments that surround computer networks, and
the virtual environments that support new social
networks. Here we have another dimension for
the new media designer to deal with; the fifth
dimension of interaction explodes to embrace

new psychological and virtual worlds.

Virtul worlds should not be seen as an alternative to the real world or a substitute, but as an extra dimension which allows us a new freedom of movement in the natural world. In other words the transcendence of physicality in the virtual world allows us to extend our mode of operation in the physical world. A new means of travel, a new form of communication, a new way of operating, a new medium of expression.

(Frazer 1995)

Reflected in the screen we can see ourselves expanding into the greater social milieu, and looking through it we can see a vista of new virtual domain. As with any conquest of a new territory there is bound to be discomfort and pain until the terrain is mapped and thoroughly explored, then it can be enjoyed. We will not learn anything by hiding behind traditional disciplines and social hierarchies, we must learn, as 'Unk' did, to enjoy the pain of transcendence.

5. A continuum of blended internal/external realities

Fascination with the body and its relationship to technology runs deep through the modernist machine aesthetic. The post-modern body freely dissolves into the technology that surrounds it, and "the plastic, if not ludicrous" (Gray 1995) distinctions between body and tool melt away. The symbiosis evident/required in the cyborg is one of meat and metal, a Léger painting manifest, not one of soul and intelligence or intuition and logic. Lying somewhere between the violent fusion of bone and metal and reductionism of 'old' HCI lies a relatively new and enlightened area of study. 'Activity Theory' articulates the subtle relationships that exist between humans and the tools they use, and explores the complex feedback loops between the impact the use of a tool has on the environ-ment and the impact the modified environment then has on the human.

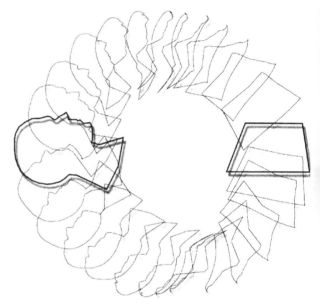

The idea is that humans can control their own behaviour – not 'from the inside', on the basis of biological urges, but 'from the outside', using and creating artefacts. This perspective is not only optimistic concerning human self-determination. It is an invitation to serious study of artefacts as integral and inseparable components of human functioning.

(Engeström 1991)

Figure 1. A continuum of blended internal/external realities.

Within this context the concept of the computer as a passive 'tool' to impact on the world or achieve a given end, seems limited and one dimensional. Transcending the mere 'tool' the computer can operate as a medium for human expression and experience, where the impact is on the psyche or mental world of the 'user'-'spectator' rather than the external world. Through the computer it is possible to blur the distinction between the 'outside' and the 'inside'; the 'outside' becomes a manifestation of the 'inside', and the 'outside' is reconstituted in the mind, a continuum of blended internal/external realities (Figure 1). Within this con-

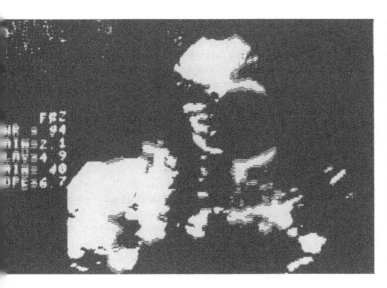

technologies that do our seeing for us. These technologies raise critical questions about the nature of the truth and knowledge they illicit, and the way in which we interpret them. Images and data generated by these systems question the way we perceive our environment and ourselves. The process of imaging says as much about the observer as it does about the observed, will these autonomous systems 'know' the 'truth' when they 'see' it? Will we recognise ourselves when seen through our artificial eyes?

*Figure 2.
Cyberbaby.*

tinuum of mutual reinforcement the inside/ outside can equally be extended to the greater social milieu on both sides of the screen. The pleasure and pain of interaction becomes a fervour, an orgy of networking.

As the computer evolves from an isolated 'artefact', through physical and social networks into an all-pervading system or process, the nature of our relationship with it will inevitably change. Activity theory articulates a sophisticated symbiosis that exists between our tools, and us, what happens to that relationship when the tools we manufacture become not only ubiquitous but also autonomous? The process of interaction begins to involve not just the 'inside' and 'outside', but also the autonomous 'other'.

Computer imaging systems have revolutionised our relationship with the 'inside' (e.g. medical imaging technology), 'outside' (e.g. security monitoring systems, remote sensing satellite images) and the 'other' (e.g. search for extra-terrestrial intelligence). Vision dominates our culture and lies at the heart of scientific and artistic endeavour for truth and knowledge. Increasingly the hegemony of the human eye is being challenged by a new generation of

6. The ultrasonic peepshow

In 1987 I sent my unborn son into Cyberspace; with the aid of an ultrasound scan, a MacPlus and several million pounds of global computer network. As part of the *Digital body exchange* project[3] it seemed an appropriate and justifiable thing to do. Indeed, he is now rather pleased at being (probably) the first baby in cyberspace. However, looking back at the process involved it seems strangely exposing. Taking a photograph of a baby is one thing, taking a sonograph (Figure 2) of the inside of the body is surely another. Now exposing the internal workings of the body seems more socially acceptable than exposing the naked body. Exposing a foetus in this way is pure technological voyeurism, to distribute it over a digital network is voyeurism on a global scale. The enabling technologies that here expose and make manifest the internal organs and bodily processes form a continuum from the ultrasound image, through the family snapshot, to the peepshow booth. They all imply 'knowing' and embody 'knowledge'; discovery, memory and carnal. Each form carries its own intrinsic politics, which is rooted in social taboo and the technology and procedures that surround it. Consider the motivations behind the ultrasonic peepshow:

> *Obstetrics is a special case because the patients are uniformly women, and are generally not ill, and it is clearly an area where male doctors can have no personal experience of the 'condition' being treated. So their claims to expertise might appear tenuous to women. Oakley argues that technology is particularly attractive to obstetricians because techniques such as the stethoscope and foetal monitoring enable male doctors to claim to know more about women's bodies than the woman themselves.*
> *(Wajcman 1991)*

Here the knowledge engendered (and 'gendered') by the technology objectifies the female form, specifically the internal form. And yet ultrasound images adorn family albums alongside first steps and first birthdays. The knowledge, or assumed knowledge, is here transmitted through low-resolution images. The resolution of the experience is extremely low. The grainy black and white image is similar in resolution to the brief glimpse of the internal workings of the body offered by the bio-feedback system, mist clearing momentarily on a scene which will remain veiled. Stare at the grey patterns emerging through the emulsion (is that a head, heart, spine?) and they draw you into a place you used to know but cannot remember.

I saw my son's face recently, as it originally appeared in those ultrasound images. They were the blurred and faded images sent back by the 1976 Viking Orbiter from the surface of Mars. They revealed little to the naked eye, until they were digitally processed, slowly revealing a skull-like face that gazes from the surface of Mars. The technology strips away the grain and fuzz and re-visions, the 'face' becames gradually un-obscured, progressively un-veiled, with

Low-resolution media does not mean a low-resolution experience

features suggestive of eyes, a ridge-like nose, and a mouth, its 'truth' emerging through the technology. From innerspace to outerspace, these processing techniques allow us to see more clearly the images we nurture inside our heads, just bringing into sharp focus the things we want to see. These tools that 'image' flatter our expectations, nurture our assumptions and reflect our own likeness.

7. The anguish of actuality

Low-resolution media does not mean a low-resolution experience. Feedback between the body and its environment, whether mediated through technology or not, always requires an internal mental manifestation for the dialogue to be complete. Consider the filtered reality of phone sex. Sexual gratification is attained using a mono-media at extreme low resolution. The 'aesthetic' of the 'form' relies on the grain in the dialogue, which may actually enhance the internal manifestation. Does the complex realisation of the 'internal' enabled through the computer's grain significantly enhance the level of such a dialogue, allowing the spectactor to transcend what Carter describes as 'existential solitude'?

> *When pornography abandons its quality of existential solitude and moves out of the kitsch area of timeless, placeless fantasy and into the real world, then it loses its function of safety valve. It begins to comment on real relations in the real world. Therefore, the more pornographic writing acquires the techniques of real literature, of real art, the more deeply subversive it is likely to be in that the more likely it is to affect the reader's perceptions of the world. The text that had heretofore opened up creamily to him, in a dream, will gather itself together and harshly expel him into the anguish of actuality. (Carter 1979)*

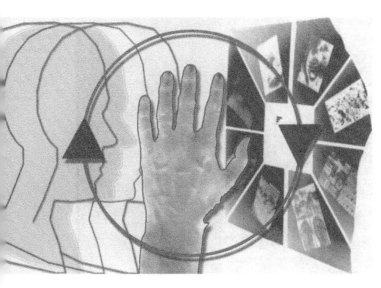

Figure 3.
'Umbilical',
biofeedback
experiments.

Now that pornography is escaping the 'placeless' and finding an interactive 'place' in cyberspace, will it gain the power to 'affect the reader's perception of the real world' or simply enhance the internal dream world? The cathartic experiences offered by an intimate interface with the computer enable complex levels of interaction with both the internal and external environment. Indeed it is this complexity within the relationships between the user / audience / observer / voyeur / participant / spectactor / actor / and interface that makes the dissolution and submission of the body so sensuous and intimate.

The cognitively induced deception of perception is a useful phenomenon for visual simulations, but why not extend the psycho-physical relationships between the real and virtual worlds and mold deadly and sensuous phenomena into the virtual dimension?
(Stenslie 1998)

The body is a three-dimensional form that occupies space. Immersive works such as *OSMOSE,*

reaffirm the central role of the subjective physical body in virtual space.
(Davies 1997)
and extend this space by revealing the spaces that occupy the body, and allowing access to new forms of space, through the merging of internal, external and mental places, in cyberspace. It is important to remember that these are spaces and not just images of spaces, and that the experience of space is the product of bodily interaction, not just visual perception.
In OSMOSE for example, instead of relying on hand-based manipulation of various interface instruments which support a disembodied and controlling stance towards the world, we developed a body-centred approach using breath and balance, enabling the participants to 'float' by breathing in to rise, out to fall, and learning to change direction. This method, partially informed by the practice of scuba diving, frees immersants from the urge to 'handle' things and from the habitual gravity-bound modes of behaviour such as walking or driving on a flat horizontal surface. Use of breath and balance was also intended to reaffirm the central role of the subjective physical body in virtual space.
(Davies 1997)

By becoming a vehicle for exploring these new places the computer transcends the tool and extends the body. It no longer needs a metaphor for interaction; it constitutes its own 'actuality' and interaction. However, with this release from the clean 32-bit world of the icon and other trappings of conventional HCI, comes the 'anguish' of this new 'actuality'. It is not the visceral welding of tissue and silicon that causes the anguish, it is the catharsis and pain of self-knowledge.

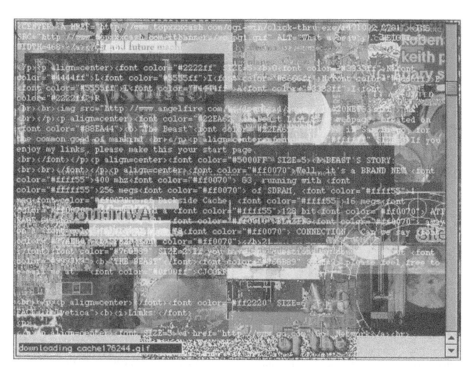

Figure 4.
Montage
machine.

8. The metaphysical fog

*Can the computer screen act as a clear-cut
barrier separating cyberspace from real space, the
space of mental inhabitation from the physical
space of corporeality? What if the boundary is
more permeable than the smooth glass finality of
the screen? What if it is no longer clear where
matter converts into information and information is reconfigured as matter or representation?
(Grosz 1997)*

The seepage from the world behind the
screen to the 'inside' and from the 'inside' to the
world behind the screen is explored through my
work with bio-feedback systems (Figure 3).
Here, with the use of simple 'psycho-galvanom-
eters' or lie detectors, the body is interfaced
directly with the soft and hardware of the
computer. The internal psycho-physical state of
the body is integrated into the computer system,
forming a tangible physical and emotional

dialogue. By using the relationship between skin
resistance and the psychological state of the
'spectactor' (here the user becomes the used) to
feed the screen display, a visceral symbiotic
dialogue is generated. The screen triggers a
response in the 'spectactor', which triggers a
response on the screen. A calm 'spectactor'
generates an aggressive image/sound/text, an
agitated 'spectactor' generates a calming image/
sound/text, and the cycle is repeated until the
'spectactor' gains control of the body, which is
extended into the digital system. With this
control comes the realisation that the
'spectactor' is aware of their own internal
processes, a sense of domination of the auto-
nomic nervous system. The insides are manifest
externally and Stelarc's 'metaphysical fog' clears
momentarily.

*We mostly operate as absent bodies. That's
because A BODY IS DESIGNED TO INTERFACE*

Figure 5.
Psalms
(1998).

WITH ITS ENVIRONMENT – its sensors are open to the world (compared to its inadequate internal surveillance system). The body's mobility and navigation in the world require this outward orientation. Its absence is augmented by the fact that the body functions habitually and automatically. AWARENESS IS OFTEN THAT WHICH OCCURS WHEN THE BODY MAL-FUNCTIONS. Reinforced by Cartesian convention, personal convenience and neuro-physiological design, people operate merely as minds, immersed in metaphysical fog.
(Stelarc 1995)

However, the resolution of this glimpse through the fog is often enough to shock and purge. Listen for a moment to your own breathing; listen to your heartbeat. Awareness brings with it catharsis … breath… pump… it hurts to know … breath… pump…as the rhythm becomes more consuming the control becomes more tenuous, … breath… pump… all senses start to turn inwards, to a 'place' they were not designed to understand and struggle to articulate. If the panic gets too much, stop!

9. The body of evidence

I had a few stomach problems several years ago, a duodenal ulcer which I had been nurturing for several years, in complete ignorance, suddenly decided to perforate an artery. After the slow fade was stabilised I saw the first views of the inside of my body, beamed back from the interior, looking something like a viscous moon landing. A cathartic experience: my internal organs exposed and laid out in front of me on computer monitors, popped inside out, on a slow journey down the oesophagus into the gut. There were several such invasions, the room of technology that surrounded me entered my body, fusing me with the architecture, a node on a network. Machines beeped as I tried to consume a few meters of cable, before trying to swallow the whole room. And there it was, my inside, emerging in front of me on the monitors as I swallowed, in full Technicolor pixel by pixel at 25 frames a second. If I had continued to swallow the whole room would have been shown there too, trapped in the digestive recursion. I half expected to feel the full glory of the cyborg fervour, but instead as this most intimate of interactions continued, a trust (or an assumed and untested trust) that I had always had in my body slowly shifted to the technology. It seemed more reliable, at least you knew when it had broken down, it couldn't pretend to be functioning correctly. Slowly, as the technology seeped into me, the unpleasantness and pain receded to be replaced by a submission and dependence. An act of faith?

There were no corpses in the time-tombs, no dusty skeletons. The cyber-architectonic ghosts which haunted them were embalmed in the metallic codes of memory tapes, three-dimensional molecular transcriptions of their living originals, stored among the dunes as a momentous act of faith, in the hope that one day the physical recreation of the coded personalities would be possible.

(Ballard 1992)

Donald Rodney died on 4th of March 1998. Ten years before, the magazine *20/20*, in a review of one of his exhibitions, announced his recent death. Rodney was not dead but dying, the premature announcement predicted the inevitable result of a Darwinian curse, which had afflicted him since birth. Sickle Cell Anaemia is a long slow degenerative disease, which resulted in Rodney's incarceration in hospitals and various technological apparatus. The result of this lifetime of physical atrophy was a creative mind that had a chillingly surgical perspective on the human condition. His physical condition provided an emotive palette

for the acute and richly disturbing creations that populated his shows, with pieces literally etched from his body. Rodney's body had, for many years, existed in a close symbiotic relationship with the medical technology that has kept him alive. How many rooms had he swallowed? This relationship left a data trail of information: photographs, X-rays, scans, measurements, data, scars, and imprints. This body of data, a body of images and measurements still exists (Figure 4).

Autoicon[4] was one of the many projects Rodney was working on at the time of his death, the intention was to integrate the body of medical data with an 'expert system' synthesised from interviews, and a rule-based montage machine that would allow *Autoicon* to carry on generating works of art. The *Donald Rodney Autoicon* is a multifaceted record of his body, a 'data' body, and a body that will now remain active in cyberspace. More importantly the *Autoicon* attempts to encapsulate the creative mind of Rodney. Whilst many of the elements for the project were in place at the time of his death, the synthesis of Donald's working process (Figure 5) and personality must now be drawn from the memories of the close group of friends (Donald Rodney plc), in collaboration with the Institute of International Visual Arts (InIVA).

Autoicon was inspired by Jeremy Bentham (1748–1832), ((in)famous for the Panopticon; or the Inspection House (1791)) who left instructions for the construction of his Autoicon. Two hundred and fifty years later his Autoicon still sits in the corridor at UCL. His body preserved in wax, his head mummified and his vital organs conserved in a pot under his seat. *Donald Rodney Autoicon* is a memoria technica, this surrogate body, the digital portfolio, provides a framework which challenges Stone's concern about leaving 'behind' the body or 'meat'.

The discourse of visionary virtual world builders is rife with images of imaginal bodies, freed from the constraints that flesh imposes. Cyberspace developers foresee a time when they will be able

to forget about the body. But it is important to remember that virtual community originates in, and must return to, the physical. No refigured virtual body, no matter how beautiful, will slow the death of cyberpunk with AIDS. Even in the age of the technosocial subject, life is lived through bodies.
(Stone 1991)

An acute statement considering the digital body is all that is left, bar the memories and the 'body' of work (a 'body' of work, which begins to fragment without the 'real' body to hold it together). Indeed, without the disease the digital body would not exist. Rodney's *Psalms* (Figure 5), an autonomous wheelchair articulates the presence or lack of presence of his body. Unable to attend his own gallery openings a wheelchair was designed to take his place. Incorporating a neural network, the chair would wander through the gallery intent on pursuing a preordained path. Its interaction with the 'real world' continually updated by motion and location sensors. Ignored and continually interrupted in its cycle of the gallery space by visitors viewing other work the system would struggle to maintain its course, pausing and renegotiating. The autonomous system represents the embodiment of the absent body.

10. Logging off

As the metaphor is left behind, the phantom of a digital *Pepper's Ghost*, an illusion created without the aid of mirrors, still hangs in the air. Before the slow fade to black a streaming body can be glimpsed through the metaphysical fog, enjoying the catharsis and fervour of a networked orgy.

Notes

1 Very old bad joke, anon.
2 Definition of 'Metaphor'. *The Collins English Dictionary 2nd edition* (1986). William Collins Sons and Co. Ltd.
3 CYBERBABY: digital body exchange (1987). Hochschule für angewandte Kunst, Vienna. Initiated by Roy Ascott.
4 *Autoicon* project can be found at <www.iniva.org>.
5 Rodney, D., with Bugmann, G. and Phillips, M. (1997) *Psalms: autonomous wheelchair*. In: *Nine nights in Eldorado*. South London Gallery, October 1997.

References

Ballard J.G. (1992) *The time-tombs. The Venus hunters*. Flamingo, London.

Carter, A. (1979) *The Sadeian woman*. Virago Press, London.

Curtis, D. (1972) *Experimental cinema*. Delta Publishing, New York.

Davies, C. (1997) Changing space: VR as a philosophical arena of being. In Ascott, R. (ed.) *Proceedings of Consciousness Reframed*. CaiiA, UWCN.

Engeström, Y. (1991) Activity theory and individual and social transformation. *Multidisciplinary Newsletter for Activity Theory* 7/8 6–7.

Frazer J.H. (1995) The architectural relevance of cyberspace: architects in cyberspace. In Toy, M. (ed.) *Architectural Design, Profile No 118*, Academy Group Ltd, pp. 76– 77.

Gray, C. et al (1995) *Cyborgology: the cyborg handbook*. Routledge.

Grosz, E. (1997) Cyberspace, virtuality, and the real: some architectural reflections. In Davidson, C. (ed.) *Anybody*. MIT Press, New York.

Harré, R. et al (1985) *Motives and mechanisms: an introduction to the psychology of action*. Methuen & Co Ltd, London.

Stelarc (1995) Towards the post-human. In Toy, M. (ed.) *Architectural Design, Profile No 118*, Academy Group Ltd, pp. 91–92.

Stenslie, S. (1998) Flesh space. In Beckmann, J. (ed.) *The virtual dimension*. Princeton Architectural Press, New York.

Stone, A. R. (1991) Will the real body please stand up? – boundary stories about virtual cultures. In Benedikt, M. (ed.) *Cyberspace: first steps*. MIT Press, London, pp.112–113.

Thimbleby, H. (1990) *User interface design*. ACM Press, New York.

Valéry, P. (1964) *Aesthetics: the conquest of ubiquity*. Trans. Manheim, R. Pantheon Books, Bollingen Series, New York.

Vonnegut, K. (1959) *The sirens of Titan*. Indigo, London.

Wajcman, J. (1991) *Feminism confronts technology*. Polity Press, London.

Mike Phillips is the director of i-DAT (The Institute of Digital Art and Technology), and deputy director of STAR (Science Technology Arts Research — one half of the CAiiA-STAR integrated research programme), University of Plymouth. He has a BA (Hons) in Fine Art - 4D, a scholarship to the University of Massachusetts, USA (1984–85), and a Higher Diploma in Fine Art (Experimental Media) at the Slade School of Fine Art, University College London (1985-87). Digital interactive collaborative work has included: pre-WWW global computer-networking projects using JANet and EARN; telematic performance work with 'UK EAT88' in Europe; audio work with Donald Rodney at the ICA (London) and TSWA 4 Cities project and South London Gallery (Psalms Autonomous Wheelchair, 1998). In 1992 he moved to the University of Plymouth to coordinate the BSc MediaLab Arts Programme, and is now overseeing the development of the On-Line MSc Digital Futures course. Current projects include Autoicon (inIVA), Spectactor (DA2), STI Project (The Search for Terrestrial Intelligence - SciArt) and a number of interactive satellite projects. These projects and other work can be found on the i-DAT web site at: http://www.i-dat.org

This article first appeared in *Digital Creativity* 11(2) 75–88 (2000).

Art practice augmented by digital agents

Ernest Edmonds

LUTCHI Research Centre, Loughborough University, UK

Abstract

Computers can be very helpful to us by performing tasks on our behalf. For example, they are very good at performing calculations, storing information and producing visualisations of objects that do not yet exist as a made artifact. Increasingly, however, a different role is being found for the computer. It is the role of a catalyst, or a stimulant, to our own creative thinking. In such cases the computer is not primarily performing a task for us and generating an answer within itself, rather it is helping us to generate answers within ourselves. The computer helps us think creatively. This role for the computer can be illustrated in the context of computer support to creative design. In order to design computer systems that support the creative process, it is important to understand that process well enough to predict what might help, rather than hinder. Given such research, we may begin to define the characteristics of what the computer must do in order to augment creative thinking. The paper explores a particular application of intelligent user interfaces — the augmentation of creative thought in artists.

Keywords: agent, art, creativity, intelligent user interface

1. Introduction

Fundamental to the argument of the paper is an understanding of how creativity in art practice works. Often, the initial creative process does not concentrate upon the surface qualities of the work, such as the texture of the paint or the quality of sound from a particular instrument. Stravinsky, for example, frequently composed at the piano and orchestrated, even in such works as *The Rite of Spring*, at a later stage.

Rather than start with surface considerations, the artist may well start with fundamental structuring considerations. The problem is to understand the concrete implications (through to the surface) of the structural decisions. This is where a significant opportunity for augmentation arises. By using intelligent agents to generate the concrete realisations of the structure decisions the artist can see the implications within very short intervals of time. The significant role of the agents in the user interface is to enable the artist to think and act in terms of the structures whilst, as a result of the agents' work, easily and quickly see the implications.

Following an introductory discussion of creative thought and the role of computer systems, the paper explores these ideas by illustrations of their significance in art practice drawn from a number of empirical studies and personal explorations. The key argument is that intelligent user interfaces can enable the artist to lift the level of concern in a way that promotes enhanced creative thinking.

2. Creative thought

Thought is not a means of solving the problems

of this world as they arise. Thought is not a problem solver but a great process of realisation that is forever transcending, transformed, changed, developed.
(Mead 1917)

One way of viewing the subject of this paper is in terms of computer creativity for creative computation. By computer creativity is meant the possibility of computers doing things that humans might consider to be creative and by creative computation is meant humans being able to do creative things with the help of computers.

Computers help us in many ways and we are used to the support they give us in performing different tasks: taking burdens away from us, doing something that is rather hard easily for us, etc. For example, they are good at doing calculations and we have spread sheets that save us from doing sums. They are good at storing and retrieving data and we use databases to save us from time-consuming searching and remembering. They are good at constructing visualisations of things which, whilst they could be constructed by an artist with pens, can be produced more easily with computer systems.

The above examples are all of tasks that are very helpful to us but they are not the primary subject of this paper. It is concerned instead with computer support that stimulates our thinking rather than that saves us work. The concern is with how to provide support that stimulates us to think in new ways and so helps, in part, our creative lives.

The formulation of a problem is often more essential than its solution, which may be merely a matter of mathematical or experimental skill. To raise new questions, new possibilities, to regard old problems from a new angle, requires creative imagination and marks real advance in science.
(Einstein and Infield 1938)

That is what creativity is about, formulating new problems or possibilities rather than solving old problems.

Often in great discoveries the most important

thing is that a certain question is found. Envisaging, putting the productivity towards the question is often more important, often a greater achievement than the solution of a set question.
(Wertheimer 1959)

Hence, in supporting creativity it is important to understand this aspect. In this context it is interesting to note the results from a study of art students who were asked to draw a still life as part of an experiment (Getzels and Csikzentmihalyi 1969). A table was produced full of items from which they could select whatever objects they wanted and arrange them in whatever way they wanted. They then had to draw the still life. The final drawings were anonymously given to experts to judge them and place them in various categories. All of the selection and drawing process was recorded.

One interesting point was the observations on manipulation and exploration. Times were taken on how long they spent on exploring the objects, and manipulating them, before they decided what to draw. So the pre-drawing process, we might say the problem finding process, where they tried to decide what they were going to draw, was measured. These times were correlated against the final results in the sense of the creativity, etc., of the result as judged by the expert panel. The results showed that originality correlated very highly with the time spent on this pre-drawing/ problem finding phase. As a matter of fact, craftsmanship does rather badly in correlating with innovation, so these things do not necessarily go together. This is, in itself, a very interesting point. Thus, psychologists working in this area came to realise that problem finding might be as important as problem solving for creativity.

3. Supporting creative users

In his keynote presentation at the *Artificial Intelligence in Design Conference* held in Edinburgh in 1991, Donald Schön discussed intelligent support for design in the context of what is known empirically about design. His analysis of the complexity of design was notable but, in particular, his stress on the roles of action and perception as well as cognition was significant. He concluded with the remarks that:

The design of design assistant is an approach that has not in the past attracted the best minds in AI. Perhaps the time has come when it can and should do so.
(Schön 1992)

In response to this challenge, a special issue of the journal *Knowledge Based Systems* was published which included Schön's address and seven responses from researchers actively investigating intelligent assistants (Edmonds 1992). The crucial point was to advocate a shift of focus away from using artifical intelligence (AI) to automate, to using it to enhance human activities, such as design. This point has been widely recognised in the Intelligent User Interface community.

Taking a more general view, creative thought, in any discipline, is hard to model. In terms of achieving benefit it can be argued, following Schön, that the most interesting avenue is to investigate support systems, or assistants. Candy (1992) drew particular attention to the distinction between creative product and creative process. It is not sufficient to be able to recognise a creative product. Rather, we wish to understand the process that led to it. In fact the research issue that is of central concern in this paper, with its concern for art, is to understand that process sufficiently to be able to provide computer support that can enhance it.

Looking beyond art or design, creative thinking in management, science, engineering

the concerns of the artist can often be with the deeper structures of their art rather than with the surface representations that make up the final artwork itself …

and other fields is mostly conducted with minimum computer support. It is only when an initial concept has been defined, such as 'Support the monitor by a wall bracket' or 'Minimise the stock held in the warehouse', that a clear enough problem has been defined for most computer-aided methods to apply. Technicians might carry out tasks according to well-specified procedures but experts are continually reflecting upon the implications of existing knowledge in the light of new circumstances (Schön 1983). In the main, experts do not work with static, tightly defined knowledge. The evolution of expert knowledge is central to how they make significant contributions to the field and, thus, gain advantage. Thus fixed systems that do not allow end users to manipulate and modify the internal knowledge are not appropriate for the support of many creative knowledge workers.

Interactive knowledge support systems (Gaines 1990, Candy et al. 1993) can assist expert knowledge workers in the more creative aspects of their work. The key advantage of such systems is that they enable experts to extend the domain knowledge of any system that supports them. The definition of that knowledge, in fact, is close to the definition of their personal expertise.

Interactive knowledge support systems, where the end user manipulates machine representations of knowledge directly (Edmonds and Candy 1993) have been applied to scientific exploration (O'Brien et al. 1992). This work has clearly demonstrated a potential for supporting creative work.

4. A study: structure in art

Before discussing the development of computer support and augmenting agents for artists it is important to take a small diversion to look at a particular aspect of art practice. The issue is the role of underlying structure in contrast with surface appearance for many artists. This section is drawn from a number of discussions, between artists and this author, as well as contributions by artists to the *Creativity and Cognition* series (Candy and Edmonds 1993, 1996, 1999). The artists quoted in this section broadly belong to the constructivist tradition. George Rickey took a catholic view of the term in his important book on the subject (Rickey 1967). He uses the term to refer to the long twentieth century theme of abstract (but not abstracted from nature) visual art. Whilst noting this point, it is important to recognise that the concerns of these artists do not differ very much, in terms of this argument, from many others and, indeed, for most music.

In January 1996 four established artists who had not previously used a computer in their art practice spent a week at an artists-in-residence on the Loughborough Campus in order to explore the potential for their art of the computer. The artists were Jean-Pierre Husquinet (Liège), Fré Ilgen (Eindhoven), Michael Kidner (London) and Birgitta Weimer (Cologne). Each artist was paired with a technical expert who worked with them, identified appropriate computer systems and drew in other experts when necessary. By the end of the week Birgitta Weimer had produced computer generated prints to her artistic satisfaction. Fré Ilgen was making virtual sculptures that resided in a void and were not subject to gravity. Michael Kidner and Jean-Pierre Husquinet had not completed new works but both had begun a new exploration that has been continued since.

The nature of the interchanges between artist and technologist as well as the artists' perspectives upon the use of the technologies and what they gained from it were recorded. Both positive and negative aspects can be observed but in all cases the nature of the art practice involved was illuminated. One example of the results to be reported is that, despite the apparent simplicity of the artists' demands, it proved to be quite a technological challenge to provide the computing support needed. It seems that very few standard computing systems can adequately support established artists such as those participating. The positive side of this observation is that, largely because of the technical support provided, one week was sufficient to overcome the initial problems that were faced.

In various ways, each artist was concerned with the structures that underlie the works produced. Also a concern for process — one might suggest the exploration of these structures — is evident. Each of these artists is involved in an exploration in which the products form a notable but not supreme part. In this sense, the computer's ability to handle structure might be quite significant. This point is illustrated by a set of quotations from the discussions held with Edmonds at Loughborough University in 1996.

Kidner: *I mean structure becomes the nature of the composition and there was a lot of discussion I think with the Russian constructivists in around 1920 as to the difference between composition and construction. They were all trying to make structures and were criticising composition.*

Well there are two things. I think one is that composition is designed to make the work attractive or interesting for the viewer to see. Well I have never thought very much about the viewer except that I am the viewer, so it seems to me that I make things and I have no idea what they will look like or very little idea. I don't really care because I am more interested in resolving my problem and seeing, confirming, my theory or not.

Husquinet: *Yes, probably the best word would be*

structure because everything is based on structure. It's built either visually or musically in structures.

If it wasn't for the process there would be no interest in the work anyway, so I wouldn't do anything. So it's clear that the process is much more important than the work itself. You can probably relate that to having a musical score that you have written, in this case it is a visual score which I have painted and every time you develop that broken space you are rebuilding another structure of course, but if you think of it in musical terms it is like, if you were thinking of a musical score again, and play it again it will wait just like jazz. They play the score and then they improvise upon the score. Every time you hear a jazz musician live he plays the same piece but differently. Its a good parallel.

Weimer: I want to find not strict rules but to have my own rules in my work, and to find basic structures in things what I experience and what I see so I always add a different angle in my work or for what I was really looking for. I think that it is an inner necessity to find rules.

I think process is important, I mean on the one hand you can say that process influences the product, for example if I had an idea and I start to realise that sometimes I find other material I choose can not do what I wanted it to do so I have to change then, this is the process which can change the back idea I had in my mind before I started to work.

Ilgen: When you see my works you have the feeling that something really argumentative — if you like a kind of order, kind of system, maybe — but you can not find the rules of the system because they are based mainly on visual experience.

> *... intelligent user interfaces may well have a significant role to play in easing the transition from those structures to the form of the artifact*

You have processes which should also reach temporarily moments of equilibrium and maybe a finished piece is that you are satisfied: your desire for making this thing reaches equilibrium.

At the same time as these studies were made, a number of other artists were involved in the 1996 *Creativity and Cognition* conference. Manfred Mohr was one of these and he made the following statement in the proceedings.

My art is not a mathematical art, but an expression of my artistic experiences. I invent rules which reflect my thinking and feelings. These algorithms can become very complex, that is to say, complicated and difficult to survey. In order to master this problem, the use of a computer is necessary in my work. Only in this way is it possible to overlay as many rules as necessary without losing control. It is inevitable that the results — that is, my images — are not readable at first glance. The information is deeply buried and a certain participation is demanded from the spectator, a readiness to interrogate this material. (Candy and Edmonds 1996 280)

Thus it is clear that the concerns of the artist can often be with the deeper structures of their art rather than with the surface representations that make up the final artwork itself. The lesson that is to be drawn from this is that intelligent user interfaces may well have a significant role to play in easing the transition from those structures to the form of the artifact. This point will be returned to after another, more specifically relevant, discussion about art practice.

5. A personal case

This section will review something of what the author has done in relation to the visual arts and computers. The production of an artwork is partly concerned with minimising the variables that one is trying to handle in order to deal with more complex things. This is similar to what many scientists do. Harold Cohen once said that someone had offered him a computer system that enabled him to use 4 million colours but he said that "the trouble was that it did not have the six colours that I wanted" (private communication).

More than thirty years ago the author used a computer for the first time to perform an art task for the construction of a work. I had a problem. I had many bits and pieces and I wanted to arrange them according to certain rules. I found it very hard. Always, when I made an arrangement, it broke one of the rules I wanted to satisfy.

However, I had access to a computer and I managed to obtain three hours of computer time which was almost enough to solve the problem for me. It is interesting, actually, because I had to switch the computer program off after three hours because someone else needed it. But I had not quite solved the problem. There was one problem remaining. but I had reduced it into something I could solve myself. So I finished the job off by hand (Cornock and Edmonds 1973).

That was good but did not excite me very much in terms of using computers. Much later it became clear that many of the structural issues that had concerned me, such as the co-existence of two colours in the same space, could be tackled by moving from static to time-based work. By this time, such work was made a possibility by the fact that computing technology had moved on and could support it in a unique way.

The use of computers in constructive art has mostly been in the production of static objects or series of objects, yet an important property of the computer is that it can handle complex activity developing in time. Indeed, computer technology has had an important impact in music from the specialised IRCAM endeavour to extensive exploitation in rock. It is true that computer-generated images and videos abound, but in so far as they aspire to art, they generally fall into the category that has become known as 'computer art', which is widely understood to refer to work that has a technological feel about it. Recent developments have often placed their strongest emphasis on constructing abstract models of three-dimensional worlds from which views are selected to make the final work. That may be too simple a description, but it certainly is the case that most of that work is not constructive, even though it might be surrealist, art. The use of the computer to feed fantasy has been dominant. This situation has been encouraged by the developments in the technology itself.

The use of computers in the handling of images has received considerable attention and there is no doubt that most of us are quite amazed at what can be achieved technically. The exploitation of these possibilities in art practice, so far, has been largely influenced by one brand of computer graphics, known as geometric graphics. In this approach, the basic elements that are manipulated in order to produce images are geometric abstractions such as lines, circles and polygons or three-dimensional entities such as spheres, cuboids and surface patches of one sort or another. We are so used to these notions that often, even mostly, we forget that they are abstract. A line, for example, has no thickness and yet when we draw one it unavoidably has one. Of course, the real line has many other qualities not attributable to the abstract one. Why else would we care about the difference between a 3B and a 2H pencil? Thus, in using geometric computer graphics, careful attention has to be given to how the abstract descriptions of images so

Figure 1.
Six stills
from Ernest
Edmonds'
'Jasper'
(1988).

constructed are realised as perceivable images. The technology itself encourages a view that the realisation of the image is only an approximation to the perfectly formed abstraction. In the early days of the use of computers in the visual arts, this approach was used in order to generate drawings produced by automatic drawing machines called graph plotters. Inevitably, when it came to producing the drawing, one of the key concerns was the particular pen to be used and how it drew, given the speed that it was driven at. Typical of modern work of this type are computer-generated video images, or sequences, showing views of imagined worlds constructed within the computer. The concrete reality of the work is, here, somewhat subsidiary to the abstract notion of it.

A quite different approach to computer graphics has been the pixel-based one. In this view, the centre of concern is the construction of the actual image as it appears on a screen. In practice, this consists of a matrix of coloured dots known as pixels and it is these that are the basis of the representations manipulated in the computer. In this way of producing images, the precise outcome is deliberately considered as part of the core concern because the actual dots that make up the image must be specified, in some way, as part of the process. In this, something has emerged that has great potential for constructive art. The computer offers a unique facility for manipulating complex systems of symbols, that is, abstract formal structures, whilst, through pixel-based graphics, precisely handling the physical reality of the images. What is more, the computer can develop and realise structures in time as is now often done in music.

A key point that must concern artists in this choice of computer graphics system is the control that they may or may not have over the underlying structure and the fine details of what they are constructing. There is little point in offering artists a computer system with a choice of more than a thousand colours if, amongst them, the six that they actually require are not to be found. The issue is not so much one of computer power but of artistic control. This is not a matter of debate in respect of most media, but somehow in the case of computers it is often compromised and may perhaps be the reason why so little 'computer art' is seen as art. In this context, the real potential is with the pixel-based graphics.

The work that I am concerned with now is what I have come to call 'video constructs'. These pieces are time-based, that is, they exist in time just as music and film do. The concrete and final destination of the images is a video monitor. In no sense whatever are the images seen on the screen a view of some other reality. They do not represent paintings or drawings any more than they relate to images seen in television news programmes. The work is concerned with precisely what exists on the monitor. However, the fact that it is generated through a computer system allows considerable attention to be paid to the structures that underlie the images, and their movement in time, but in contrast to much of the geometric-based work, the image is not a view of an abstract world. In video constructs, the logic in the computer provides the underlying structure that leads to the form of the work. The image on the screen is the concrete reality.

To take a specific example, the video construct *Jasper* (Figure 1) is based upon a number of overlapping squares of reducing dimensions, each of a different grey tone. The work starts with the grey levels stepping evenly from black to white, starting with the largest square and ending with the smallest. This order is disrupted at the beginning and the work proceeds in a search for a new resolution, and it is the search itself that is the basis of the work. The image pulsates as the tones shift between the static squares in a way that is, perhaps, closer to the so-called minimalist music than normal video material.

In a later example, *Fragments version 5* (Figure 2), a matrix of squares is explored in a

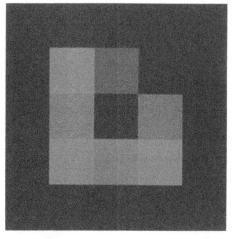

Figure 2. Still from Ernest Edmonds' 'Fragments version 5' (1989).

similar way, except in colour. Here, the piece moves through a portion of the colour space. Whilst the local rate of change can be fast, with some specific images only lasting for a fraction of a second, the general shift of colour is slow enough for the work to be quite different in the mid-afternoon to mid-morning. This work, therefore, cannot be seen very satisfactorily in the context of, for example, film. Rather, it is a changing exhibit having, perhaps, more in common with light dappling on water as the sun slowly rises and eventually sets than with the simple geometry that is, at first sight, its basis.

What has become clear is that a very detailed technical control of the computer system is as important in producing video constructs as control over oil paint is when producing oil paintings. Having control is largely a matter of the availability of descriptions that are clear and brief enough to be understood. The most exciting element of the constructive video is, perhaps, the careful and very terse way in which a specification of what occurs in time is possible. The brevity of the specification is extremely important in the development of ideas. The inevitable exploration is so strongly supported by this aspect of the use of the computer that new ways of

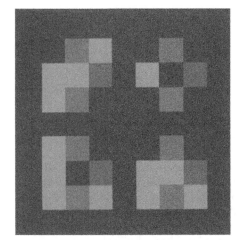

*Figure 3.
Three stills
from Ernest
Edmonds'
'Sydney'
(1995).*

thinking about work emerge in their very construction.

The exploration of time-based constructive work made possible by modern computer technology is more than a new way of doing something. The conceptual development that goes along with the art practice is something new that has implications beyond video constructs. The new understandings will inevitably influence drawing, painting and construction as much as they are influencing the video.

The point is that what the computer enabled me to do was to express, at a much higher level than I was used to, what I was after: so I could talk about structures.

What one could do with the system was express structure and have the system generate the implications of that structure which one can then look at and think about and evaluate. What that means is that one can start to think about the implications of the structures in ways that were not possible without computers. Generating time-based work of this kind was transformed by the computer. It was not just a matter of a speeded up process but one that was changed in kind.

Figure 3 contains three stills from one of these time-based works, *Sydney* (1995). The structures provided to the system specified the colour and physical relationships that can be used in any single still, the transformations that can be used between stills and the strategy for progressing through time. The system has knowledge built into it that can be used to move from these structures to the actual realisation of a work. (Edmonds 1988).

This work developed into a specific approach to the use of computing to augment creativity in which the expression of knowledge in the system and the interactive development of that knowledge was seen to be very important (Edmonds 1993).

6. Agents for artists

Any attempt to build a creative computer program will necessarily be knowledge-based in three areas: what the program needs to know about the things it seeks to represent; what it knows about its own performance; and how to do the things it decides to do. [Cohen] demonstrates through his AARON program that what the program knows and what it can do are closely interdependent.... Feedback is central to creativity, both in the long sweep of the individual's career and in the stepwise construction of new material, and we should therefore expect any attempt to build a creative program to be rule-based. Rules are informed by criteria, which are not simply standards of performance but standards of performance with respect to specific issues.

(Cohen, in Candy and Edmonds 1999 14)

The program written by Harold Cohen produces images without his direct intervention in any way. See, for example, Figure 4. Although Cohen does not talk in terms of agents, his program can be thought of as a hierarchical set of just such objects. One might say that it contains agents that know about hands, faces and so on. It has agents that know about bodies and others that know about the relationships between bodies in space. Other agents know about spatial and colour composition etc., etc. In the case of AARON, the goal is to have the program do all of the work of generating the image. Of course, AARON can only do what it does because of the knowledge that Cohen has built into it. Taking this work as a clear proof that programs can be constructed to perform the extremely complex task of, at least in some sense, making art let us consider a slightly more modest possibility. AARON works from a very high level but even not going that far real new avenues of creative exploration exist.

Now we can come to the main point of the paper. What is the method of augmentation that is being promoted? The translation from the fundamental structural ideas to the physical realisation is not the hard problem for the artist. The key point is that this transformation can be explained, expressed and modelled in a computational way. Hence, an agent can do it. The advantage of this possibility is that the speed of the artistic exploration (problem finding, transformation and development) can be changed to a degree that implies a change in kind for the artistic process.

The work briefly referred to above, particularly by Mohr, Edmonds and Cohen, all relies on computer processes of this kind. The key added dimension that is now being offered by the concept of an agent is embodied in its small modest ability to perform small modest tasks. A collection of agents can offer the artist a kind of pallet of realisation opportunities.

So, what are the problems with this approach to augmenting the artist? The first and foremost is the fact that only the artist has the knowledge that such agents need. Hence we need artists to make the agents, in some sense. More of a problem is that each artist develops important individual knowledge in this area. The answer then must be that the augmenting agent cannot simply be an off-the-shelf product for an artist to use. The reality is quite the contrary. The agent is a technological type that needs to be made available in a form that the artist can instruct, modify or construct in order to meet their particular creative requirements.

7. Conclusion

True co-operation between human and machine in the context of creative tasks must involve the manipulation of knowledge in the system at quite a deep level. In particular, domain-specific expertise must be explicitly addressed in a way that allows the expert user to modify and extend it. Knowledge support systems, which allow end users to manipulate knowledge represented in the system, are therefore proposed as the way forward for the support of creative thought.

Figure 4.
Original
screen image
produced by
Harold Cohen's
ARON (1999).

In the view of the author, augmenting the artist by agents does not make life any easier for the artist, but it might make it more interesting. Further advances in our understanding of creativity, and in the development of computer systems that enhance creative skills, can only be made by the bringing together of ideas and understandings from all of the relevant fields. Thus the relevant research must be multi-disciplinary. That includes art!

Acknowledgements

Thanks are due to all of the artists mentioned, who gave their time and effort, both freely and enthusiastically, to the studies. Linda Candy made much of the work possible and a number of the ideas included in the paper have an origin in discussions with her. Some of the work was supported by Loughborough University and by the EPSRC. A shorter earlier version of this paper was an invited keynote at the *International Conference on Intelligent User Interfaces*, published by ACM Press, New York, 2000 (Edmonds 2000). Some of the words draw partly from an earlier publication by the author (Edmonds 1989).

References

Candy, L. (1992) Modeling the creative product versus supporting human creativity. *AISB Quarterly* 81 31–34.

Candy, L. and Edmonds, E. A. (eds.) (1993) *Proceedings of Creativity and Cognition Conference.* Loughborough University, UK.

Candy, L., O'Brien, S.M. and Edmonds, E.A. (1993) End user manipulation of a knowledge based system: a study of an experts practice. *Int. J. Man-Machine Studies* 38(1) 129–145.

Candy, L. and Edmonds, E. A. (eds.) (1996) *Proceedings of Creativity and Cognition Conference.* Loughborough University, UK.

Candy, L. and Edmonds, E. A. (eds.) (1999) *Proceedings of Creativity and Cognition Conference.* ACM Press.

Cornock, S. and Edmonds, E. A. (1973) The creative process where the artist is amplified or superseded by the computer. *Leonardo* 16 11–16.

Edmonds, E. A. (1988) Logic and time-based art practice. *Leonardo*, Electronic Art Supplemental issue. Pergamon Press, Oxford, pp. 19–20.

Edmonds, E. A. (1989) Constructing with computers. *Art Monthly* 129 12–13.

Edmonds, E. (ed) (1992) Artificial intelligence in design. *Knowledge Based Systems* 5(1).

Edmonds, E. A. (1993) Knowledge based systems for creativity. In Gero, J. and Maher, M-L. (eds.) *Modeling creativity and knowledge-based creative design*. Erlbaum, Hillsdale, New Jersey, pp. 259–271.

Edmonds, E.A. & Candy, L. (1993) Knowledge support for conceptual design: the amplification of creativity. *HCI International '93*. Elsevier, Amsterdam, pp. 350–355.

Edmonds, E. A. (2000) Agents augmented by artists. In Lieberman, H. (ed.) *International Conference on Intelligent User Interfaces*. ACM Press, New York, pp. 68–73.

Einstein, A. and Infeld, L. (1938) *The evolution of physics*. Cambridge University Press, Cambridge.

Gaines, B. (1990) Knowledge support systems. *Knowledge Based Systems* 3(4) 192–201.

Getzels, J. W. and Csikzentmihalyi, M. (1969) Aesthetic opinion: an empirical study. *Public Opinion Quarterly* 33 34–45.

Mead, G. H. (1917) Scientific method and the individual thinker. In Dewey, J. (ed.) *Creative intelligence*. Holt, New York, pp. 176–227.

O'Brien, S. M., Candy, L., Edmonds, E. A. and Foster, T. J. (1992) Knowledge acquisition and refinement using end-user knowledge manipulation systems. *Proc. Applications of Artificial Intelligence and Knowledge-Based Systems Conference*. Orlando, Florida.

Rickey, G. (1967) *Constructivism*. Brazilier, New York.

Schön, D.A. (1983) *The reflective practitioner*. Maurice Temple Smith, London.

Schön, D.A. (1992) Designing as reflective conversation with the materials of a design situation. *Knowledge Based Systems* 5(1) 3–14.

Wertheimer, M. (1959) *Productive thinking*. Harper and Row, New York.

Ernest Edmonds has used computers in art practice since 1968. His recent work has concentrated on logic-based generative digital videos, known as video constructs. He first exhibited a video construct in London in 1985 and has since shown them, and related works, in Moscow, Sydney, Rotterdam, Liège, Vervier, Budapest, Koblenz, etc. He has published more than 160 research papers on human-computer interaction, creativity and computer support systems. His book with Linda Candy, Explorations in art and technology, was published in 2002. He was leader of the UK DTI's mission to Japan - The Interaction of Art and Technology, is a member of the UK Arts and Humanities Research Board's Visual Arts and Media research panel and a member of the Art and Technology Advisory Board at the ATR Laboratories, Kyoto. He is also Chairman of the ACM SIGCHI Creativity & Cognition conference series and is Director of the Creativity and Cognition Research Studios, Loughborough University, UK.

This article first appeared in
Digital Creativity 11(4) 193–204 (2000).

Emergent constructions: re-embodied intelligence within recombinant poetic networks

Bill Seaman

University of Maryland, USA

Abstract

Computer-mediated networks present an artistic medium that heightens the potential for an inter-mingling of the knowledge of the viewer with the 're-embodied intelligence' of an author or authors. Given that computers can house 'recombinant' digital elements of image, sound and text, how can the artist become an 'author' of responsive, self regulating systems which enable 'intelligent' emergent poetic responses to viewer interactivity via the encoding, mapping and modelling of operative poetic elements?

Keywords: emergent, interactive, network, re-embodied intelligence

Computer-mediated networks present an artistic medium that heightens the potential for an intermingling of the knowledge of the user with the 're-embodied intelligence' of an author or authors. We will consider 'networks' in an all-inclusive manner, from the scale of a network of poetic elements housed within a single computer, to that of the distributed housing of the World Wide Web. Such computer-mediated environments can potentially facilitate new forms of inter-authorship. These environments enable the user to engage with the 'artefacts' of the consciousness of the author. Central to this interaction is an emergent experience that is unique for each subsequent participant. Given that computers can house 'recombinant' digital elements of image, sound and text, how can the artist become an 'author' of responsive, self-regulating systems that enable 'intelligent' emergent poetic responses to user interactivity via the encoding, mapping and modelling of operative poetic elements? How can such an environment enhance or trigger particular 'states' of consciousness in the user? To what extent can we 're-frame' aspects of the consciousness of the artist, via specific modes of 'translation' of operative poetic processes and poetic elements of image, sound and text, within functional computer-mediated networks?

I am interested in interactive art works that exhibit 'intelligent' responsiveness to user input. Aleksander and Burnett state:

> *Rather than becoming embroiled in the controversies which surround the nature of human intelligence, the practitioners of artificial intelligence have generally chosen to define their goals in empirical or operational terms rather than theoretical ones...*

Figure 1.
Worldgen 27.

(Aleksander and Burnett 1987 13)
The researcher simply chooses a task that seems to require intelligence (playing chess say or recognising visual images) and tries to build a machine that can accomplish it.
(Aleksander and Burnett 1987 108)
This definition becomes extended or blurred in terms of responsive 'intelligence' in a work of art. We must be careful to differentiate the kind of 'intelligence' exhibited by such an artistic mechanism, to that examined through the Turing test. Thus the value of the Turing test to determine 'intelligence' may be seen as relevant to particular contexts but, for the purposes of art content, it may be completely irrelevant. An artwork may explore any approach that the author (or authors) finds appropriately 'intelligent'. Thus a system may appear to be non-functional, silly, ironic, stupid, humorous, tragic, overtly sexual, etc. — any form that is appropriate to the individual's aesthetic. The artist is not trying to 'fool' someone into believing the machine is thinking. The artist is attempting to 'intelligently' translate particular kinds of responses and/or behaviours into computer-based environments so that, during interaction, the mind-set of the programmer/ artist can be experienced by the user in the service of experiential content.

My research explores computer-mediated, re-embodied 'intelligence' in the context of a new form of poetic construction and navigation that I call 'recombinant poetics'. Artworks which explore recombinant poetics are characterised by the interaction of a user with a system of content exploration which carries potential meaning constructed of language, image and sound elements, within an authored technological environment. The term recombinant poetics was created by the author in 1995.

Re-embodied intelligence can be defined as the translation of media elements and/or processes into a symbolic language that enables those elements and processes to become part of an operative computer-mediated system.

In seeking the origins of the concepts

which have come to enable this art practice, we can make a 'genetic' analogy to the principles which enabled the functioning of the Jacquard loom. One can trace the genealogy of the computer from the initial patterns of weaves facilitated by this particular loom to the fabric of contemporary communication — images and texts comprised of pixels. Recombinant poetic works are embodied within systems which propagate the inter-authorship of the programmer and artist via symbolic logic. The result of this endeavour is finally manifest on the outermost level of the system of representation as recombinant configurations of light and sound. Modular visual and textual elements which are operative within this technological system have a punning function in relation to that system. Outwardly they communicate artistic content to the user, while inwardly they perform as the functional connection to encoded symbolic logic.

A computer language is a notation for the unambiguous description of computer programmes. Such languages are synthetic in their vocabulary. Punctuation, grammar, syntax and semantics are precisely defined in the context of a particular operating system. They suffer from an inability to cope with autonomous expression — an essential attribute of an organic language. The poetic of computers lies in the genius of individual programmers to express the beauty of their thought using such an inexorable medium. (Hamilton and Bork 1997)

One can see the seeds of re-embodied intelligence within the Jacquard loom, which has been described as exhibiting "the selective powers of the human brain and the dexterity of living

fingers" (Blum 1970 41). The person who encodes the punch card 're-embodies' an aesthetic conception into a language which the analogue machine can read. Blum states:

This intricate process actually starts when an artist draws a sketch. When finished, it must look like the pattern will appear in the cloth ... it is transferred by a draftsman to a ruled sheet similar to those used by engineers to show curves and graphs. Each tiny block or square sheet represents a tiny section of the fabric to be woven ... With the design blocked out on the ruled sheet directly in front of him, the card-cutter works his way through the bewildering network of lines, paths of colour — a perfect maze of passages and tracks, punching holes in the oblong cards. Each of these holes controls eight threads in a weave arrangement over the passing shuttle. Each has a meaning as to weave effects and colour selection, and these all have to be translated so that the loom understands them. (Blum 1970 44)

This description shows one early relevant example of the translation of aesthetic practice to a machine-mediated process. We can extrapolate this idea in terms of contemporary computer-art practice, making a direct analogy to the punch cards functioning as 'conceptual machines' within the analogue mechanism of the loom to the software/hardware paradigm in computers, where the code functions as a vehicle of the translated aesthetic conceptions of the artist. The computer enables not only the production of an image, but of entire artistic processes — the writing of a poem, the construction of a virtual world, the navigation of a poetic environment, etc. Once a chosen 'intelligent' process has been translated, the

Recombinant poetic works are embodied within systems which propagate the inter-authorship of the programmer and artist via symbolic logic

machine can perform 'intelligent' functions in the manner of the author, producing unique new works of art in conjunction with the interaction of a user. Thus the machine functions as an extension of the author's sensibility, presenting an environment for another mode of inter-authorship via user interaction.

We can look at the computer code in recombinant poetic works in terms of a series of layers, on a number of levels. We start at the bottom, with assembly language. We then have various other logical layers which enable the construction of an upper or outer layer of code that floats on the surface of the system, presented via images, sound and text. A graphical user interface can potentially function in a non-hierarchical and non-linear manner in relation to the presentation of artistic content. Such code may also embody paradox, nonsense, play, etc. — any quality of aesthetic phenomena. I am examining computers as being expressive vehicles, housing and enabling the exploration of operative poetic elements via this series of interdependent levels of responsive 'code' authoring. In terms of the connectivity of computers and the potentials of distributed interactivity, such processes may function on various levels from the local to the international. The network of poetic elements can be housed on a single computer, or can be distributed via numerous machines which are networked.

In terms of user interactivity with computer-mediated artworks, we are moving in the direction of computers functioning as 'sensing' and 'responding' devices. Such systems were envisioned by the founders of AI. In his discussion of an automatic computing engine, Alan Turing refers to 'input' and 'output' organs (Turing 1986 36), suggesting notions of sensing. He also projected the possibility of computers playing chess — an intelligent, rule based, combinatorial process.

The goal is to have the computer function as a mediated extension of focused perception, both in terms of 'sensing' and

'responding'. The output of the system is not known in advance by the author, but is an emergent product of the interaction of the user with particular 'recombinant' elements and processes authored into the system. The construction and navigation processes have also been translated and encoded, enabling inter-authorship.

Computer-mediated environments facilitate 'states' of authorship. In computer-mediated interactive artwork, a user can intermingle with the operative elements of the system and interact with them via authored feedback mechanisms. The user can enter into a conceptual 'dialogue' with 'artefacts of thought' that the initial author has encoded in the system. These media artefacts and processes enable the exploration of particular states of consciousness which are triggered within the experiential environment.

In tracing the genealogy of ideas related to recombinant poetics, the *Notes* of Ada Lovelace prove central (Menabrea 1843). Her work with Charles Babbage's Analytical Engine in the 1800s explored the manifestation of symbolic logic via the encoding of punched cards, a direct outgrowth from the Jacquard loom. The punched cards of the Analytical Engine function as a 'translation' and encoding of symbolic language, and can function as a conceptual machine within a 'physical' one. This is again analogous to the hardware/software paradigm. Lovelace wrote:

We may say most aptly that the Analytical Engine weaves algebraical patterns just as the Jacquard-loom weaves flowers and leaves. (Babbage 1961 249)

Lovelace also remarked that:

The Analytical Engine is an embodying of the science of operations, constructed with particular reference to abstract number as the subject of those operations... Again, [the Analytical Engine] might act upon other things beside number were objects found whose mutual fundamental relations could be expressed by those

Figure 2.
Worldgen 255.

of the abstract science of operations, and which should be also susceptible of adaptations to the action of the operating notation and mechanism of the engine. Supposing for instance, that the fundamental relations of pitched sounds in the science of harmony and of musical composition were susceptible of such expressions and adaptations, the engine might compose elaborate and scientific pieces of music of any degree of complexity or extent... It may be desirable to explain that, by the word operation, we mean any process which alters the relation of two or more things, be this relation of what kind it may. This is the most general definition and would include all subjects in the universe.
(Babbage 1961 249)

In Lovelace's *Notes* we see a number of foci related to the salient characteristics of both recombinant poetics and re-embodied intelligence — that of the ability to perform multiple operations upon chosen abstract entities as well as the potential of those entities to be aesthetic in nature, i.e. that the machine might act upon

and compose and perform 'music.' Also relevant to recombinant poetics is the pun in Lovelace's use of the word 'translator' in her title. It could refer to her being the literal language translator of L. F. Menabrea's text, or a 'translator' of thought into readable code as in the analytical engine, or the translator of Babbage's ideas about the analytical engine into an understandable as well as extended form.

From the perspective of the present, also relevant to these areas of research is the potential of the computer to enable 'generative' music, as coined by Brian Eno. Also related is the notion of modular recombinational music structures: 'Recombinant' music as coined by Seaman. This music is based on sonic variables and parameters entered into the system, as well as operative processes which act upon those variables, producing various sonic output. Such a system is activated and experienced via the interaction of the user. Ada continues:

In abstract mathematics, of course operations alter those particular relations which are

involved in the considerations of number and space, and the results of operations are those particular results which correspond to the nature of the subjects of operation. But the science of operations, as derived from mathematics more especially, is a science of itself, and has its own abstract truth and value; just as logic has its own peculiar truth and value, independently of the subjects to which we may apply its reasonings and processes. Those who are accustomed to some of the more modern views of the above subject, will know that a few fundamental relations being true, certain other combinations of relations must of necessity follow; combinations unlimited in variety and extent if the deductions from the primary relations be carried on far enough.
(Babbage 1961 249)

These ideas are central to the functioning of recombinant poetic works. This enlightened *Note* was published in 1843, almost 100 years before Turing would pick up on its potential ramifications.

Figure 3.
Worldgen 272.

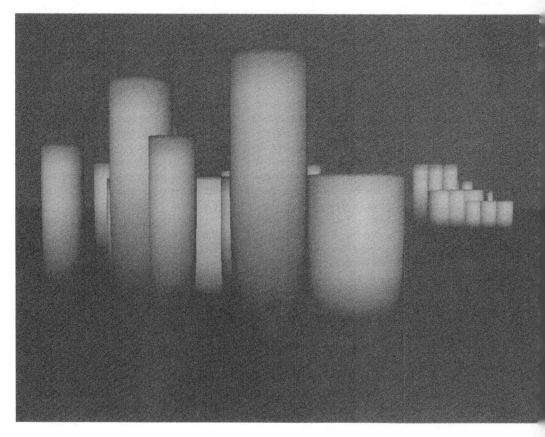

Acknowledgements

The graphics were generated during use of the virtual reality work entitled *The World Generator / The Engine of Desire* © 1996/97, Bill Seaman with Gideon May, Programmer.

This work empowers users to construct virtual worlds in real time using a new interface metaphor. One menu option enables the user to instantly generate an entire world, including a series of media elements: sound objects, poetic texts, digital movies, digital stills, 3D objects, texture maps and attached behaviours, exemplifying re-embodied intelligence. The work was most recently shown at the InterCommunication Center in Tokyo, networked to the ZKM (Center for Art and Media) in Karlsruhe, Germany. Thus two participants could be in the same virtual space at the same time, both building and exploring an inter-authored virtual environment. A video avatar showed the relative position of each participant (vuser). They could also converse with each other about their experience via video phone.

References

Aleksander, I. and Burnett, P. (1987) *Thinking Machines: The Search For Artificial Intelligence.* New York: Alfred A. Knopf.

Babbage, C. (1961) *Charles Babbage And His Calculating Engines: Selected Writings.* New York:

143

Dover.

Blum, H. (1970) *The Loom Has A Brain*. Littleton, New Hampshire: Courier Printing Co. Fifth Printing.

Hamilton, R. and Bonk, E. (1997) *The Typosophic Texture In Politics/Poetics: Das Burch Zur Documenta X*. Cantz.

Menabrea, L.F. (1843) *Sketch Of The Analytical Engine Invented By Charles Babbage ... With Notes By The Translator, A.A.L. [i.e. Augusta Ada King, Countess Lovelace]*. London: R. & J.E. Taylor.

Turing, A. (1986) *A. M. Turing's ACE Report Of 1946 And Other Papers*. The Charles Babbage Institute Reprint Series For The History Of Computing, 10). Cambridge: MIT Press.

Bill Seaman received a PhD from the Centre for Advanced Inquiry In the Interactive Arts, University of Wales, Newport, 1999. He holds a Master of Science in Visual Studies degree from the Massachusetts Institute of Technology, 1985. His work explores text, image and sound relationships through technological installation, virtual reality, linear video, computer controlled laserdisc and other computer-based media, photography, and studio based audio compositions. He is self-taught as a composer and musician. His works have been in numerous international festivals and museum shows where he has been awarded prizes such as the Prix Ars Electronica in Interactive Art (1992 and 1995, Linz, Austria); International Video Art Prize, ZKM (Karlsruhe, Germany); Bonn Videonale prize; First Prize, Berlin Film / Video Festival, for Multimedia (1995); and the Awards in the Visual Arts Prize. Seaman is a Professor in the Department of Design | Media Arts, UCLA where he is exploring issues related to the continuum between physical and virtual/media space.

This article first appeared in
Digital Creativity 9(3) 153–174 (1998).

Artistic communication for A-life and robotics

Naoko Tosa and Ryohei Nakatsu

ATR Media Integration and Communications Research Laboratories, Japan

Abstract

A computer-generated poet, MUSE, conveys short poetic words and emotions to a person using the "Renga" format. "Renga" is generated by multiple people as a combination of short Japanese poems such as the "Waka" or "Haiku" which were created in the ancient era and have been used as a medium to express Japanese spiritual emotions. By hearing these words, the person is able to enter the world of that poem and, at the same time, he or she is able to speak to MUSE with poetic words.
Through this process of exchanging poetic words, the interactive poem allows the user and computer to work together to build the world of an improvised poem filled with inspiration, feeling, and 'emotion'.

Keywords: cross-cultural understanding, computer poetry, emotion recognition, sensitive communication, spiritual interactive art

1. Introduction

Humans cannot live alone. A human is basically a creature who longs for communication with humans and things. By showing affection to someone or something, teasing someone, or personalising things, a human is spiritually satisfied. In the future, humans will tend to love or hate the computers that will fill our lives. In order to co-exist with computers, we are forced to change our lifestyles. In our life today, however, it is nearly impossible to avoid communication with computers. That is why sensitive communication with computers becomes important. Although computers are essentially unfriendly, they can be made friendly by the skilful design of computer software and hardware. In this paper, we introduce an AI computer system featuring an interactive theatre in which a person can create an impromptu poem and participate in a play while communicating with AI characters capable of sensing human emotion.

2. Interactive poem

We propose a new type of speech-based interaction system called *Interactive Poem* (Figure 1). A human and a computer agent create a poetic world by exchanging poetic phrases, thus realising emotion-based communications between computers and humans. As a first step toward emotion-based communications between computer agents and humans, we have developed several computer agents such as Neuro Baby (Tosa 1994), MIC and MUSE (Tosa and Nakatsu 1996). These are computer characters that are capable of recognising several emotions

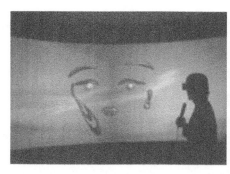

in speech and reacting to them by changing their facial expressions and body motions. Fortunately, these agents have been very successful and have been demonstrated at various exhibitions. As a next step toward the realisation of feeling-based communications between computer agents and humans, we selected the 'poem' as a means of communication. There are several reasons for this approach. The main reason is that in a poem not only the meaning of words or phrases but also the rhythms and moods created by their sequence plays an essential role. Therefore, the poem is intended to transmit feeling information such as mood and sensitivity rather than logical information. The second reason is that poems were originally expressed by oral reading rather than in writing. This means that a poem is suitable for interaction between computers and humans. Recently, researchers have shown increased interest in the realisation of feeling-based interactions and communications between computers and humans (Maes et al 1995, Perlin 1995, Bates et al 1992). However, only a few have worked on voice communications, despite the fact that voice is an essential means of feeling-communications. This is the third reason for our interest in developing communications based on an uttered poem. This paper next explains the basic principles of the *Interactive Poem* system we have developed based on the above concept. The software configuration and hardware configuration are then described in detail. Finally, a typical installation of the *Interactive Poem* system is introduced.

Interactive Poem is a new type of poem that is created by a participant and a computer agent collaborating in a poetic world full of inspiration, emotion and sensitivity. A computer agent called MUSE, who has been carefully designed with a face suitable for expressing the emotions of a poetic world, appears on the screen. She will utter a short poetic phrase to the participant. Hearing it allows him/her to enter the world of the poem and, at the same

time, feel an impulse to respond by uttering one of the optional phrases or by creating his/her own poetic phrase. Exchanging poetic phrases through this interactive process allows the participant and MUSE to become collaborative poets who generate a new poem and a new poetic world.

3. The concept of interactive poem

My interest is in how to generate feeling in communication between people and intelligent characters. Also, I'm interested in creating an intelligent character's consciousness. The computer-generated poet, MUSE, can make a poem with you interactively and in real time.

Figure 1.
Interactive
poem.

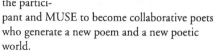
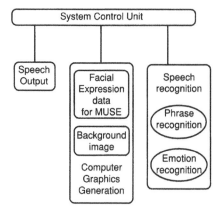

Figure 2. Block diagram of the interactive poem.

Interactive poetry has its roots in old Japanese culture as a type of poem called "renga". Renga is a kind of haiku. Haiku was created in the Edo era (beginning in the 1600s) and is a typical expression of Japanese sensibility. Renga is a combination of short poems and generated by multiple people. For example, one person makes the first short poem, and another person makes the second short poem.

3.1 Software configuration

The system used to create the interactive poem consists of four main units: system control, speech recognition, computer graphics generation and speech output (Figure 2). The system control unit manages behaviour of the whole system by utilising the interactive poem database. In this system, the most important issue is

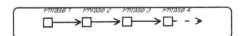

Figure 3a. Construction of a conventional poem.

Figure 3b. Construction of the interactive poem. (a)

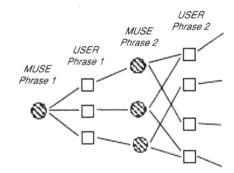

Figure 3c. Construction of the interactive poem(b)

constructing the interactive poem, so we must first explain how the interactive poem database is constructed. A conventional poem is considered a sequence of poetic phrases. In other words, the basic construction of a conventional poem can be expressed by a simple state-

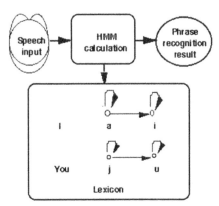

Figure 4. Phrase recognition.

transition network where each phrase corresponds to a given state, and for each state there is only one successive state (Figure 3a). The basic form of the interactive poem is expressed by this simple transition network, but it differs from a conventional poem in that phrases uttered by the computer agent and phrases uttered by a participant appear in turn. This corresponds to a simple interaction where the computer agent and the participant alternately read a predetermined sequence of poetic phrases (Figure 3b). Reaction of the computer agent to utterances of a participant is expressed through her speech and by images. In the speech output unit, speech data for each phrase to be uttered by the computer agent is digitally stored and generated when necessary. The computer graphics generation unit controls the image reaction of the computer agent. Image reaction consists of two kinds of images: facial expressions for the computer agent MUSE and various scenes. The facial expressions of MUSE express her reactions to the emotional state of the

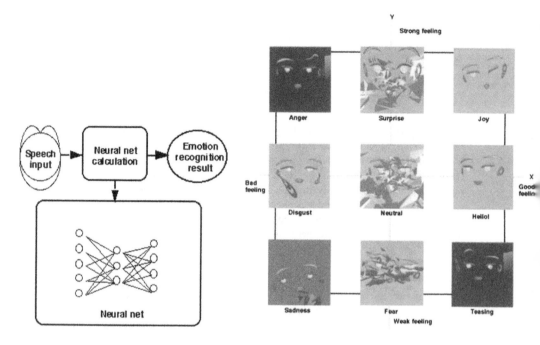

Figure 5. Emotion recognition.

participant. These images are represented by keyframe animations, each of which corresponds to the eight emotions (Figure 6). To express the atmosphere of the interactive poem, several kinds of scenes are digitally stored. Each scene image corresponds to a group of states in the transition network, and each correspondence is carefully determined in advance.

3.2 Hardware configuration

This mainly consists of several workstations and a PC: a workstation for computer graphics generation, a workstation for both system control and phrase recognition, a workstation for emotion recognition, and a PC for speech output. For the participant's convenience, optional phrases that may be uttered following an utterance of MUSE appear on the display. The participant can choose one of these phrases based on their feelings and sensitivity, or they can create their own poetic phrase. Regardless, the emotion recognition function can produce a result. In addition, the phrase recognition function selects the pre-existing phrase that most closely resembles the uttered phrase. Therefore, the participant feels as if the interactive poem process continues in a natural way (Figure 7).

4. Interactions

The interaction mechanism operates as follows.
(1) When MUSE utters a phrase, the recognition process is activated. A participant then utters a phrase and it is recognised by the phrase recognition function, which uses the lexicon subset corresponding to the next set of phrases in the transition network. At the same time, the emotion contained in the utterance is recognised by the emotion recognition function.
(2) Based on information pertaining to recognition and the transition network, the system's reaction is decided. The facial expression of MUSE changes according to the results of emotion recognition, and the phrase MUSE utters is based on the results of phrase recognition and the transition network. The background scene changes as the transitions continue.
(3) In the above manner, poetic phrases between MUSE and the participant are consecutively produced.

5. Interactive cinema with emotion recognition

As a media artist, I've always been fascinated by the idea of entering the world of movies I created myself. In interactive art, one can

Figure 6.
MUSE's
emotional
expression.

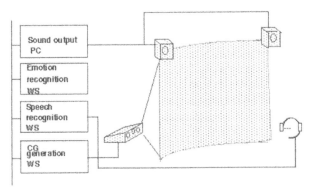

Figure 7.

Interactive poem — hardware configuration.

interact with movies in virtual reality. My vision was to create a work in which I can talk to characters of my own creation as if they were alive and feel the excitement of dramatically changing a virtual reality world. One could say this experience resembles the world of dreams. In a dream, we autonomously communicate with the characters and objects we encounter, and the world is a series of fragments of images with or without context. Characters in a dream fascinate us with their mysterious behaviour. What happens in a dream resembles being emotionally involved with movies in a movie theatre. The difference is that we are more autonomous in dreams. We have begun research on this electronic daydreaming as the next generation of cinema. In this paper, we introduce the design of attractive characters that are capable of recognising emotion from the tone of a human voice.

6. Interactive character design

MIC is a male child character. He has a cuteness that makes humans feel they want to speak to him. He is playful and cheeky, but doesn't have a spiteful nature. For example, he is the quintessential comic character.

6.1 Emotion

MIC recognises the following emotions from intonations in the human voice. An asterisk indicates how the user should make intonations. The physical form of intonations is called prosody.

a. Joy (happiness, satisfaction, enjoyment, comfort, smile)
  * exciting, vigorous, voice rises at the end of a sentence
b. Anger (rage, resentment, displeasure)
  * voice falls at the end of a sentence

c. Surprise (astonishment, shock, confusion, amazement, unexpectedness)
  * screaming, excited voice
d. Sadness (sadness, tearful, sorrow, loneliness, emptiness)
  * weak, faint, empty voice
e. Disgust
  * sullen, aversive, repulsive voice
f. Teasing
  * light, insincere voice
g. Fear
  * frightened, sharp, shrill voice

6.2 Communication

In most cases, the content of a media transmission conceals the actual functions of the medium. This content is impersonating a message, but the real message is a structural change that takes place in the deep recesses of human relations. We aim for this kind of deep communication. People use a microphone when communicating with MIC. For example, if the participant whistles, MIC's feeling is positive and he responds with excitement. If the speaker's voice is low and strong, MIC's feeling is bad and he gets angry.

6.3 Processing

This section describes the principles and operational details for the recognition of emotions included in speech. It also explains the generation process of Neuro Baby's reactions, which correspond to the emotions it receives.

6.4 Basic principle

Neuro Baby (NB) has advanced from its original version through several stages (Tosa 1994, 1995) to MIC and MUSE. In our present research, we tried to realise higher-level processing that can achieve more sophisticated interactions between NB and humans. For this purpose, we have emphasised the following issues in our work.
(1) Treatment of various emotional expressions
How many and what kinds of emotional expressions to be adopted are both interesting

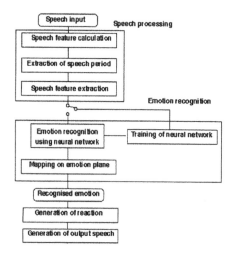

Figure 8. Block diagram of the processing flow.

and difficult issues. In our previous study, we investigated four emotional states [1]. Based on our experiences of demonstrating the first version NB to a variety of people and on the belief that an increased number of emotional states would make the interaction between NB and humans richer, this study encompasses the seven emotional states described later.
(2) Speaker-independent and content-independent emotion recognition. Speaker independence is an important aspect of speech/emotion recognition. From a pragmatic viewpoint, a speaker-dependent emotion recognition system requires a tiresome learning stage each time a new speaker wants to use the system; therefore, it is not easy to use. Moreover humans can understand the emotions included in speech, as well as the meaning conveyed by speech, even for arbitrary speakers. Also, content independence is indispensable for emotion recognition. In daily communication, various kinds of emotions are conveyed by the same words or sentences; mastering such nuance is the key to rich and sensitive communications among people. Therefore, by adopting a neural network architecture and by introducing a training stage that uses a large number of training utterances,

we have developed a speaker-independent and content-independent emotion recognition system.

6.5 Block diagram of the processing

Figure 8 is a block diagram of the processing flow. The process mainly consists of three parts: speech processing, emotion recognition and generation of reactions. In the speech processing part, feature parameters of input speech are extracted in real time in the feature extraction stage. Then, by observing the speech power, the period where speech exists is extracted. From the extracted speech, feature parameters are extracted and arranged as an output of the feature extraction stage. This output is fed into the emotion recognition part, where two-stage emotion recognition is carried out. In the first stage a combination of plural neural networks, each of which is designed and trained to recognise a specific emotion in speech, receives feature parameters and carries out a recognition

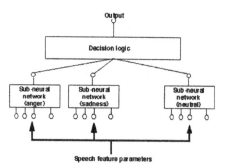

Figure 9. Configuration of the emotion recognition part.

process. In the second stage the multiple output of the first stage is processed through a specialised logic, and the emotion recognition results are expressed as points on a two-dimensional space on which eight emotions including neutral state are displayed according to our criteria listed earlier. The result's position on the emotion plane and its movement determine the reaction of Neuro Baby, including its facial expressions and actions. These facial expressions and actions were previously created by an intuitive design process developed by one of the authors. These reactions are visualised with computer graphics along with appropriate speech output.

Configuration of the neural network

The neural network for emotion recognition is a combination of eight sub-networks (Figure 9). The decision logic stage combines the outputs of these sub-networks and outputs the final recognition result. Each sub-network is tuned to recognise one of seven emotions (anger, sadness, happiness, fear, surprise, disgust, and teasing) and neutral emotion. Basically, each sub-network has the same network architecture (Figure 10). It is a three-layered neural network with 150 input nodes corresponding to the dimension of speech features, 20 to 30 intermediate nodes and one output node.

Neural network training

To recognise emotions, it is necessary to train each of the sub-networks. Since our target is speaker-independent and content-independent emotion recognition, the following utterances were prepared for training:

Words: 100 phoneme-balanced words

Speakers: five male speakers and five female speakers

Emotions: neutral, anger, sadness, happiness, fear, surprise, disgust, and teasing

Utterances: Each speaker uttered 100 words eight times. In each of the eight trials, he/she uttered words using different emotional expressions. Thus, a total of 800 utterances for each speaker were obtained as training data.

Using these utterances, we carried out various preliminary training tests. It turned out that preparing two kinds of networks for each emotion, one for male speakers and the other for female speakers, is better than preparing only one network to handle both male and female utterances. In other words, the emotional

expressions between males and females are somewhat different and cannot be handled together. The reason for this is not clear and will require further research.

Emotion recognition by a neural network

In the emotion recognition phase, speech feature parameters extracted in speech processing are simultaneously fed into the eight sub-networks and trained as described above. Eight values,

$$V = (v1, v2, ..., v8),$$

are obtained as the result of emotion recognition.

Mapping on an emotion plane

As described above, the output of the emotion recognition network is a vector $V=(v1, v2, ..., v8)$ and the final recognition result should be obtained based on V. In our previous study, we expressed the final emotion state by a point on a two-dimensional plane. Based on the experiences of previous research, in the present study the positions of the eight emotions have been rearranged on emotion plane E (Figure 11). It is necessary, therefore, to carry out the mapping from V onto E. Let m1 and m2 be the first and second maximum values among v1, v2, ..., v8, and also let (xm1, ym1), (xm2, ym2) be the emotion positions corresponding to m1 and m2, respectively. The final emotion position (x, y) is calculated by

$$x = c{*}xm1 + (1\text{-}c){*}xm2$$
$$y = c{*}ym1 + (1\text{-}c){*}ym2$$
(c: constant value).

6.6 Generation of reaction and selection of output speech

The structure of animation

There are four emotion planes, all of which use the same x, y data (Figure 11).

a. Plane *a* generates facial animation by choosing the three key frames closest to the (x, y) data point. The computation of a weighted mean frame is done as follows. Let A be the area formed by the three key frames, and a1,

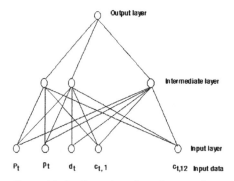

Figure 10. Configuration of a sub-network.

a2, and a3 the areas shown in Figure 6. Accordingly, the three weights for each key frame are A/a1, A/a2, and A/a3, respectively. The interpolated frame is then calculated by a weighted average of the three key frames.

b. Plane *b* generates an animation of the character's body by mapping each (x, y) data point on the plane to a body key frame.

c. Plane *c* is a mapping of each (x, y) data point to camera parameters such as zoom, tilt, and pan.

d. Plane *d* is a mapping of each (x, y) data point to background tiles.

Selection of output speech
From a mapping from the (x, y) data points of the emotion plane to 200 sampled speech utterances, one of the utterances is selected as the output speech. A personal computer is used to play the selected sounds.

6.7 Reaction of the characters
The reactions of MIC could be carefully designed and were visualised with computer graphics. Several examples of emotional expressions by MIC are shown in Figure 12.

7. Conclusion

This paper describes two new areas of applied research in artificial life: the *Interactive Poem* created by the interaction between a human and an anthropomorphic computer-generated poet named MUSE; and, as part of next-generation interactive movies, the design of characters that can sense human emotions based on computer graphics. Research in these areas is now expanding into a movie description system consisting of an interaction manager, scene manager, script manager and other functions that enable character scenes and stories to change dynamically. Here, while the properties of anthropomorphic artificial-life characters are often set by internal design, they may also turn 'good' or 'bad' according to environmental settings and the scheme adopted for communicating with humans. The internal design of characters depends heavily on artificial-life technology, and the ability to communicate requires that an environment be established in which emotions can be introduced naturally. The ultimate objective of combining art with artificial-life research is to achieve works that impact viewers in a new and powerful manner. In this regard, the time is coming when artists and researchers must develop a sharp sense of the best techniques for efficient artistic expression, or in other words, the means of achieving a bridge between technology and creativity.

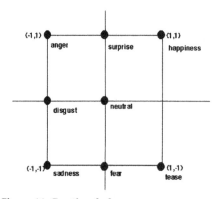

Figure 11. Emotional plane.

References

Bates, J., Loyall, B. and Reilly, S. (1992) An architecture for action, emotion, and social behaviour. *Proceedings of the Fourth European Workshop on Modelling Autonomous Agents in a Multi-Agent World.*

Maes, P., Darrell, T., Blumberg, B. and Pentland, A. (1995) The ALIVE system: Full-body interaction with autonomous agents. *Proc. of the Computer Animation '95 Conference.*

Perlin, K. (1995) Real-time responsive animation with personality. *IEEE Transactions on Visualization and Computer Graphics,* 1(1), pp.5–15.

Tosa, N. et al. (1994) Neuro-Character. *AAAI'94* Workshop, AI and A-Life and Entertainment.

Tosa, N. et al. (1995) Network Neuro-Baby with robotics hand. *Symbiosis of Human and Artifact.* Elsevier Science B.V.

Tosa, N. and Nakatsu, R. (1996) Life-like Communication Agent — Emotion Sensing Character 'MIC' and Feeling Session Character 'MUSE'. *Proceedings of the International Conference on Multimedia Computing and Systems,* pp. 12–19.

Naoko Tosa is Artistic Director and Researcher in the Interactive Movie Project, ATR Advanced Telecommunications Research Laboratories, Associate Professor at Kobe University and Lecturer at the Department of Media Arts and Science, Musashino Art University

Figure 12.
Example of interaction between MUSE and participant.

This article first appeared in
Digital Creativity 9(1) 53–61 (1998).

Technological latency: from autoplastic to alloplastic

dECOi Architects

Paris/London

Abstract

Digital technologies can bring about a paradigm shift in architecture that reflects the ongoing cultural adaptation of society to an electronic environment. To achieve this we must consider current technical developments in psychological as much as technical terms. The concept of 'trauma' is important: it refers not to a strategic dis/re-orientation, but to a suspension of the possibility of orientation.

The paper speculates on the relations of trauma to the patterns of creativity propagated by digital technology, in order to counter the re-incorporation of electronic technologies within traditional ideological frameworks. One might characterise this as a shift from an autoplastic (a self-determinate operative strategy) to an alloplastic (a reciprocal environmental modification) mode of operation.

Three projects are described. The Pallas House project hints at new possibilities of numeric craft and decoration. In Aegis the surface deforms according to stimuli captured from the environment, which may be selectively deployed as active or passive sensors. The Paramorph is imagined as a series of tessellated aluminium surfaces which act as host to interactive sound sculpture, sound deployed in response to the passage of people moving through the form.

Keywords: architecture, disorientation, reciprocal environments, surface deformation, trauma

1. Introduction

> *Hyper-*   *excessive, overmuch, above, from Greek huper- over, beyond e.g. hyperbole — a figure of speech which greatly exagerrates the truth hypercritical — too critical, esp. of trivial faults*
>
> *Hypo-*   *below, under, deficient, from Greek, hupo-, hup- under e.g. hypocritical — of or characterized by hypocrisy a pretense of false virtue, benevolence* (Vattimo 1992)

The evident formal capacity of new generative media in architecture to produce complex or non-standard form(s) is perhaps as nothing compared to the shifts in cognition that such technical change engenders in a subliminal but widespread sense. For what has been claimed as a 'paradigm' shift in architecture is not so much the sudden utilisation of CAD by architects, but the ongoing cultural adaptation of society to an electronic environment. If we consider that 'technology' constitutes the base textile of a culture (its *ge-stell*, or *en-framing*, in Heideggerian terms — its base language) the impact of any new development is most pertinently measured as the degree to which such terrain is reconfigured in the implication of a new technical weft.

In presenting the work of dECOi in terms of digital creativity, we will therefore consider current technical developments in psychological as much as technical terms, considering shifts in general patterns of cultural (not just architectural) production but also reception. This will suggest a transition from a mode of shock (Heidegger's *stoss*) to a more subtle one of sustained dis/re-orientation — almost a suspension of shock — which we will consider in terms of trauma. Here we will draw in particular from Sandor Ferenczi's reconsideration of Freud's analyses of trauma to suggest a move from an autoplastic to an alloplastic cultural mode. Implicitly this will shift emphasis to consideration of hypo- rather than hyper-surface(s) as the prescient (in)forms of electronic genera(c)tion in architecture.

2. Latency

In *The transparent society*[1], Gianni Vattimo suggests that contemporary cultural production relies no longer simply on shock but on an effect of sustained disorientation — almost a suspension of shock. For Vattimo the effective event/work is one that endlessly differs/defers cognitive assimilation, marking a shift which I will here characterise in psychological terms as trauma (the mind struggling to comprehend a lack). The term latency is used within psychology to describe the lack of incorporation that attends trauma — that it is founded on an insistent yet unassimilable event — which I will here consider in terms of the effects engendered by/in a digital medium.

Vattimo's text is concerned with the cultural effects of technical change, tracking shifts in the base 'psychologies of perception'; here I will extend this to a consideration of architectural production/reception in its attempts at incorporation[2] of a new technology.

Vattimo's insight

The psychological shift ... requires not simply the incorporation of a new technology, but a quite fundamental re-evaluation of the very manner of cultural creativity and receptivity that it engenders

suggests a quite marked shift in cultural aptitude — a sharp contrast to Gombrich's *The sense of order* (1979), for instance, (subtitled *a study in the psychology of decorative art* circa 1960) in which he continually asserts that cognitive disorientation cannot be tolerated and will quickly be grounded by a representative predilection (the mind short-circuiting the difficulty). Gombrich is certainly fascinated by artworks and patterns that confound perception, but he seems to allow that this can only be a momentary disorientation before the mind exerts an order in absentia, as if this were somehow a preordinate and natural 'representative' capacity of the mind.[3] Vattimo's suggestion that the effectiveness of strategies of shock seems to be giving way to "softer, more fluid" modes of operation, fluid in their dissolution of representative certitude, corresponds to current strategies throughout the arts. These I would characterise as being ones of precise indeterminacy, as precisely calibrated forms of disorientation, which Gombrich, for one, might struggle to account for.

Such thought has been provoked in large part by my attempt to register the bewildering effects of William Forsythe's Frankfurt Ballet, where he asks his dancers to 'represent loss', 'sustain the reinscription of forms', 'capture an absent presence', etc. — strategies of sustained and deliberate absenting.[4] Articulating this in terms of trauma draws from Heidi Gilpin's suggestive essay *Aberrations of gravity* where she characterises the charged effect of disappearance such dance engenders in terms of trauma, as "the staging of that which does not take place" (Forsythe), a "traumatic absence" (Gilpin 1997). But having worked with the Frankfurt Ballet in their production of *Sleepers' guts* and having witnessed the creation of *Eidos/Telos* I realised that both production and reception, which for Forsythe are very much extensions of one another, are traumatically implicated in that both operate with no a priori, no representational dictat. "We work free of idea", he suggests, preferring an open processural creative drift to the determinism of ideological constructs.[5] The creative process, that is, is highly implicated in the resultant effect — it embraces disorientation in its very process — a crucial aspect in such strategies of cultural latency.

As we begin to operate in a fully electronic creative environment in architecture, which offers the possibility of quite open-ended and fluid creative processes, such strategic yet non-linear creative strategies of dis-incorporation seem prescient. The psychological shift hinted at by Vattimo, that is, requires not simply the incorporation of a new technology, but a quite fundamental re-evaluation of the very manner of cultural creativity and receptivity that it engenders.

3. Shock

Shock has long been considered the modus operandi of the Modernist arts, writers from diverse fields (Heidegger, Benjamin, Barthes, etc.) all accounting for the effectivity of artworks in terms of 'the shock of the new' and the dis/re-orientating wrench that it engenders. For Benjamin this marked the shift from 'aura' to exhibition-value of artworks: henceforth art would no longer derive its meaning by being somehow replete with pre-ordinate significance, but in its capacity to actively reorient cognition through its interrogation of extant cultural pattern (Benjamin 1969). His prognosis seems with hindsight to have been an accurate one: that art has moved off its pedestal to come into

much more direct contact with the world, deploying new genres of effectivity — most significantly (for Benjamin) as strategies of shock.

But in considering the effects of a profligate and radical new productive electronic media that rapidly infiltrates all aspects of the current cultural field — an "art in the age of electronic de-production" as it were — one senses a general dissipation of shock-effectivity. For it seems that different patterns of cultural registration are emerging, engendered by an electronic medium which reconfigures the field subliminally. For shock implies reference for it to be effective, the resulting dis-orientation figured consciously as a strategy of reactivity (frequently as a strategy of re-orientation, also). But much contemporary work, in its genera(c)tive profligacy, disenfranchises comprehension in an absence or over-abundance of evident reference, the trace of its coming-into-being 'digitally' indeterminate.

The ensuing disorientation differs from that of shock in its very indeterminacy: no longer is it simply a strategic dis/re-orientation, but it acts as a suspension of the possibility of orientation. It does not rely, that is, on a memorialised circuit for effectivity — in fact, quite the inverse — it stimulates through its very denial of incorporation. Frequently this seems to take the form of/as an endless transformation of the same, engendering a range of effects propitiated in the struggle for an endlessly absented comprehensibility. Here I am thinking of art-works such as Michel Saup's *Supreme particles* — an endless reconfiguration of two floating objects distorted sharply by an improvisational violinist who responds to each distortion as a new reading event — a quite hallucinogenic patterning-in-time which sends the mind reeling spatially in its continual reconfiguration. Such works, that is, evidently 'work' according to an entirely reconfigured psychological circuit.

4. Trauma

Psychological accounts of trauma are varied, but generally it is characterised as stemming from a moment of incomprehension or cognitive incapacity. At a moment of severe stress, for instance,

> there is a frequent shut-down of the conceptual apparatus (as if for protection), which creates an anxiety of reference.

Cathy Caruth, who has written extensively on the relations of trauma and memory, suggests that

> in its repeated imposition as both image and amnesia, the trauma thus seems to evoke the difficult truth of a history that is constituted by the very incomprehensibility of its occurrence.

(Caruth 1996 18)

Trauma, that is, develops not as a direct response to (a) shock, but through the very inability to register it conceptually – through the absence of its assimilation and the struggle of the mind to account for this cognitive incapacity.

> While the traumatized are called upon to see and relive the insistent reality of the past, they recover a past that enters consciousness only through the very denial of active recollection. The ability to recover the past is thus closely and paradoxically tied up, in trauma, with the inability to have access to it… an event that is constituted, in part, by its lack of integration into consciousness.

(Caruth 1991 187)

Freudian psychoanalysis is effectively predicated on trauma in its belief that neuroses are constituted as unconscious traces which are palpably 'there' but repressed or forgotten, inaccessible to the conscious mind (the very conscious/unconscious divide was posited by Freud to account for this).[6] Psychoanalysis then sets itself the task of recovering such traces for consciousness, permitting their assimilation and comprehension: it works by re-establishing representative linkage and causal lineage. In positing trauma as a now effective cultural trope, one would then be working against the Freudian grain and against any simple causal sequence, creative or receptive, posing the question of "how one might learn to write the way the Wolfman spoke". Forsythe seems to me a creative practitioner who operates in just such manner, working with primary memory which he never seeks to entirely recover for consciousness: there is no ideological incorporation.

What seems incontestible is that the representative indeterminacy that resides in trauma is no longer, as Gombrich might have it, intolerable: modes of productivity and receptivity increasingly seem to operate in an indeterminate (electronic) milieu where absence is deployed with cultural effectivity. 'Understanding' here seems to be replaced by 'effect'. My interest is to speculate on the relations of trauma to the patterns of creativity propagated by digital technology, in order to counter the re-incorporation of electronic technologies within traditional ideological frameworks.

5. Transformation

Evidently such technical development may be considered through a variety of conceptual frameworks (psychological (Freud/Fenenczi), philosophical (Derrida), art historical (Benjamin), etc.), but perhaps most simply as the apparent break-up of representative strategy. This shift I would characterise as moving from a notion of origin to one of transformation, the most evident effect of which is to implicate time in an activated sense. The link with electronic production seems evident here: that as we enter a mode of creativity that implicates time in multiple ways, to the extent that the generative patterns of creativity are left as indeterminate traces of transformative process – transformation displaces origin and disperses its vertical legitimacy to a now limitless electronic horizon. In this the notion of trauma seems redolent: cognition searching restlessly for an endlessly absented referent.

Trauma, like shock, then needs to be

thought of in terms other than those of simple debilitation (even in medical terms trauma functions as a strategy of survival). In trauma the very lack of cognitive assimilation from which it derives produces a variety of effects, such as an immediate compulsion to account for that lack (a stimulus) coupled with a heightening of bodily awareness; as if the very absence of cognitive assimilation dispersed thought throughout the sensorium. Trauma, that is, tends to stimulate neglected modes of cognition as an intense 'sampling' of experience as the mind deploys its full cognitive capacity to account for the unfamiliar pattern.

This raising of the body to a cognitive level, a chemic as well as optic mode of thought, metonymic as much as metaphoric, Forsythe characterises as a proprioreceptive mode of production/reception, "a thinking with/in the body"[5]. The current generative environment, in which "the image becomes primary"[7] (develops a life of its own, begins to lead creative endeavour) dislocates familiar patterns of comprehension and the referential strategies they seem to imply. The turmoil this engenders for determinate creative strategy — both productive and receptive — then poses profound questions for cultural (and not simply technical) activity. Most essentially, perhaps, it forces thought back within the body, interrogating the privileging of the senses in relation to conceptual thought, loosening the hegemony of optic sense (on which the linear, causal, memorialised representative circuit largely relies).

6. Autoplastic / Alloplastic

Drawing from Ferenczi's analyses of trauma, one might characterise this as a shift from an autoplastic to an alloplastic mode of operation. Autoplastic is defined as a self-determinate operative strategy, and alloplastic as a reciprocal environmental modification. Classically in trauma autoplastic response is predetermined by the inertia and indifference of the environment:

for trauma to have effect, no effective 'alloplastic'

action, (that is, modification of the environmental threat) is possible, so that 'autoplastic' adaptation of oneself is necessary.[8]

If, then, trauma becomes culturally operative, we might then characterise it in these terms as a shift from an autoplastic to alloplastic mode, both in a productive and a receptive sense. Creatively we operate within an alloplastic 'space' as one begins to work in a responsive, conditional environment, sampling and editing the proliferating capacity of generative software: it is a transformative creative medium, by its very nature. But increasingly this also extends even to physical contexts, which through the (over-)deployment of electronic systems, become interactively malleable, our very determinacy being placed in flux. In the new electronic environment there is a reciprocal negotiation between self and environment — an interactive 'allo-plasticity'. Asked what his ideal theatre might be, Forsythe suggested that it would be an indeterminate architecture in which the surfaces themselves would ceaselessly reconfigure, even the floor offering differential resistance and support impelling the dancers to continual recalibration and requalification of movement strategy. The physical plasticity that such suggestion implies need not be taken literally (although this is the point of departure for the *Aegis* project described below), the essential challenge being the more general one of deploying alloplastic strategies in both creative and receptive registers. *The Pallas House*, the *Aegis* and the *Paramorph* projects described below each in its own way has developed as a speculation on such alloplastic potential. As such they are vehicles for foregrounding current operative design strategies, exploring dynamic and static aspects of open-ended transformative process.

7. The Pallas House
(in collaboration with Objectile)

The Pallas House attempted to capture an energetics in material form. The house was

Figure 1.
The Pallas
House: final
form.

a fluid trapping of thickness – the perforations opening and closing according to orientation, as a sort of frozen responsiveness – there is the actualisation of a new logic at work: an entirely non-standard and complex surface. As variable electro-glyphs incised in a subtly curving plane, the project hints at new possibilities of numeric craft and decoration, and a sort of meltdown of expressivity: what we felt might be an 'active inert'.

The implicit suggestion embedded in the project is that the cathode-ray scanning of a screen might be translated to a numeric-command machine (routing, milling, etc.) in order to apply complex calculus derivatives directly to material surfaces, with the resulting data-form to be routed accurately in plywood and cast in aluminium or plastic. Here calculus becomes the operative, creative medium, our design function being displaced to that of a sampler or editor of endless computational patterning. In this sense the skin was no longer conceived as a model or representation of fixity, but was suspended as a norm-surface, responsive to parametric input from the client, the engineer or the architect: an elastic and flexible matrix of possibility.

In generating the surface we began by trapping, or mapping, lines on animating amorphous forms, generating sequential traces of displacement or movement. This created a fluid, cyclical series of three-dimensional glyphics as decora(c)tive trace-forms or spatial patterning. Morphing the original gave rise to infinite series of distorting analphabets, which offer an infinite potential to achieve a hitherto unimaginable formal complexity, born of a process which relaxes its control.

Here we might consider the essay *Hystera* by the feminist philosopher Luce Irigaray, which is a beguiling rereading of Plato's myth of the cave (Plato's *Hystera*) as a sort of defining moment of cultural form – specifically, for her, the definition of masculine form. The move out of the cave, the leaving behind of the cavern, or womb, with its fluid indeterminacy – the

commissioned by a developer who, fascinated by the latest developments in technology, asked that we try to attain the formal sophistication of product design. This suggested an approach utilising generative software which is linked directly to automated manufacturing techniques. The design then developed as an attempt to take to 'architectural' scale the experimental research of Objectile (Cache/Beaucé) in their development of software which permits surfaces and forms to be generated mathematically in formats which are suitable for direct manufacture by CNC (numeric command machining). But our interest lay much more in the implied drift of the design process into calculus-imagining, and the release of the open-ended generative potential implicit in such a working method.

The complex external skin of the house was imagined as an arabesque screen acting as a filter to the harsh climate. It evolved as a series of formulaically derived complex-curved shells, incised with numerically generated glyphs which capture the trace of a curve differentially mapped on a rotating solid. At first glance this subtle morphing is barely noticeable – virtually a standard cladding surface, albeit one of syncopated rhythm. But at the level of detail, where the surface captures a movement and develops as

Figure 2. The (Paramorph) site modelled as a 'fluid' trace of moving particles.

Figure 3. Site-sound used as a distorting formal generator.

Figure 4. Site-sound applied to the emergen form.

stepping out into the clear light of day – being a quite decisive (masculine) rationalising gesture. Irigaray interprets this as an allegory of the elevation of the visual sense with its linearising tendency to cognitive supremacy (the hard-eyed masculine gaze as a denial of the fluid rhythms of the body).

Irigaray's language is vague, meandering around its subject, as one might expect of a discourse that traces the outline of an 'other' state, a fluid state, at the moment of deconstructive return. We seem to have reached such a moment, a moment of fluid, or bodily, swell, a realm repressed by the linearising strictures of rational thought, but released by our machines of proclivity and our restless imaginations in front of them. In this transitional mental state we sense the emergence of a mechanics of fluids — a re-entry of the hystera, or a raising of the bodily senses to a cognitive level. For if the eye promotes linearity and causal rationality, the body is cyclical and fluctuating – it goes with the flow: the endless meanderings of process, or, one might say, processors.

The Pallas House skin may then be thought of as a *hystera protera* (the masculine form of which means an inversion of natural or logical order), which offers an image of a fluid and process-based mental realm straining for release. This we might term, following Irigaray, a 'hyster(a)ics', an emergent form of radicalised practice.

8. Aegis

Aegis was devised in response to a competition for an art piece for the Birmingham Hippodrome (UK) — specifically for the cantilevered 'prow' which emerges from the depth of the foyer to extend over the street. The brief simply asked for a piece which would in some way portray on the exterior that which was happening on the interior — that it be a dynamic and interactive art work.

The resulting project is simple in its conception: one might even say that it is nothing or that it highlights the nothing — the everyday events which occur in the theatre around it. It is a plain architectural surface — metallic and facetted — just one of the walls of the prow which penetrates from exterior to interior as a gently curving surface. But it is a surface which carries dynamic potential and in response to stimuli captured from the theatre environment it can dissolve into movement — supple fluidity or complex patterning. As such it is a sort of visceral 3-dimensional screen, capable of rapid and detailed surface

Figure 5.
CAD drawings
of the site
context.

reconfiguration driven by a matrix of thousands of electronically-controlled pistons. It plays the fields of art and architecture, alternating between background or foreground states.

The resolution and speed of the wall surface will emerge from the actual parameters of the device — both physical and electronic — but subject to those parameters it will be capable of registering any pattern or sequence which can be generated mathematically. The surface deforms according to stimuli captured from the environment, which may be selectively deployed as active or passive sensors. It will be linked in to the base electrical services of the building which are to be operated using a coordinated bus system, such that all electrical activity can feed into its operational matrix, allowing it to register any aspect of electronic capture. But additional input from receptors of noise, temperature and movement will be sampled by a program control monitor which responds by selecting a number of base mathematical descriptions, each parametrically variable in terms of speed, amplitude, direction, etc. producing a near infinite series of changing permutations which overlap continually, drifting in and out of sequence.

Aegis is then effectively a translation surface — a sort of synaesthetic transfer device, a surface-effect as cross-wiring of the senses. As a translation surface it is in principle readable, a form of glyphism, but now as a real-time event laced programmatically with causal triggers/disruptors. Like the hieroglyphs it drifts between pattern and writing, proffering and deferring a promise of meaning but as a sensual

Figure 6.
Early sketch
for exit form
(perspective)

and rhythmic form of tectonic electronic writing.

The surface is therefore not designed or determined as such: it is genera(c)ted by a random sampling, a deployment of electronic sensory-input from the immediate environment. In its creation as in its reception it suggests an alloplastic rather than autoplastic logic, the designer's role becoming that of editor or sampler of a proliferating range of effects. *Aegis* is perhaps therefore not a 'form' at all, since it escapes 'design' ideology, conceived much rather as a matrix of the possibility of form: is, in fact, the becoming/absenting of form-in-pattern.

The design process, which implicated many people from a variety of fields, threw up a further possibility: that of qualitative filtering. The mathematician generating the formulas began assigning them names which coloured or stained the abstract formulation — gave them a human dimension. We enjoyed the congenital breach of abstract codification, the mischief of a mathematics let loose: "large aspirin in a foil packet", "cat under the mat", "go right (go right dammit!)". From this we began to devise alphabets of patterning, and categories of deformation as emotive lists. These then offer a further selective filter which may be introduced into the generative matrix, such that visiting companies can select, say, three categories which capture in some manner the mood or artistic direction of the company adding modes of damping or inflection to the patterning. As a device of translation upon translation, the project highlights the extent of writing systems in their utter saturation of the cultural field,

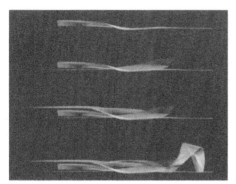

Figure 7. *Combination of elements which make up the gateway.*

writing now become primary. The basic premise of the project — to capture a technical shift in cultural experience by foregrounding the extent to which writing and translation mechanisms figure in contemporary processes (that we are wrapped by endless writings) — suggested a creative process that itself involved translation and multiple writing. Interactivity is predicated on mechanisms of translation — the evident or instant transfer from one medium to another (movement to sound, sound to light, etc). *Aegis*, conceived through the translation between multiple writings will then operate in response to many other forms of writing — musical scores, flow charts, temperature scales... But the project seeks to emphasise the irreducibly human aspects of such iterative processes, playing on the slippages between domains and the pleasures of forms of notation (the 'elegance' of programmatic description, for instance).

9. Hyposurface

The surface is poised between physical states, undecideable not only as a writing-effect, but in its physical statelessness — its oscillation between solid and fluid. As such it may be held to be in a smectic state, that point of liquid-crystal indeterminacy at immanent crystallisa-

tion or meltdown — the fluctuating limit-case of objectivity. This smectic surface is neither object nor image, but haunts both territories: it follows, in an architectural register, the logic of LCD imaging, be it the latest flat-screen technology or vitreous plate-glass opacity-switching, all of which rely on the ferroelectric reversibility of the interstitial molecular structure of certain smectics. Here, though, it is not an imagery which derives from a physical indeterminacy, but the collapse of physical determinacy into processing: we generate neither object nor image, but effect, transformation displacing the notion of origin (of representative a priori). The piece tries to capture the sense of contemporary technologies which propitiate entirely new cultural forms, processes... Our previous *Pallas House* was developed as an investigation of the demise of representative priority in numeric design process, marking a release of chance-calculus imagining. The name of the project refers back to the emblematic *Palladium*, fashioned by Athena in memory of the double she had murdered (Pallas), a figurine which lies at the heart of all problems of representative doublature.[8] The anxiety of the *Palladium* relates to the uncertainty of originality, both in terms of the originary sin it represents, but thereafter in its endless repetition (originally in order to protect the 'original' from plunder). Athena, haunted by the ghost of duplicity, can be seen as the very figure of eidetic ambiguity — poised between *eidos* (form) and *eidolon* (phantom) — abstraction and rationality latent within her glittering form (the very image of optic priority).

The genera(c)tive development of the *Pallas House*, calculated as a series of non-standard (and therefore non-repetitive) glyphic motifs, marks a transition to the 'primacy of the image': a process, as it were, that needs no Palladian sanction — becomes indeterminate. In this sense the skin of Pallas carries an enigmatic, absent quality — an endless deferral of serial (in)significance – it, too, an eidetic

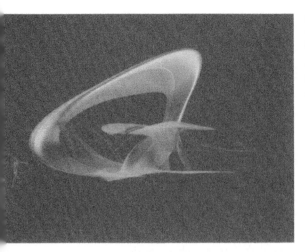

Figure 8. Entrance elevation of the final gateway form (Waterloo).

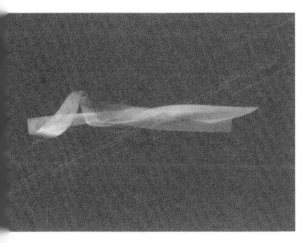

Figure 9. Plan of the final gateway form showing the viaduct above.

image... An aegis is implicated in both instances that Pallas figured in the life of Athena, and both encounters involved duplicity. It was the moment that the childhood Athena stood stock still, spear in hand, confronted by her own likeness in the form of her friend Pallas that Zeus, sensing a danger, threw down his aegis (originally the skin of the monster with fiery breath, Aegis). The momentary distraction released Athena's spear which mortally wounded Pallas, whose body the remorseful twin fashioned in timber and wrapped ambiguously in her own aegis, placing it in her own place next to her father, Zeus. The adult Athena then encountered the giant Pallas who lured her to an attempted rape by pretending to be her father. Athena, slaying the giant, added his scaly skin to her aegis, as she was always adding to it trophies of her adventures. The enigmatic surface, alternately hard and soft, both warning device and defensive shield, fused with the figure of Athena, the rational female-warrior. The aegis, then, as the very figure of inflection, a beguiling surface of reciprocity, harbours a latent memory, is significantly alternate — mute or vociferous — a device of trapping (in the double sense of both capture and decoration). We then select this image/object as ambiguous appellation for the subliminal hyposurface which unfurls around us in the interstices of technical expressivity, eidetic image of a reciprocal environmental calculus...

10. Hypo-surface

Trauma, as we've noted, is not marked by an overfullness or excess of significance, but by an absence of conceptual registration. This suggests that the prefix hypo-, which is characterised by deficiency and lack, by a subliminal incapacity, might be more appropriate in considering the effect of such numerically-generated surfaces than hyper-, which denotes excess or extremity. In engendering a sort of inexpressive plasticity in its languid surface distortions *Aegis* would seem to mark a shift to

Figure 10.
Parametric
model
showing
serial
deformation
of constraine
geometric
forms.

the sublimity of hypo-surface. As a surface of variable significance, a literal distortion of reference fluctuating between hypnosis and hallucination (the limit cases of optic sense) it will be interesting to guage the displacement of conceptual registration that results and to inquire as to the possibility of an emergent genre of hyposurface.

11. Paramorph

In response to a competition to design a gateway to the South Bank in London, we have differently pursued such alloplastic potential. For the project has been devised as a *Paramorph* — as a body that may change its form but whose fundamental property remains the same — in this case its geometric character. Here, though, the 'dynamic' final form is static, but has been derived from a paramorphic process inhabited by variance.

Our gateway derives from a series of different mapping strategies — sound and movement models in particular — which have each been pursued openly as generative processes (i.e. as environmental 'samplings' with no particular goal in mind). In this we concentrated on non-visual aspects of the site, producing mappings which revealed its dynamic rather than static character, time becoming actualised in the exploratory process. This derived a constantly-evolving formal solution for a gateway-in-depth, genera(c)ting series upon series of sheaths, sheets, shell-forms, etc. — a quite open process of discovery which condensed a 'final' form as a sort of collapsing vortex. The mappings were revelatory and dynamic, a series of strategies which were aimless but cogent in deriving a series of

coherent and precise formal solutions, each of which propagated the next. The 'final' form folds down from the scale of the public plaza (Sutton Place) to the quite constrained passageway beneath the viaduct (Sutton Passage) as a languid spatial compression.

The *Paramorph* is imagined as a series of tessellated aluminium surfaces which act as host to interactive sound sculpture, sound deployed in response to the passage of people moving through the form, morphings the site-sound. These will be 'floated' through the form by temporal relay such that the generative process continues into the actual architectural effect — one of an endlessly distorted redeployment of the dynamic aspects of the site itself. Such transformation of 'nothing' — of the ambient environment registered electronically — feeds back into that same environment as a temporal condensation and a heightening of sensory effect.

12. Parametric process

The developmental process of the Paramorph was accompanied by the creation of customised parametric models of geometric constraint (Mark Burry at Deakin University) — i.e. as 'elastic' models of precise descriptive geometry. This effectively embeds a geometric property into a descriptive model as a sort of inviolable genetic code — in this case that all surfaces be

Figure 11.
Parametric
model
showing
'fluid'
deformation
of ruled
surfaces.

describeable by straight-line geometry (therefore as derivatives of hyperbolic paraboloids) — which then informs the various reiterations of the form that we apply. I.e. no matter how we distort the form (here 15 hoops were controlled by 157 variable parameters) the surfaces are always derived from straight-line description (and hence can be fabricated by straight lengths of extruded aluminium). In fact, the model allows us to facet, rule or nurb the surface offering transformative reiterations of the form, each self-similar but different.

Again here we have created not so much a form as the possibility of (a) form, embedding specific parameters which are latent within a quite open creative system. It is this latent 'forgotten' character which, we feel, gives the object a 'precisely indeterminate' quality, and which stimulates yet denies incorporation. The form seems fluid but is highly constrained the tension of which can be somehow sensed visccrally. The form derives from and propagates the absenting psychologies of trauma, preferring an open and speculative transformative process to a reactive ideological determinism. If such forms seem to offer a fluid potentiality for both production and reception, it will be in the liquification of the linearity of extant 'design' processes (verification and refinement now collapsed into the base parametric description) that is most suggestive of modes of fluidity to come...

Acknowledgements

dECOi
  Mark Goulthorpe, Gabriel Evangelisti, Matthieu le Savre, Karine Chartier, Arnaud Descombes, Oliver Dering, Felix Robbins, Gaspard Giroud, Greg More
with:
Deakin University
  Prof Mark Burry
  Grant Dunlop
  Andrew Maher
Objectile (Pallas House)
  Bernard Cache, Patrick Beaucé
UCL Mathematics Dept
  Prof Keith Ball
  Dr Alex Scott
Peter Woods (programming)
Chris Glasow (systems engineering)
Univer (pneumatic systems)
Consultant Engineers
Ove Arup & Partners
  David Glover (Structural Engineering)
  Andy Sedgewick (Electrical Engineering)
  Sean Billings (Facade Engineering)
Aegis for PACA / Birmingham Hippodrome

Notes

[1] See for example, *Art and oscillation* : *"the aim of this is not to reach a final recomposed state. Instead, aesthetic experience is directed towards keeping the disorientation alive"* (Vattimo 1992 512).

[2] Here I use the term in its psychological sense, used by Freud to denote cognitive assimilation.

[3] For example, *"no jolt should take us unawares ... the most basic fact of aesthetic experience is the fact that delight lies somewhere between boredom and confusion... a surfeit of novelty will overload the system and cause it to give up..."* (Gombrich 1979 95).

[4] My knowledge of William Forsythe and the Frankfurt Ballet derives from study of their work over a number of years, and many discussions with them. See my essay *An architecture of disappearance* (*Un architecture de la disparition*) in *Contredanse*, 1998.

[5] These experiments were carried out during rehearsals of *Eidos/Telos*, 1995, which I studied whilst running Intermediate Unit 2 at the Architectural Association.

[6] The 'classic' texts on trauma are those of Sigmund Freud which deal largely with the neuroses associated with vividly disturbing events. Sandor Ferenczi offers a more subtle interpretation, extending Freud's thought to a wide range of everyday events, in effect using the discourse on trauma as a means of developing a generalised psychological theory. In my view such 'extension' does not imply opposition to Freud's basic thought — rather, a requalification — and in seeking to extend Ferenczi's thought to consideration of cultural reception I would note the basic similarities of both thinkers in their descriptions of trauma. A

good account of their respective differences is given by Frankel (1998).

[7] This is an expression of Bernard Cache (1995) describing the extent to which the computer image is no longer a representation of something prior, but begins to develop a life of its own — to become primary, or generative, in the creative process.

[8] Ferenczi 1955, p.221. This is the third volume of his collected notes and papers, published posthumously.

[9] Here I borrow from Roberto Calasso's (1994) insightful re-interpretation of Classical mythology.

This essay is formulated from two previously published papers : 'The active inert : notes on technic praxis' in *AA Files 37* Autumn 1998, and 'Hypo-surface, from alloplastic to autoplastic tendency' in *Hypersurface 2, Architectural Design* vol 69-10/1999 Profile 141.

The **dECOi** atelier was created by Mark Goulthorpe in 1991 as a forward-looking architectural practice. dECOi has received awards from the Royal Academy in London, the French Ministry of Culture and the Architectural League of New York, and has represented France at the Venice Biennale and the United Nations. They were selected by the *Architects Design* journal in its international survey of thirty 'Emerging voices' at the RIBA in London, and were awarded second place in the BD Young Architect of the Year Competition, 1999. Most recently they have been invited as international representatives at the Venice Biennale 2000, and to curate/participate in an exhibition of technology and architecture (*The new architecture genera(c)tion*) at the RIBA in 2000.

References

Benjamin, W. (1969) The work of art in the age of mechanical reproduction. In Arendt, H. (ed.) *Illuminations*. Schocken Books, New York.

Cache, B. (1995) *Earth moves : the furnishing of territories*. MIT Press, Cambridge, MA.

Calasso, R. (1994) *The marriage of Cadmus and Harmony*. Cape, London.

Caruth, C. (1991) *Unclaimed experience : trauma and the possibility of history*. Yale French Studies 79, Literature and the Ethical Question, p. 187.

Caruth, C. (1996) Freud, Moses and monotheism. In Caruth, C. *Unclaimed experience*. The John Hopkins University Press, Baltimore, p.18.

Ferenczi, S. (1955) Notes and fragments. In Ferenczi, S. *Final contributions 1930-32*. Hogarth Press, London.

Frankel, J.B. (1998) Ferenczi's trauma theory. *The American Journal of Psychoanalysis* 58(7).

Gilpin, H. (1997) *Aberations of gravity*. Parallax, The John Hopkins University Press, Baltimore.

Gombrich, E. (1979) *The sense of order: a study in the psychology of decorative art*. Phaidon Press, Oxford.

Vattimo, G. (1992) *The transparent society*. Polity Press, Cambridge, UK.

This article first appeared in *Digital Creativity* 11(3) 131–143 (2000).

Autonomous architecture

Ted Krueger

Rensselaer Polytechnic Institute, USA

Abstract

Krueger (1996) argued for an intelligent and interactive architecture conceived of as a metadermis,
a socially inhabited body, referencing recent work
in the fields of robotics, intelligent structures and
skins, and interactive materials. These developments serve both as a source of technical information and as a methodology by which architecture
may develop capacities, which are currently available only within the organic realm.

The present paper extends the characterisation of
architecture as a body to consider the evolution of
an independent entity. Recent developments in artificial intelligence research indicate that increasingly
complex behaviours can be obtained only with an
increase in the autonomy of the agent — that func-
tionality comes at the expense of control. It is argued that goal-directed behaviours on the part of
the agent imply a degree of self-awareness and that
this awareness is given by the sensing capacity of
the organism. The availability of a wide range of
sensing technologies suggests that the kind of
awareness developed by architectural entities may
be foreign to human experience.

Keywords: architecture, biomimetics, robotics,
  subsumption, sensors

1. Behaviour-based AI

Autonomous mobile robots as a method for
investigating intelligence grew out of a critique
of the state of academic AI research as it had
developed through the mid-1980s. Much of the
carefully crafted research that had been undertaken in the academic laboratories was incapable
of making the transition out of them. In part,
this was due to the desire to achieve human level
intelligence. In order to do so, researchers had
started with what they 'knew' about the human
experience of intelligence through introspection.
They had begun by attempting to emulate
higher-order phenomena without first building
an appropriate substrate. This lead Searle
(1980) to observe that while such systems were
capable of some measure of symbolic processing,
they would be inherently incapable of apprehending meaning in the task.

An alternative approach was to begin by
producing machines based on a physical-
grounding hypothesis. Intelligence was decom-
posed into behaviour generating modules that
had a strong interrelation with the 'real world'.
These behaviours were linked in a layered
hierarchical organisation called Subsumption
Architecture (Brooks, 1985). Complexity was
built from the bottom-up and intelligence was
measured by the capacity for appropriate
behaviours. A modular approach allowed for the
testing and debugging of a number of simple
behaviours which, once perfected, could be left
unmodified as attention was turned to higher
order structures. These new structures were
concerned with the mediation or coordination
between simpler behaviours in an effort to
produce more complex activity. It was assumed

that there would be conflicting information, missed communications, and the occasional failure of a mechanism or behavioural module. Failures at an upper level of organisation left the machine to interact at a more primitive level, but would not halt the robot entirely. Modularity and robustness, situatedness and embodiment are central to this approach.

2. Architecture and subsumption

While there are ideas here that are of interest to the development of intelligent systems in architecture, the transfer of strategies from robotics to architecture may initially seem inappropriate. Even allowing that a significant number of effectors may be incorporated into a structure, the architectural artifact is static in comparison to a mobile robot. This is so only from the standpoint of an observer, however, as a sensor is capable only of registering a change of state. Therefore developments founded on mobility will be applicable in any context where there is a significant dynamic. In architectural contexts, this dynamic may be the result of programmatic as well as environmental or structural variables.

If one assumes architecture as a built project, particularly using the metaphor of a body, situatedness, embodiment and behaviours are to the point. The methodology is an incremental and iterative strategy that yields useful behaviours at frequent points along the way. Once a behavioural module is developed it is exportable to another context. Higher level behaviours assume the existence, but not the authorship, of simpler behaviours. Some of the lowest level sensor-actuator couplings are already developed and in place in mechanical, lighting and security systems and other more sophisticated systems exist within most appliances. Standards are under development that allow these devices to intercommunicate. There is no need to integrate all systems into a unified network, but only to establish an asynchronous

intercommunication between them as the need arises. This sets a context where higher level behaviours can be developed. The fact that useful behaviours result from each layer of integration provides a motive for an increase in sophistication. An ideology of utility and the entrepreneurial imperative in contemporary economics guarantees this kind of development. That the system degrades gracefully in the event of a failure is advantageous as well - the lights stay on and the elevators still work.

Behaviour-based approaches are not without difficulty however. It is unclear as to how well the reactive strategy will scale and the extent to which the philosophical ban on representation will limit higher order behaviours. The ability of emergence to generate complex behaviours such as consciousness in synthetic environments is unknown. While it may exist as a possibility, it may not exist as a requirement. Maes (1991) notes that emergent behaviour, even at relatively simple levels, requires that the designer set an interaction loop between an agent and the environment that results in a convergence on the desired behaviour. In this case, emergence is less a function of magic and more a function of craft. It is remarkably efficient and robust for simple tasks. Its effectiveness and efficiency for complex tasks is as yet undemonstrated.

As the system scales and the probability of conflicts between behaviours increases, either a subsuming module must be written for these conflicts or the conflicts will begin to interfere with the functioning of the machine. Obviously the first alternative is to be preferred, yet with increases in complexity the programmer must anticipate a combinatorial explosion in the set of possible interactions.

Architecture as an extended object with a large number of behaviours running concurrently is a prime candidate for this kind of complexity. One of the fundamental concerns of design — architectural, robotic or otherwise — consists in the mediation of conflicting require-

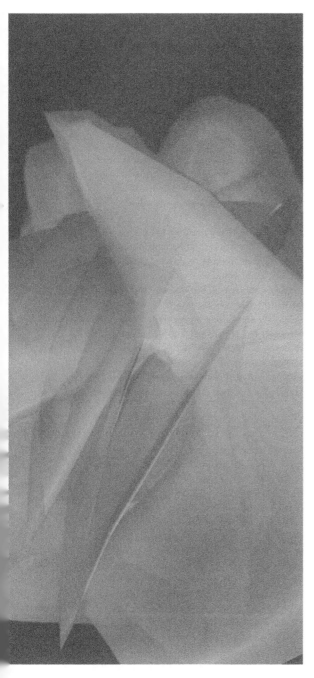

Figure 1. *Architecture will develop qualities that are currently obtainable only in the organic realm.*

ments. These conflicts carry through beyond design into the operation of the artifact. Technology may supply new means to address — but cannot eliminate — these problems.

3. Robotic imagination and desire

Harnad (1995) suggests that in order to produce an artificial mind that could be equated with a human one, a method of grounding its symbolic capacities must be employed. This possibility arises when the symbols are organised relative to contact with the world, and their interrelations are established through experience rather than by pre-processed rule structures. The mind must be embodied if it is to escape from Searle's Chinese Room.

Brooks (1991) acknowledges that the behavioural and symbolic approaches may in fact be complementary. The extent to which behaviour-based systems can integrate and ground symbolic ones remains an empirical issue. The deepest levels of integration will arise from situations in which the representational systems are derived from the experiential. They may have a development and structure that is closely related to the behavioural parameters from which they originate.

Stein (1991) has undertaken some development which is particularly intriguing in this regard. In her study of the implementation of imagination in a behaviour based robot, the machine was capable of recognising places it had encountered by virtue of a signature 'feel' or representation of the place as encoded by its sensory apparatus. These perceptions were stored for future reference. The researcher was able to feed the robot a corresponding representation of a place it had not visited and but which it would recognise when the sensory stimulus came into the proper configuration. It was found that the robot could explore the world and recognise places that it had not previously visited but which it had been told about and for which it had, in a sense, an image in its imagination.

While it has been suggested that the logical and symbolic capacity of the human mind is a serial process riding on top of the parallel structure of the unconscious, Stein's approach was not to place the representational capacity atop the behaviour-based substrate, but to run the two in parallel. The physical structures of the machine were emulated on one of the robot's computers and the robot could explore these virtual spaces using its simulated sensors.

This parallel strategy may be able to be implemented such that the virtual representation results from transformations of the current physical sensor readings with a subsequent evaluation by the simulated sensors. That is, from the machine's perspective, "if I would do *this*, it would feel like *that*". A further extension suggests that several scenarios may be produced and evaluated for the best course of action.

At this point, the question of the basis of those evaluations will arise simultaneously with the issues of which scenarios to generate and how many to produce as well as an evaluation of the number of steps into the future to continue the exercise. The constraints faced by the responding system must be anticipated either by a programmer or by rule structures imbedded in the agent. Here again, we are again up against the combinatorial wall. The range of permutations may be circumscribed by reference to goals.

Goals not only bias or restrict the range of choices but also make possible the allocation of resources such that several simultaneous objectives may be addressed or approached through a single action. Typically, goals are not isolated, but rather a nested series of interrelationships that provide a guide for action at many scales simultaneously. As Maes (1991) notes, goals are a crucial ingredient of self-consciousness and a precondition for effective learning. One of her contributions to research in

this area has been to develop autonomous agents that are capable of setting their own goals in the face of conflicting requirements. A measure of autonomy must be granted to the machine in order to be able to effectively deal with the complexity of its interactions with the environment.

In order for a machine to have goals it must have some notion of its capabilities, (if a building decided that it wanted to paint like Kandinsky, it would be a very interesting development indeed, but one which it would have little chance of carrying out), further it must have an understanding of the things that are under its control. Self-knowledge comes only from the delimitation of the self through the agency of the senses and from the capacity to effect a change of state in the environment. The knowledge of which is again a sensory function.

4. Sensor technologies

Sensor technology is currently undergoing a revolution equivalent to that of other computational devices. It is now possible to fabricate a wide range of sensors using chip production technologies and facilities and to include calibration, processing and communications circuitry along with the sensor on the same device. Unit and implementation costs are rapidly decreasing while reliability increases. This has lead to the widespread incorporation of sensing technology into automobiles and appliances. These devices are incorporated because of a favourable cost-benefit ratio. There need be no philosophical underpinnings and no overall development strategy.

A wide range of sensor technologies has been developed. These technologies enable both a sensing of things that are readily available to us as well as a sensing of things that are not apparent. The first instance enables machines to gather information as we would; the second allows them sense things that we cannot. Typically we re-map this extended range of sensing into our native modalities. Much work in scientific visualisation is an effort to do so. Machines will not need this conversion, as they will be built to directly access the stimuli. Just as our minds have developed and have been shaped in response to the information that we have about the world as given by our senses, so the structure of artificial minds will be formed in response to their sensory input. What are the qualia associated with proximity sensing?

Steels (1993) notes a clear distinction between efforts to understand phenomena based on computational models and those based on artificial models. He illustrates with a simulation of a bird in flight and notes that even with a highly accurate and sufficiently detailed computational model one would in the end not have real flight. Whereas with an artificial model, the test of the theory embodied by the model would be given by its performance. Note, however, that you still don't have a bird. This is problematic only to the extent that making a bird was the point of the exercise. Clearly it was not. Yet we make this same mistake if we look for a 'human emulation mode' in an architectural entity.

Efforts to produce human level competence in a robot may justifiably attempt to build an android and concern itself with sensing strategies such a foveated binocular vision systems and methods of compliant pressure transduction.

We are concerned here not with human level cognition, intelligence or consciousness, but rather with the question of what could be the consciousness of an architectural artifact modelled on biological phenomena? The attempt is not to build a habitable golem, but to understand and anticipate the potential and inherent qualities of the architectural being.

References

Brooks, R. (1985) *A robust layered control system for a mobile robot.* A.I. Memo 864, M.I.T. Artificial Intelligence Laboratory, Cambridge, MA, pp. 1-25.

Brooks, R. (1991) Elephants don't play chess. In Maes, P. (ed.) *Designing autonomous agents: theory and practice from biology to engineering andback.* Bradford/MIT Press, Cambridge, MA, pp. 3–15.

Harnad, S. (1995) Does mind piggyback on robotic and symbolic capacity? In Morowitz and Singer (eds.) *The mind, the brain and complex adaptive systems.* Santa Fe Institute Studies in the Science of Complexity - Volume 22. Addison Wesley, Reading, MA, pp. 203–220.

Krueger, T. (1996) Like a second skin. In Spiller, N. (ed.) *Integrating architecture.* Architectural Design Profile 131. Academy Editions, London, pp. 29–32.

Maes, P. (1991) Designing autonomous agents. In Maes, P. (ed.) *Designing autonomous agents: theory and practice from biology to engineering andback.* Bradford/MIT Press, Cambridge, MA, pp. 1–3.

Searle, J. (1980) Minds, brains, and programs. *Behavioural and Brain Sciences* 3(3) 417–457.

Steels, L. (1993) Artificial life roots of artificial intelligence. *Artificial Life* 1(1&2) 75–110.

Stein, L. (1991) *Imagination and situated cognition.* A.I. Memo 1277, M.I.T. Artificial Intelligence Laboratory, Cambridge, MA, pp. 1–8.

Ted Krueger directs a Laboratory for Human Environment Interaction Research in the Informatics and Architecture program at Rensselaer Polytechnic Institute's School of Architecture.

.

This article first appeared in
Digital Creativity 9(1) 43–47 (1998).

Vibrating tectonics: gestural trajectories, energy mappings and self-conditioning design strategies

Pawel Szychalski

School of Architecture, Lund University, Sweden

Abstract

The transposition from abstract painting to archi-tecture from two-dimensional entity to a spatial struc-ture, became the core idea of a project designed for the students of architecture to encourage them to examine the possibilities of abstract expression in the conceptualisation of architectural ideas and strategies. A series of tasks were created to enable them to identify full expression and physical pres-ence of movement in an abstract painting as trans-ferable into architecture. There were then other tasks oriented towards discovering, investigating and recording various types of spatial conditions as potentially architectural.

Fundamental issues related to Jackson Pollock's philosophy of painting are now finding a new dimension in the digital domain of 3D model-ling techniques, supplying them with the tool capa-ble of not only projecting the release of pure energy in virtual space but also of recording endless se-quences of free gestures in time and space. These can then be rewritten in the form of a computer pro-gram as well as being controlled on a higher level of architectural design.

Keywords: abstraction, architecture, design, digital, teaching

1. Introduction

Architecture of today tends to expose the process of constructing, of grouping and balancing a myriad of unstable elements and units of architectural matter. A vibrating body of the architectural structure under construction is left in a phase of disequilibrium and indefinition in order to open new possibilities for us to be involved in the process of living with or within it, to get the other coherency of architectural work in favour of the needs of individual expression.

It suggests that we can constantly observe and interfere with the process, rather than only its effect. This is achievable due to the openness and multiplicity of formal narration which was searched for in the project, the development of the process simultaneously generating form, construction and program.

Fundamental issues of Jackson Pollock's philosophy of painting are now finding their new dimension in the digital domain of 3D modelling techniques, supplying them with the tool capable of not only projecting the release of pure energy in virtual space but also recording endless sequences of free gestures in time and space. These can then be rewritten in the form of computer programs as well as being control-led on a higher level of architectural design.

2. Abstract expressionism

Through the visual and structural material of an abstract painting, the initial exercise of this teaching programme was to provide students with the vastness of an emotional and intellectual springboard to stimulate and generate architectural concepts. Articulated as a spontaneous succession of forms, the complexity of gestural, intuitive painting was to be a storehouse of a graphic language that could be taken

Figure 1. By Linda Camara. An abstract painting that should trigger associations with the complexity of the urban texture.

out of its context and transposed from one medium to another, from painting through drawing to architecture. This investigation had as its base a comparison of the abstract image and the urban setting, of the geometrical composition (Figure 2) versus the architectural record (Figure 3). Paintings and drawings, being two-dimensional entities, were then explored and redefined in relation to the student's own urban and architectural preconceptions or/and their alterations, rediscovered through this procedure. This was possible through the analytical, geometrical works and the use of techniques of an architectural record such as sections (Figure 4), invented and introduced in this project, 'viewing-sections sample models' (Figure 5) and made upon their images, photographic collages (Figure 6).

Ultra-individual artists representing the 'New York School' of American painting or abstract expressionism were the originators of gestural abstraction in painting. They wanted to turn art into real life with its deepness, importance, and full expression. This specifically subjective manner made them look for and use new tools, materials and media. But the most radical was Jackson Pollock's decision to eliminate every possible tool — splashing and spreading paint on canvas. Gesture itself became a tool and catalyst of all idealistic and hypothetical assumptions and the executive means of expression. While executing the painting, the space of gesture appeared fulfilling the necessity of controlling space yet constructing painting's new dependence on space (see Le Corbusier 1946).

Pollock's action paintings can be interpreted as projections of the paradigm of configurations of volume and void in space onto a flat, horizontal surface. So the surface of the painting becomes loaded with the information on space and movement, which then might be unfolded into a new paradigm of form, space and time. Pollock, with his gestures, carved out and captivated certain fragments of space. So does Frank O. Gehry[1] . The former left the

records of space or rather
records of time and space in

Figure 2. By Linda Camara. Every overdraw-
ing taken out of the painting is supposed to
peel by layers its texture. At the same time,
qualities like harmony, proportions and
rhythm are being derived and modulated.

Figure 3. Map of the city of Malmö. Every urban plan such as
this city map has been constituted by such orders (harmony,
proportions and rhythm), yet as it augments in time, these
orders become disrupted, violated and redistributed.

his action paintings, whereas the latter recreated them in sketches, models and finally in a real space — the space of the building.

Gehry's architectural sketches and Pollock's paintings are both projections of a gesture in space and/or projections of space of a gesture onto a surface. Labyrinths of paths produced of thin streamlets of paint poured by a painter are but a record of space demarcated and defined by trajectories of the artist's moves while acting on the stage of the canvas of his painting[2]. While sketching, Gehry with a single, uninterrupted gesture of a draughtsman is projecting on a surface the trajectories of architectural struc-

ture. It is moving and winding during the act of creation, being in the phase of eruption and transmission of an architect's most creative thought. It reminds us of a fluid substance which congeals for a short while in the form of a 'flattened' drawing on paper only to explode again and again in the next sketches. A series of such projections makes possible the rendering of the spatial model of structure frozen in motion. Just like cinematic recomposition or reconstruction of the flow of certain fraction of motion out of numerous separate frames, vague and blurred photographic images, being only its partial, disjoint and disarranged record. Things

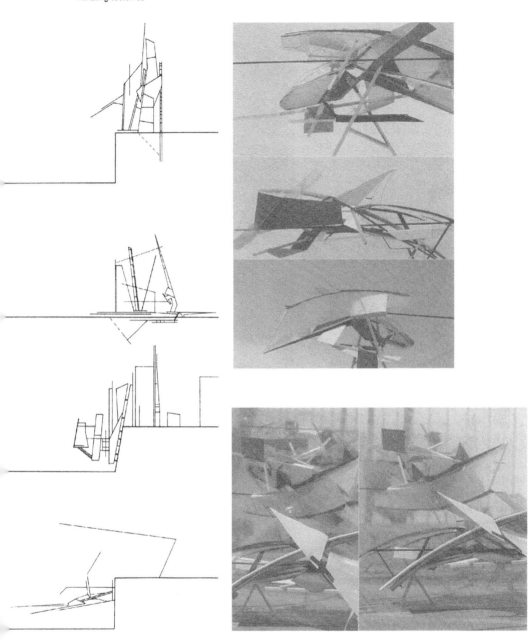

igure 4 (left). By Gabriella Gustafsson. Sections. Imagined geometrical compositions derived
om the depth of 'the painting's texture'.

igure 5a (right top). By Caroline Olsson. Three examples of sample models of textural/
chitectural compositions constructed upon sections.

igure 5b (right bottom). By Caroline Olsson. 'Viewing-sections-model'. An apparatus which
as supposed to compose and recompose samples of the future architectural composition.

which are observable in singular architect's linear sketches become imperceptible elements in the continuum of architectural vision.

3. Student painting

Such transposition from abstract painting to architecture, from two-dimensional entity to a spatial structure, became the core idea of the project designed for the students of architecture who were supposed to examine the possibilities of abstract expression in the conceptualisation of architectural ideas and strategies. A series of tasks were developed to identify full expression and physical presence of movement in an abstract painting as being transferable into architecture. Then other tasks were oriented towards discovering, investigating and recording various types of spatial conditions as potentially architectural.

The investigated and redefined complexity of students' own paintings (their first task), born out of intuitive and semi-automatic acts[3] , became a spatial instrument in their hands. Multiple and manifold use of this instrument was supposed to stock up a conceptual and formal paradigm of spatial and finally architectural enclosures. Perceived as a storehouse of forms, this paradigm became a vehicle for conceiving and modelling 'ineffable spaces'(Le Corbusier 1946) , whereas recognised as a conceptual principle it became an opportunity to overcome architectural limits.

Providing the students with the emotional and intellectual catalyst for the generative search-to-discover design process was the principal intention of the procedure. Articulated as a spontaneous succession of spatial compositions, harmonies and orders, these strategies were supposed to serve as a tool for students to invent their own architectural syntax. The process initialised by the act of decomposition (and the dissolution of the definition) of architectural space, represented by the task of abstract painting and its analysis, had to be

Figure 6. By Caroline Olsson. Photo-collages were supposed to test and reveal more of architectural and urban qualities of 'viewing-sections-models'.

Figure 7.

By Linus Pettersson. Photo-collage. Constructing urban space out of several images of sample models with 'the worn man from Tibet'.

Figure 8.

By Linus Pettersson. Photo-collage constructed in the same manner as Figure 7; this time with 'the Russian chess players'.

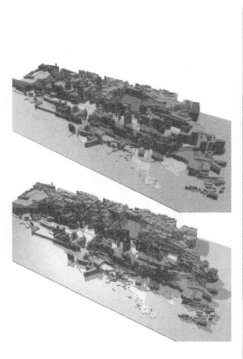

Figures 9a and 9b.

By Linus Pettersson. Printable city. A series of computer rendered probable cityscapes of a chosen site of the former harbour and shipyard, Malmö, Sweden.

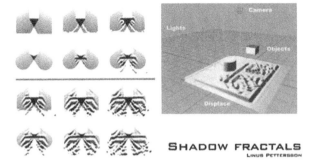

SHADOW FRACTALS
LINUS PETTERSSON

Figure 10.

By Linus Pettersson. This simple 3D computer-modelling experiment is the first trial to enclose and control some processes discussed in the project, such as simple and readible orders developed into highly complex ones or enriching compositional harmonies in a seemingly random and chaotic, yet controllable, way.

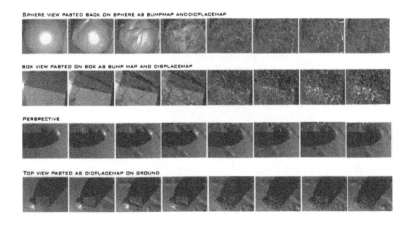

Figure 11.

By Linus Pettersson. More refined and elaborated 3D modelling experiment continues to discuss the same processes aiming at self-evolutionary architectural design processes.

Figure 12.

By Vasco Trigueiros. This set of images compares initial abstract paintings with their overdrawings, while the last pair illustrates the origination of the concept of architectural matter being modulated in relation to time and the sun's position.

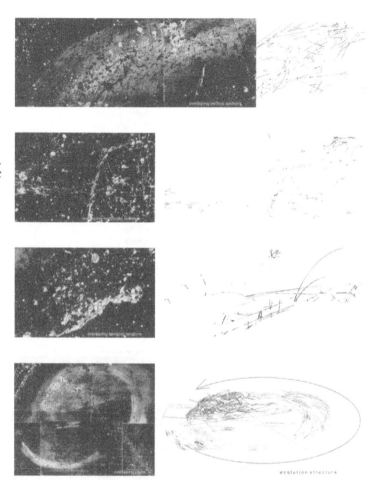

accomplished by a much longer and much more strenuous process of recomposition, and the re-interlocation of architectural matter with its other qualities, demands and requirements.

4. Digital tools

The objectives of the project itself were first developed in 1991, at that time anticipating the utilisation of digital tools. Yet, year by year, the project has been evolving along with an immi-nent development of 3D modelling techniques (not to mention computer technology in general), towards the situation in which digital tools are not only recommended in some of the assignments, but also inspire the students to reconsider: the concept of the architectural design process in general; the architecture and its possible use; the concept of urban design; and, finally, the very specific aspect of time in architecture which might be called 'occurring architecture'.

Figure 13.

By Vasco Trigueiros. The image shows overdrawing derivations of plan layers distributed vertically and rendered in 3D modelling application.

Since "architecture, sculpture and painting are specifically dependent on space, bound to the necessity of controlling space, each by its own appropriate means"(Le Corbusier 1946) , then the digital techniques open up new possibilities of joining up and finding ways of controlling space, no longer "each by its own appropriate means", but with only one, comprising all specific features of all three of them. It may result in the rapid shift in the conceiving and receiving architecture.

5. Student projects

In the 1999 edition of the project the problems of the process and its engagement of time were specifically observed and taken into consideration. The process of designing architecture, the possibility of architecture (or architectural matter itself) which is in a constant state of occurring, as its new innate feature, was investigated.

Figure 14.

By Vasco Trigueiros. This sequence of nine images represents three different levels of development of architectural matter in time and space.

The upper row of images shows top views of the site with transforming architecture. The middle row shows the close-ups of 'skin-layering'. The bottom row shows the side-views of the site.

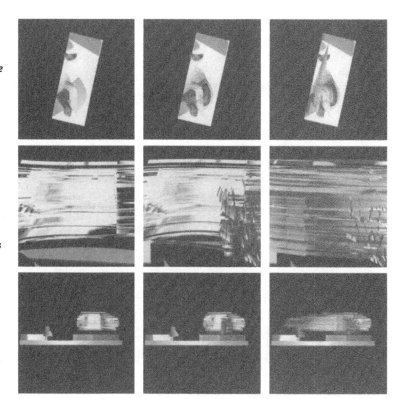

Can we aspire to architecture that has the same relation to time as the one that is held in music, where an architect-composer writes the score, yet for architecture to occur the score has to be interpreted and performed ('played')? Due to the digital technology, music can be programmed, and its subjection to the performer can be controlled and guided, sampled and distributed in time. This is the concept of architecture that has been approached by some of the students from the project. This is the architecture that resembles the sailing-vessel where the form is mutable and stretchy and the function flexible and dependent upon the wind force and direction.

The following three works of students represent a creative approach not only in terms of architecture and the use of 3D-modelling and rendering applications, but also in overcoming their most common features. They found new aspects of creative interrelations between form, construction and function. All the three students decided to go on with the project inspired by the digital possibilities they discovered during its earlier stages, arriving at the higher and higher levels of intellectual and technological advancement.

Figure 15.

By Vasco Trigueiros. Three photo-collages showing the life of and the inside of the 'body' of space-time architecture.

Figure 16.

By Cord Siegel. Two digitally rendered images depicting the concept of landscape/building 'big roof' structure in relation to the 140m. high crane existing on the former shipyard site in Malmö, Sweden.

Figure 17.

By Cord Siegel. A comparison showing the abstract painting and its digitally rendered 'spatial overdrawing'.

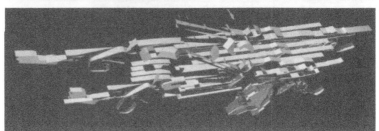

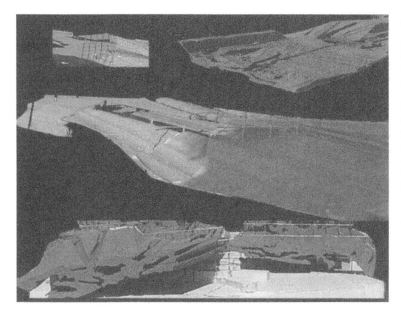

Figure 18.

By Cord Siegel. A set of study models of the 'big roof' landscape structure rendered in traditional architectural models materials (e.g. foam, wire, plaster).

5.1 Work and text by Linus Pettersson

5.1.1 The Kockums shipyard crane as a 3D printer

While working on the project, in its final part, I found two images (the worn man from Tibet (Figure 7) and the Russian chessplayers (Figure 8)) that led me to a new idea that was stronger than just the shipyard crane in Malmö as a 3D printer.

The knowledge about how the intelligent cameras work and the neural network concept was also the input to the new idea .

The new idea was the following:

1. Cameras can read structures and images can be used to remake virtual 3D objects.

2. A town can be defined as spatial structures.

3. If a town can be defined as spatial structures and a camera can record these structures and a computer remix them, then a 3D printer could print town-like structures (Figures 9a and 9b).

4. The 3D printer can take away material as well as print.

5. A feedback system gives feedback on human practical structures.

6. If a system can give feedback about successful and unsuccessful structures in relation to humans, the computer that remixes town-like structures can together with the cameras that read these and other structures, remake the unsuccessful structures until they are, according to the feedback system, successful ones.

A system that works like this would be a self-developing city where the meaning of space would be the practical usage of space. Structures no longer in use would be remade until they have a practical meaning. There are of course questions that are very hard to answer. How would one define a successful structure? Where would it be possible to remake structures if people live close to a non-successful structure? From this new idea I wanted the whole area to be printed and skip the borders between printed housing area and not printed commercial area.

5.1.2 The fractal building

The next notion that came on my mind was the concept of the fractal building. I came up with the idea of feeding images with their own images. I was thinking of a fence giving shadow, and the shadow of the fence gave explanation to the next fence.

I didn't dare to try it out on a computer. Two days later I was trying to figure out the third step in shadow experiment, but I found it impossible. I just couldn't. I had to head for the school computers and try it out. Three hours later I had the images of shadow fractals (Figure 10) and my heart was taking extra beats. Although it didn't seem to be fractal, only chaotic, I knew I could easily turn it into well known fractals.
I knew that one important thing was that the fractals as self-similar, they would remember what they had been through, since they were feeding themselves. Yet, I didn't connect this to a practical usage until two weeks later.

After this first shadow fractal image, there came a period of doing all the experiments I wanted to do. One of the first experiments was to determine that I could do fractals. I used the shadow to explain holes in the same box that made the shadow. I did this for something like eight times and it really looked like an iteration process. I was very pleased to find fractals. It didn't surprise me this time and I could continue without exaltation.

5.1.3 The box and sphere experiment

The next important step was to arrive at the box and sphere experiment (Figure 11). The sphere sees itself and changes according to its own image. The box sees itself and does the same. The ground follows the same principle. Within no time the box surface becomes self-evolutionary. The sphere seems chaotic, as does the ground. With this, after eight iterations, I zoomed all cameras and I wanted to see if it could forget what it had been through. It didn't forget, even if it looked rather dream-like. The

square seems to forget in the long run. The box has a very strange behaviour so I don't dare to make a prediction.

While working on my presentation text, finally the connection was made how to use the remembering feature of a fractal. If you have the conditional set of light, object and camera and roll the fractal iteration, the changes of the object will be smaller and smaller as the iteration process goes further. Providing you have fractally stable conditions and not chaotic. If the light is changed to be a moving object and the movement is of the sun, the object will have a small memory of the morning in the afternoon, because it is self-similar and remembers the shadow changes.

What I have is a thing that can express the movement of the sun. It can be self-evolutionary and it remembers changes from any parameter set to another (because it brings the old parameters in its own body, to the new set). I believe this is something very powerful and useful.

With this technique combined with a filter to human needs, there is one open door to create the 'growing' building that develops itself upon human needs instead of ordinary environmental restrictions.

During recent investigations, I have found the great concept of evolutionary algorithms that are just waiting for architects to be used.

5.2 Work and text by Vasco Trigueiros
5.2.1 Part 1 / Gestural abstraction

After studies and analyses of the action paintings and overdrawings (Figure 12), an interpretation with the site data was made to obtain the primal forms for the modulation.

The plan layering

The plan density contra projected shadow density on each plan corresponds to light and dark space in relation to time and sun's position (Figure 13). This allows you to determine the boundaries of the skin, and together with the sections, you obtain the whole skin-layout, in each generation.

To gain a variation in space and light quality, the skin must be adjusted to this density pattern.

The skin layering

The technique used to reach the skin of the main four architectural bodies (Figure 14), involves the study of various sections (analysed and cleaned overdrawings from the action painting) and the plan layering map. The skin of each body is then transformed into horizontal section layers to create translucid and vertical flexibility.

The four bodies will create their own space-time by their activities, and will work as a stabile dynamic organism (Figure 15).

5.3 Work and text by Cord Siegel

5.3.1 A big roof

I chose to work with digital media because I strongly believe that in the future we will be able to control biological processes, and as a consequence to build up landscape, buildings and forms.

In the project I tried to achieve this kind of future form, a form that would express this intention and create the desire for it. I created a landscape-like structure in Vasterhamn, a big roof (Figure 16), built up in a context of needs for big structures and social places, keeping at the same time historical impacts. Having in mind the climate of Sweden and Malmö today, I wanted it to be a dynamic place (Figures 17 and 18).

According to old law of the city planning, first of all one has to make sure that social places are protected. So, let's take the top surface! The historical shipyard buildings could be integrated in the roof , as it would be hard to pull them down, and even if you do that there will always be a kind of visible wound. The top

surface would be sunk 20 metres in the water, as well as 20 metres over the water. The vital microclimate will be developed, and the area could be well used with the help of the computer and a smart gardener.

5.3.2 A shadow-catcher

The shadow-catcher would be formed out of shadow and other roofs. It would be constituted by an impact from the real world, light and shadow. It would be an example of a databody. It was a great thing to print the shadowcatcher, and then only glue the parts together and to hold this computer model in my hands.

Acknowledgements

I would like to express my gratitude to the faculty of the Department of Theoretical and Applied Aesthetics, School of Architecture, Lund University, Sweden, especially to Professors Janne Ahlin and Abelardo Gonzalez for inviting me to the School of Architecture and providing me with the opportunity to carry out and develop my experimental teaching project and their much appreciated advice; to Lars-Henrik Stål, Gunnar Sandin and Mats Hultman for their academic support, generous assistance and willingness to discuss the issues of my interest. Many thanks to Horst Kiechle for his encouragement and for showing his works and sharing ideas. And to my wife Bozena, without whose assistance, patience and aid my work would not have been possible.

Notes

1   Californian architect, known e.g. for his Guggenheim Museum in Bilbao, Spain, accomplished in 1997.

2   *My painting does not come from the easel. I hardly ever stretch my canvas before painting.*

I prefer to tack the unstretched canvas to the hard wall or the floor. I need the resistance of a hard surface. On the floor I am more at ease. I feel nearer, more a part of the painting, since this way I can walk around it, work from the four sides and literally be in the painting…

from *Possibilities I*, (Winter 1947–48), reprinted by permission of Wittenborn Art Books, Inc. and ARS N.Y./Pollock-Krasner Foundation, 1988. Reprinted in Shapiro and Shapiro 1990, pp. 356–357.

3 Walter Benjamin wrote:

The work of craftsmanship becomes an artwork as far as it is able to contain and transmit the spontaneousness of automatic art. (Benjamin 1969)

References

Arnell, P. and Bickford, T. (eds) (1985) *Frank O. Gehry. Buildings and projects.* Rizzoli International Publications, New York.

Ashton, D. (1973) *The New York School: a cultural reckoning.* Viking Press, New York.

Benjamin, W. (1969) The work of art in the age of mechanical reproduction. In Arendt, H. (ed.) *Illuminations.* Schocken Books, New York.

van Bruggen, C. (1998) *Frank O. Gehry, Guggenheim Museum, Bilbao.* Guggenheim Museum Publications, New York.

Le Corbusier (1946) Ineffable space (L'espace indicible) l'Architecture d'Aujourd'hui, January 1946. Reprinted in Ockman, J. (ed.) (1993) *Architecture culture 1943–1968.* Rizzoli International, New York, p.66.

Gehry, F. O. (1999) Frank O.Gehry: the architect's studio. Louisiana Museum of Modern Art.

O'Brien, J. (ed.) (1986) *Clement Greenberg: the collected essays and criticism.* Beacon Press, Chicago.

Rosenberg, H. (1959) *The tradition of the new.* Thames & Hudson, London.

Seitz, W. C. (1983) *Abstract Expressionist painting in America.* Harvard University Press, Cambridge, MA.

Shapiro, D. and Shapiro, C. (eds.) (1990) *Abstract Expressionism: a critical record.* Cambridge University Press, Cambridge, UK.

Stiles, K. and Selz, P.(1996) *Theories and documents of contemporary art. A sourcebook of artists' writings.* University of California Press.

Stangos, N. (ed.) (1985) *Concepts of modern art.* Thames and Hudson, London.

Treib, M. (1997) *Space calculated in seconds: the Philips pavilion. Le Corbusier Edgar Varese.* Princeton University Press.

Tyler, P. (1986) Jackson Pollock: the infinite labyrinth. In Shapiro and Shapiro (1990) *Abstract Expressionism: a critical record.* Cambridge University Press, Cambridge, UK, pp. 365–367.

Pawel Szychalski is an architect, designer and an academic teacher who lives in Kalisz, Poland. He has an MSc in Architecture from the School of Architecture, Poznan Technical University in Poznan, Poland, and studied graphic, industrial and interior design at the Fine Arts Academy in Poznan. From 1991 to 1999 he ran an architectural design studio at the School of Architecture in Poznan. He teaches architectural studio at the School of Architecture, University of Lund, Sweden where currently he is also pursuing his PhD research on contemporary architecture and its relations to art.

This article first appeared in *Digital Creativity* 11(3) 173–189 (2000).

Quake® goes the environment: game aesthetics and archaeologies

Aki Järvinen

University of Tampere, Finland

Abstract

Computer and video games are blurring the boundaries of such categories as play, narrative, space, entertainment and art. Games are, if anything, a form of popular art. They present us with a particular kind of problematic regarding narrative and aesthetics. The article discusses computer and video games in the context of the cultural history of the moving image. The focus is on one type of games in particular. This is the game genre known as 'first-person shooter' (FPS), which became hugely popular with Doom (1994) and has spawned numerous other popular games (e.g. the Quake and the Unreal series).

Pre-cinematic devices and techniques, special effects, 'cinema of attraction', and theories of visuality serve as points of reflection. The differences between games and narratives are also discussed. Games are situated between the paths of two aesthetic disciplines: aesthetics of the moving image (film, television, video) and aesthetics of the environment (landscapes, architecture, space). The formulations presented in the article help us to understand the inter-dependent nature of virtual environments and their users. In this way, they light the way towards understanding new media from an aesthetic perspective.

Keywords: computer games, design, digital aesthetics, digital cinema, media history, video games

1. Introduction

Computer and video games stand at a crossroads. They are blurring the boundaries of such categories as play, narrative, space, entertainment and art, for instance. My focus is especially on the questions of game aesthetics. Traditionally aesthetics, and the philosophy of art, has been concerned with the relationship of man and beauty, especially in the so-called fine arts. Aesthetic theories have also provided artists with theoretical guidelines and knowledge. From a broader perspective, aesthetics discusses our relationship to the environment in general. In recent years environmental aesthetics has indeed presented new objects and fields of study for aesthetic criticism. In this paper I present some notes on what aesthetics could be regarding digital games and the environments represented in them. I will examine games as a form of popular art and argue the need for an aesthetically-conscious approach towards studying and designing new media products. I will situate digital games at the crossroads of two aesthetic disciplines: aesthetics of the moving image, and aesthetics of the environment.

I use the term 'aesthetic' with two meanings: on one hand, in the sense of an artistically conscious, theoretical approach with which to offer guidelines for new media studies and design. On the other hand, the term serves to focus the reader's attention on certain emotive dimensions of our interactions with digital media, games in particular.

I believe that the 'gaming situation' is fundamentally an aesthetic situation. As popular artefacts of global media culture, games give birth to countless aesthetic experiences day in, day out. This is one of the biggest reasons why we need game criticism. Studying games and their aesthetic dimensions is necessary in order to deepen our understanding of digital media in general. The inherent mutability of digital images and sounds is an aspect that would benefit from a carefully thought-out and culturally informed theory of digital aesthetics. This article presents some routes and premises for such an approach.

2. Games as popular art

Computer games challenge the traditional notions of constructing, realising and enjoying a work of art. Games are, if anything, a form of popular art. Games' aesthetic dimensions are appreciated among the gaming audiences in various ways. Even a quick look into the gaming communities (websites, magazines, newsgroups, etc.) helps one to realise that the audio-visual design and output of games is valued extremely high among gamers. A certain kind of 'aesthetic consciousness' exists among game audiences. In addition, there is no reason to rule out artistic and aesthetic intentions from game design and production.

The individual ways and preferences of aesthetic appreciation vary. Therefore, only by the means of a common context can a concept like aesthetic appreciation be of any analytical value. I use the term 'art' in a common and everyday sense of the word, referring to the quality of experience that is associated with the media product in question. In this way, a certain concept of art is recognisable for the game audiences in a shared context of game playing. A theorist of the popular arts and their aesthetics, Sung-Bong Park, has argued that aesthetic as a concept is always at hand, even when it is not written with a capital 'A', as with the fine arts. Park elaborates:

whenever we attempt to intensively actualize, completely realize and consciously articulate the

quality of experience, there is always the concept of the aesthetic whether we are aware of the term 'aesthetic' or not.
(Park 1993 12–13)

This accounts for the fact that games do foster what Park calls 'aesthetic situations': moments where aesthetic dimensions of things rise to the surface (Park 1993 63, 66).

'Playability' and 'usability' are familiar attributes and concepts from new media and interface design, but they do not fit the fine arts very well. In fact, during modernity a work of art pretty much required a 'bad interface' to be accepted into the canon of the fine arts. Park (1993 59) has stated that whereas the popular arts have been 'easily accessible', the fine arts have been 'difficult to access'. Successful game designs are both easily accessible, playable and have a high degree of usability. Although games require certain playing skills to start with, one can play and consume them 'wherever' and 'whenever', outside institutionalised practices. This is an aspect that is familiar from enjoying popular culture in general. Therefore, I see no real use in trying to fit the virtual gameworlds into the analytic traditions and contexts of the 'art world'. An approach like this would rather lead away from qualities essential to games than help to understand them.

Whether computer and video games are a form of popular art, or maybe a future artform in their own right, aesthetic questions regarding games are certainly not irrelevant. As I intend to show here, aesthetic theory can help us in grasping such questions as "What elements make a good game?", or "What constitutes a satisfying gaming experience?". Answering these questions can, in the shape of theory and critical vocabulary, give useful tools for game criticism, development and design. What makes this especially relevant is the fact that whereas appreciating a work of art takes place within the artistic context and the artist (more or less), appreciating and enjoying games relates to the context of design.

3. Questions of game archaeologies

It is easy to get blinded by the novelty of digital technologies. When this happens, new techno-logical innovations and their contents appear to us as ahistorical: without traces and counterparts in history. However, if we try to uncover the historical roots of a practice like game-playing as a form of media use, we need to look farther into history than the date when the first computer game was programmed or the first game console was released to the market. In what follows, my intention is to present the reader with some ideas about the historical counterparts and precursors of contemporary digital games and the virtual spaces represented in them. I will call this kind of approach game archeology.

The approach outlined here originates from Finnish film and cultural historian Erkki Huhtamo's concept of 'media archeology', which he defines as follows:

> I would like to propose it [media archeology] as a way of studying such recurring cyclical phenomena which (re)appear and disappear and reappear over and over again in media history and somehow seem to transcend specific historical contexts. (Huhtamo 1994 131)

Thus, we should also question the supposed novelty of digital games and trace their origins into history. In addition, playing games is a case of media use. Therefore, by uncovering historical parallels between media technologies, media use and, in this case, media audiences' aspirations for virtual realities, we can shed light on the reasons why digital games are so popular.

4. Games as everyday virtual reality

It is useful to take note that digital games are perhaps the most diverse media genre until now. It is extremely problematic to make general assumptions about 'computer games' – what might ring true about adventure games (such as *Myst*) seldom qualifies for games like *Tetris*. In order to avoid these kinds of generalisation, I am focusing on one type of games in particular. This is the game genre known as 'first-person shooter' (FPS), which became hugely popular with *Doom* (Id Software 1994) and has spawned numerous other popular games (e.g. the *Quake* and the *Unreal* series, *Half-life*, etc. See Figure 1). These games mainly consist of running down corridors, dungeons, and other environments and shooting everything that moves with big guns.

The distinctive quality of the FPS genre is its mode of representation. The game-world is represented from the first person viewpoint, much like the numerous virtual reality (VR) prototypes (with headsets and gloves) intro-duced in the past. The 'technique of the observer' in these games reminds one of a continuous cinematic tracking shot, with the player controlling the camera. The point, of course, is similar to VR, to create an illusion of another reality. Regarding digital technologies, it has become common to call this kind of 'losing oneself' in these spaces as 'immersion' (see e.g. Murray 1997).

It is important to point out here the fact that although it might appear to be so, immer-sion is not solely a technological solution –

Figure 1.

The special-effects (un)reality of virtual reality.

Quake 3: Arena. Id Software, 1999.

readers, listeners and audiences of fairy tales, novels and cinema have been immersing into fictional stories (and the spaces represented in them) for centuries. Rather, immersion is a state of mind, closely related to the 'willing suspension of disbelief' familiar from discussions concerning other media and other kind of games, namely the 'second-order realities' that children immerse themselves while playing. However, it is evident that with spaces that one can manoeuvre through, digital technologies make new degrees of immersion possible. The contexts of immersion are often familiar from the imagery of popular culture (science fiction, fantasy, sports, etc.).

A supposed step towards a higher degree of immersion is that the function of the subjective viewpoint in FPS games is its immediacy, i.e. the disappearance of the interface and the computer as medium (cf. Bolter and Grusin 1999 23–24). This is strengthened by the use of the so-called 'Renaissance perspective' in constructing the player's view of the game-world. But, in the end, the optics represented in the game are based just as much on the binary code of the software as the senses of the player. This is the handicap of today's games when we compare them with both their archaeological predecessors, for example panoramas and amusement park installations, and their future platforms, VR cubes and such.

Taking your average first-person shooter as everyday virtual reality, as I suggest here, is relevant to cultural and media studies which focus on everyday and widespread media use, and the construction of culture in this sense. From this viewpoint, the high-tech VR 'cubes' and 'caves' found today around the world's media laboratories are not that interesting because they are available only for an esoteric group of designers and engineers. Of course, from the perspective of design the latest technology with its potential can be fascinating enough, but I argue here that without relevant knowledge of the tradition of media technologies and the cultural history of the moving image, it is quite easy to get stuck into unimaginative recycling of formulas and ideas from existing media. If games are to conquer the throne of the number one entertainment form of the 21st century, theoretical knowledge of the traditions of audio-visual media must be implemented into the more practically orientated work of programming and design. One way to pursue this agenda is by digging deeper into the prehistory, or 'media archaeology' of computer and video games.

5. Screenshots from the past

In his *Digital Aesthetics*, Sean Cubitt has argued that certain Baroquesque qualities are re-articulated in digital culture. He writes:

The rendition of space as spectacle, whether in baroque ceilings or in immersive VR systems, is a complex specularisation of the dialectic of reason and twining of art and science, and which illuminates the central role of the commodity form in the development of digital cultures. (Cubitt 1998 77)

So, our wanderings around the game-spaces of media commodities such as *Doom* and *Quake III: Arena* and other 3D games can be understood as echoes of the landscapes and the fantastic, found already in the panoramic paintings of the Baroque. The positions of the viewer constituted before them and their distinctive aesthetics have been transformed by historical developments in media technology. These range from pre-cinematic devices, such as magic lanterns and panoramic theatres, to stereographic devices and phenakistiscopes (see e.g. Crary 1991, Friedberg 1994), and early experiments with film known as 'the cinema of attraction' (e.g. the films of Georges Méliès). Another point of reflection is the 'phantom train' films, which have found their contemporary equivalents in roller coasters and computer-animated 'ride movies' of amusement parks. In their mode of representation, the games dis-

Figure 2.

The aesthetics of speed.

Supreme Snow Boarding.
©Housemarque /Infogrames, 1999.

one of shock aesthetics, as discussed by Walter Benjamin in the 1930s in relation to modern urban existence. Gunning has made a connection between this and the aesthetics emerging with early cinema:

> *Shock becomes not only a mode of modern experience, but a strategy of a modern aesthetics of astonishment. Hence the exploitation of new technological thrills that flirt with disaster.*
> *(Gunning 1995 128)*

Thinking about games and playing in general, this aspect finds a suitable context from Roger Caillois' study of different games. Caillois writes about *ilinx*, a subcategory of games that produces a feeling of tumult and vertigo:

> *The last kind of game includes those which are based on the pursuit of vertigo and which consist of an attempt to momentarily destroy the stability of perception and inflict a kind of voluptous panic upon an otherwise ludic mind. In all cases, it is a question of surrendering to a kind of spasm, seizure, or shock which destroys reality with sovereign brusqueness.*
> *(Caillois 1961 23)*

And he continues:

> *It is not surprising that the Industrial Revolution had to take place before vertigo could really become a kind of game. It is now provided for the avid masses by thousands of stimulating contraptions installed at fairs and amusement parks.*
> *(Caillois 1961 25–26)*

And with digital technology, and games in particular, these contraptions have been domesticised. The vertigo and sense of speed offered by games of *ilinx* have been virtualised in games such as *Supreme Snow Boarding* (see Figure 2). In a sense, aesthetic experience has been packaged and stamped with a trademark (see Welsch 1997 1–2).

6. The games of attraction

Tom Gunning has introduced the label 'cinema of attraction'. He has indicated that cinema of

cussed here represent a continuation of these traditions. The ability to 'move the frame'; to control the perceptible view – the 'Albertinian window' of art history – as one does when playing *Doom*, for example, was already embedded in the panoramas of the 1800s (cf. Hillis 1999 30), and the well-known *Viewmaster* toys, but in games this ability has been transformed into the shape of playable digital entertainment. The game industry has begun to offer this distinct aesthetic experience in the shape of media commodities.

Here we encounter games as a form of thrill-seeking. As film historian Tom Gunning has noted, the early films with on-rushing trains

> *combined sensations of acceleration and falling with a security guaranteed by modern industrial technology.*
> *(Gunning 1995 122)*

In games these sensations are re-invented and transformed towards the fantastic. This is tied to the spectator's relationship to reality, which has been transformed by an increasing amount of media technology in our everyday surroundings. We are bombarded by different mediated symbols and messages from billboards and such, and in games' hectic and aggressive environments this happens quite literally. This reminds attraction was basically a series of early, one-reel experiments with telling a story using moving images. In other words, it was a search for narrative conventions; a phase of 'showing' rather than telling with the means of cinematography. The narrative conventions of cinema as we know them (Hollywood-style) were established later in the 1910s and 1920s. (Gunning 1995 121)

From Gunning's idea of the 'aesthetics of astonishment', we can find many media-archaeological parallels to the phase of development where digital games stand today. Gunning writes:

Rather than being an involvement with narrative action or empathy with character psychology, the cinema of attractions solicits a highly conscious awareness of the film image engaging the viewer's curiosity. [...] This cinema addresses and holds the spectator, emphasising the act of display. In fulfilling this curiosity, it delivers a generally brief dose of scopic pleasure.
(Gunning 1995 121, emphasis mine)

These observations will serve as my point of reflection when discussing the ways in which games re-articulate and expand the aesthetics of attraction and the role of the spectator. In other words, the degree and nature of scopic pleasure is made more concrete and somatic as it becomes interactive in a material sense, that is, when it becomes dependent on the actions of the player by the means of the game controller (joystick, mouse, keyboard, etc.).

Television, video, and now computers and game consoles with their digital games have more or less followed cinematic conventions and appropriated them to their own strengths and limitations. We can construct the following parallel between the development of early cinematic techniques and digital games: because the digital technology develops at a faster pace than camera technology at the beginning of the century, game authoring and design is
a) a process of continuous adapting, and
b) experimenting with familiar conventions from

other media, and thus producing new formulas of narrative discourse and modes of representation.

Games nowadays emphasise action, spectacle, special effects ('attractions') and spatiality instead of narration. This argument is illustrated by Tom Gunning's statement about the cinema of attraction:

This is a cinema of instants, rather than developing situations.
(Gunning 1995 123)

Games offer instant action, instant pleasure. The doses of pleasure are delivered according to a game mechanism. This is created by the designer, who allows/constructs things to happen in the game environment, but also by the player who achieves pleasure by successfully executing the actions that the game requires in order for the game to continue.

The pre-historical occurrences and degrees of virtual reality outlined above can be seen as digital games' act of remediation, as discussed by Jay David Bolter and Richard Grusin (1999). Remediation accounts for the means of re-purposing narrative techniques and modes of representation from historical forms of media, and also co-evolving with the existing ones. Rather than mediating messages between people, media begin to mediate each other.

The starting points for game archaeology are similar to the ones of remediation, but at the same time, broader in scope: different card, board, and parlour games have been a part of the everyday leisure of men and women for centuries. In the last forty years, along with the development of digital technology, these phenomena and impulses have respectively gained new subjects and objects in digital games as entertainment and consumable media artefacts. With the approach outlined here, there is no need to force the well-known puzzle-game *Tetris*, for example, into existing categories of narrative or media, because it obviously does not fit them very well. Instead we can reflect this particular game against the historical continuum that different outlets for people's play-impulses form. Mechanical toys, such as the *Rubik's cube* and other puzzles, and moreover, technological forms of *ilinx* (amusement park installations), have previously been fostering these impulses. *Tetris* is the *Rubik's cube* remediated by the means of digital technology. In *Tetris*, figuring out the colourful cube and restoring its 'harmony' have been topped with a digital interface, game-like rhythm, and mutability. Snow and skate boarding, car racing games and the 'deathmatches' in multiplayer FPS games present other examples of remediating *ilinx* by digital means. On the other hand, narrative elements in games (cinematic cut-scenes between game levels, character development, etc.) are used to create narrative contexts for the gameplay itself.

7. Towards kineaesthetic spectacles

Although the concept of remediation is useful in situating new media in historical contexts, it has its shortcomings as well: when applied to games, looking only for similarities might leave the most significant and attractive qualities of games unexamined (cf. Aarseth 1997 22–23). Evaluating games only by the standards of other media cannot get us to their essence and popularity. This kind of blindness is at times evident in Bolter and Grusin's views on games' remediative strategies: they use rather conservative types of adventure games as their examples (e.g. *Myst*, *The Last Express*), where remediations of narrative devices, namely cinematic conventions, are quite easy to spot. I think it is more interesting to see how contemporary movies are incorporating

I think it is more interesting to see how contemporary movies are incorporating game-like elements and aesthetics

game-like elements and aesthetics: e.g. the fighting scenes of *The Matrix* and scenes in David Fincher's *The Game* where the protagonist is thrown into game-like situations. *Starship Troopers* reminds one of a shooting game, and in *Speed* Keanu Reeves' character is basically playing a driving game and David Gronenberg's *eXistenZ* is a game-movie par excéllence. With these films, or remediations, Hollywood is trying to evolve and co-exist with the needs of the game audience. Then again, the audio-visual 'style' (for the lack of a better term) of an up-coming game *Max Payne* (from Remedy Entertainment, see http://www.maxpayne.com) is clearly influenced by Hong Kong action movies and *The Matrix*.

So we see that special effects represent the modern-day 'attractions' for movie audiences. There is a certain family resemblance in these two particular realms: both answer to an aesthetic desire for action-packed spectacles, or 'the sense of wonder' attributed to science fiction. One should remember, however, that Hollywood-movies are not games but narratives. Playing games takes place 'live', and therefore it has performative instead of narrative aspects, not unlike media art that uses computer technology (cf. Saltz 1997). This doesn't mean that games cannot incorporate narrative elements, such as cut-scenes, prologues, and literary depictions (as they often do), but these elements do not constitute the game itself; they are not what 'gameplay' is about.

At the moment, playing games incorporates and automates mainly vision and visuality, but one cannot underestimate the importance of sounds in creating an immersive gamespace. Although games' haptic aspects are still rather restricted, it is important to note that the person playing the game does guide (with the means of the gamepad, joystick, keyboard, wheel, etc.) the 'virtual camera' which brings the game environment and its representations visible to us (cf. Binkley 1997 113). The dynamic viewpoint, where human agency is "placed at the center of the dynamics of sight" (Hillis 1999 38) is an important point of departure when we think of other media (film, television). It is the groundwork for a sense of interaction with the game environment.

Timothy Binkley has pointed out another difference. This is the 'vitality' of digital creations. Binkley writes:

> If images make their subjects present to us, digital representations make us present to them. (Binkley 1997 108)

This observation is quite accurate when we think of games. It is characteristic of digital games that the antagonists and objects of the game environment react to the 'sight' of the protagonist (the player). Everyone who has ever tried *Doom*, or even *Pac-Man*, can testify to this. This is also a concrete example of the 'event-time' that the player enacts during gameplay (cf. Aarseth 1999 37).

In any case, discussing only one modality (e.g. visuality) of digital media is not sufficient in order to produce aesthetic criticism. Applied to game aesthetics, this means taking into account the virtual game-world as a whole, multi-sensual and senso-motoric experience, as one would when analysing experiences in an environment that is natural and 'real'.

8. Environmentquakes

We find digital games, then, between the paths of two aesthetic disciplines, aesthetics of the moving image (film, television, video) and aesthetics of the environment (landscapes, architecture, space). The first path illustrates where game aesthetics are coming from. The second gives an idea of where game aesthetics are, what they are heading towards in the future, and to what realms we should relate the aesthetic experiences games provide. One cannot separate these from the experiencing subject, his/her personal histories, beliefs and the contexts of game playing in general. Therefore, the above-mentioned disciplines should be complemented in future research with the aesthetics of play, or more simply, the study of playful media use that attracts aesthetic situations. These are the points of departure for game aesthetics.

Working with theory, it is easy to forget how central aesthetic judgments and questions of taste are to our everyday consumption of media products. The discourse of leisure and pleasure is crucial here, regardless whether the aesthetic enjoyment results from action, suspense, horror, comedy, role-playing and/or the visual and aural splendour in games. In the end, games too are played because they are entertaining and fun. Aesthetic analyses can help us to make the decisions into what media artefacts we spend our time, energy and money in order to find this pleasure we are seeking. From the perspective of design, game aesthetics can produce historically conscious and culturally informed approaches to game development and production.

Here we should note Allen Carlson's ideas on the key questions of environmental aesthetics and especially the relationship of the perceiving and experiencing subject and the environment s/he is observing. I believe the following citation helps us to understand the connections between environmental aesthetics and the game aesthetics I am proposing here.

> The 'object' of appreciation, 'the aesthetic object' is our environment, our own surroundings, and thus we are in a sense immersed in the object of appreciation. This fact has the following ramifications. We are in that which we appreciate, and that which we appreciate is also that from which we appreciate. If we move, we move within the object of our appreciation and thereby

change our relationship to it and at the same
time change the object itself. Moreover, as our
surroundings, the object impinges upon all our
senses. As we recide in it or move through it, we
can see it, hear it, feel it, smell it and perhaps
even taste it. In brief, the experience of the
environmental object of appreciation from which
aesthetic appreciation must be fashioned is
initially intimate, total and somewhat engulfing.
(Carlson 1992 142)

Of course, we have to make several
reservations regarding games here, and especially
their limited multi-modality compared to the
experience of a natural environment. Still, I
would argue that the similarities are more
significant than the differences. The 'engulfing'
experience of a natural environment turns into
the 'immersive' of virtual game environments.
As Lev Manovich has noted, with the help of
digital technologies, space becomes a media
form (Manovich 2001). From the perspective of
aesthetics, this means that the two aforementioned disciplines (moving image and environment) converge. It is the nature and construction of this kind of game environment that I
propose we can understand more thoroughly
with the help of environmental aesthetics.

This also brings us to the question of
cybernetics, namely the interaction of man and
machine during game-play. Whereas a natural
environment changes at will, in games the
virtual and mediated game environment reacts
to the actions of the player. The causal relationships that exist within a natural environment
have been substituted in virtual environments
with computational algorithms. A cybernetic
loop is formed between the player and the
environment, the architecture of sounds and
images, that is. As Espen Aarseth has put it:

The player plays the game, and, at the same
time, the game plays the player.
(Aarseth 1997 162)

How this kind of cybernetic loop is constructed,
is a question of design.

9. Game over

It is also the task of aesthetic criticism to present
judgments of the objects of study. In game
aesthetics, tools are created to understand the
nature and function of game experiences. These
can be situated into larger contexts by studying
the history of game and play impulses and their
re-articulations and new horizons in contemporary digital games. This includes the effort of
trying to uncover the archaeology of digital
games from the histories of media technology
and media use. These have been the goals of this
essay.

Regarding aesthetics, a formalistic
approach – guidelines of design, or design
principles – is not enough. The building blocks
of aesthetic experiences are just as much
dependent on the individual contexts of media-
use and the personal preferences of audiences as
they are on the work of designers. Game
aesthetics cannot be separated from the contexts
of game-playing: the material and ideological
resources and the life-world of the player, or the
'user', a familiar but not very useful term from
the rhetoric of new media design. I believe it is
here that the biggest challenges for digital
aesthetics lie in the future. The formulations
presented in this text help us to understand the
inter-dependent nature of virtual environments
and their users. In this way, they light the way
towards an aesthetic approach to new media
studies and design.

References

Aarseth, E. (1997) *Cybertext. Perspectives on ergodic
literature*. Johns Hopkins University Press, Baltimore.

Aarseth, E. (1999) Aporia and epiphany in *Doom* and
The Speaking Clock. The temporality of ergodic art.
In Ryan, M-L. (ed.) *Cyberspace textuality. Computer
technology and literary theory*. Indiana University
Press, Bloomington.

Binkley, T. (1997) The vitality of digital creation. *The Journal of Aesthetics and Art Criticism* 2(55) 107–116.

Bolter, J. D. and Grusin, R. (1999) *Remediation. Understanding new media*. MIT Press, Cambridge, Massachusetts.

Caillois, R. (1961) *Man, play and games*. Trans. Barash, M. The Free Press of Glencoe, Inc., New York.

Carlson, A. (1992) Environmental aesthetics. In Cooper, D. (ed.) *A companion to aesthetics*. Blackwell, Oxford, pp.142–144.

Crary, J. (1990) *Techniques of the observer. On vision and modernity in the nineteenth century*. MIT Press, Cambridge, Massachusetts.

Cubitt, S. (1998) *Digital aesthetics*. Sage Publications, London.

Darley, A. (2000) *Visual digital culture. Surface play and spectacle in new media genres*. Routledge, London.

Friedberg, A. (1994) *Window shopping. Cinema and the postmodern*. University of California Press, Berkeley, Los Angeles.

Gunning, T. (1995) An aesthetic of astonishment: early film and the (in)credulous spectator. In Williams, L. (ed.) *Viewing positions. Ways of seeing film*. Rutgers University Press, New Brunswick, New Jersey, pp.114–133.

Hillis, K. (1999) Towards the light 'within'. Optical technologies, spatial metaphors and changing subjectivities. In Crang, M., Crang, P. and May, J. (eds.) *Virtual geographies. Bodies, space and relations*. Routledge, London, pp.23–43.

Huhtamo, E. (1994) From kaleidoscomaniac to cybernerd. Towards an archeology of the media. In Tarkka, M. (ed.) *ISEA '94*, The 5th International Symposium on Electronic Art Catalogue, University of Art and Design, Helsinki, pp. 130–135. Also available: http://www.isea.qc.ca/symposium/archives/isea94/pr501.html.

Manovich, L. (2001) *The language of new media*. MIT Press, Cambridge, MA.

Murray, J. (1997) *Hamlet on the holodeck. The future of narrative in cyberspace*. MIT Press, Cambridge, MA.

Saltz, D. Z. (1997) The art of interaction: interactivity, performativity, and computers. *The Journal of Aesthetics and Art Criticism* 55(2) 117–127.

Park, S.-B. (1993) *An aesthetics of the popular arts. An approach to the popular arts from the aesthetic point of view*. Acta Universitatis Upsaliensis, Uppsala.

Welsch, W. (1997) *Undoing aesthetics*. Trans. Inkpin, A. Sage Publications, London.

Aki Järvinen has worked both as a concept designer and a researcher in the field of new media. He has written several articles and columns on digital media culture, focusing especially on computer game studies. He is currently employed as an Assistant Professor at the Hypermedia Laboratory in the University of Tampere, Finland. He is working on a PhD on computer and video game aesthetics.

This article first appeared in *Digital Creativity* 12(2) 67–76 (2001).

Remediating theatre in a digital proscenium

Steve Dixon

University of Salford, UK

Abstract

The paper examines and evaluates the transposition of live theatre performance into a digital multimedia environment utilising QuickTime (or equivalent) movie software for use on standard PCs. Writers such as Brenda Laurel have discussed the close correspondences between theatre and computers, and CD-ROM authoring software such as Director clearly adopts theatrical paradigms and terminology. The differences between attending a performance in a theatre and viewing a recording on a computer screen are outlined, and how these two experiences differ in what is expected from the audience/user. The distortions inherent in any video recording of a theatre event are explored, with particular reference to differentials in performance scale. The flickering, low-resolution picture typifying video playback on CD-ROMs is then argued to be a positive virtue in the remediation of theatrical footage, and far preferable to full-screen video recordings. A number of reasons are proposed which explore ideas around documentary realism, visual and aesthetic convention, totemic fetishisation, and Brecht's alienation theory. It is suggested that the small-window digital movie placed within the larger multimedia screen where other graphical codes and images can co-exist and interact with the video footage, creates a dual proscenium that is poetic, evocative, and inherently theatrical.

Keywords: digital performance, QuickTime, remediation, theatre CD-ROM

1. Introduction

The word 'remediation' has been common coinage in the waste disposal industry for some time. The term is finding increasing usage within cultural studies and postmodern theory, to indicate not only a recycling of material, but also the transposition, reworking or deconstruction of texts into different forms or media. This paper explores the effects of the remediation of live theatre into a digital CD-ROM format for standard domestic personal computers, using QuickTime or equivalent video playback software. In recent years, CD-ROMs examining plays and theatrical performance have been produced both as teaching and learning resources within academic contexts, and as commercial home 'edutainment' packages. This paper attempts to evaluate the particular qualities and drawbacks that result from the metamorphic remediation of live theatre to computer screen.

2. Digital = dramatic

Though non-linear, hypermedia is nonetheless a quintessentially dramatic/ theatrical form, as Brenda Laurel has discussed extensively in her seminal Computers as Theater (1991). The most engaging and effective multimedia applications, whether art, education or entertainment-based, invariably adopt dramatic paradigms just as computer games rely heavily upon performative elements - clearly defined characters, empathy, dramatic tension, surprise, melodrama, conflict and resolution. Successful multimedia programmes create new and exciting 'worlds' in the computer screen proscenium just as theatre performances do within their own stage frames.

The audio-visual design conception also plays a pivotal role in the success of both multimedia applications and theatrical spectacles. Equally, both can work effectively using either sparse ('poor' theatre/ minimalist graphics) or expansive (opera/ complex graphics and layering) design strategies.

It is significant that the industry-standard authoring software currently employed for CD-ROM production is called Director — clearly relating the role of multimedia author to the key creative individual in theatre, film or television production. Director's screen interface and language also places dramatic metaphor and terminology firmly at its core. Like a theatrical impresario, the multimedia designer assembles 'cast members' (also called 'puppets') that take the 'stage' according to rehearsed and pre-set cues.

3. Re-viewing performance

Whilst attending theatre performances and viewing multimedia applications can both be conceptualised as performance 'events', they are quite different experiences. Theatre is a communal experience reliant on a captive audience in a normally darkened auditorium, where all attention is tightly focussed on the stage action, with minimal external distractions. Home computer CD-ROM experiences are normally private and unstructured events, where distractions or breaks may occur. Unlike going to the theatre, the computer user exploring remediated theatre does not dress up, make an effort to travel somewhere, and then sit still and quietly in the dark for several hours. The experience is de-ritualised, there is no sense of the

Whilst attending theatre performances and viewing multimedia applications can both be conceptualised as performance 'events', they are quite different experiences

user entering a 'sacred space', and most crucially, no restriction on the user actually stopping and starting the show to go to the toilet, make a cup of tea, or fly to Paris for the weekend. In such an environment the live event can never be adequately simulated or replicated — nor should it be.

When the computer remediates theatre, paradoxically, the computational proscenium returns drama to its traditional roots within a fixed box frame, whereas the current trend in non-mainstream theatre and performance tends more towards a fluid, immersive and environmental space (remediating non-theatrical space). The transposition of theatre to computer screen thus lends video footage of performance a nostalgic quality, putting it back into a box. It restrains its liveness and immediate presence, yet used creatively a different, but equally powerful presence and theatrical 'magic' can be achieved by manipulation of the new double-proscenium: the small QuickTime window placed within the wider screen area that surrounds it. Graphical elements, sound, still imagery and photomontage can be used dynamically to frame, mirror, transpose, emphasise, change meaning, and otherwise interact with the moving pictures. The conjunction of theatrical movie file footage with other visual elements can create rich, expressive and haunting environments, interfaces and dramatic experiences. (See Figures 1–6).

It is nonetheless ironic that since the viewing of theatrical CD-ROMs normally takes place alone, the futuristic computer may ultimately serve to archive and remediate theatre in a

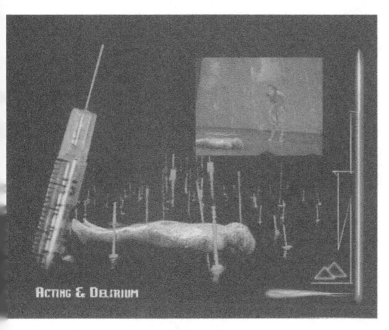

Figure 1.
Elements of
the theatrical
mise-en-
scene are
transposed
and reworked
to create
hybrid set
designs
within the
computer
proscenium.
(Chameleons 2)

Figure 2.
A simple
design
strategy
encapsulates
the funda-
mentals of
theatre:
performers
within a
space.
(Chameleons 2)

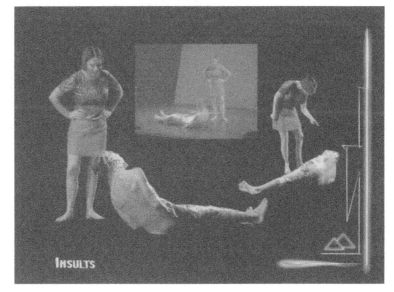

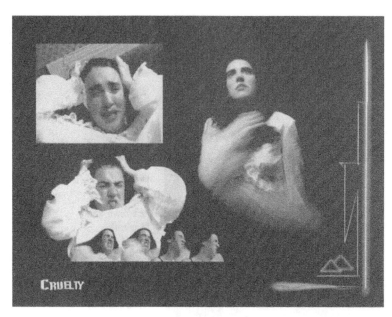

Figure 3.
Frozen
images taken
from the
video footage
(top left)
build up and
repeat on
screen to
highlight and
emphasise
dramatic
themes.
(Chameleons 2)

Figure 4.
The split-focus
multimedia
elements
illustrated in
the video
footage of
the Chamele-
ons 2 theatre
production
(top left) are
closely
mirrored in
the screen
interface
design.
(Chameleons 2)

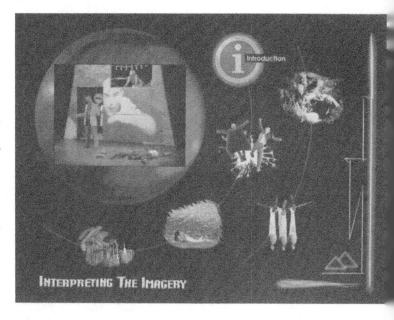

The screen-shots that illustrate this paper are taken from two CD-ROMs produced by the author, which remediate live theatre productions by The Chameleons Group, a company he directs. The group devises multimedia theatre that is inspired by surrealism and the theatrical writings of Artaud. Both CDs are public domain, and gratis copies can be obtained by writing to: S.Dixon@salford.ac.uk

Figure 5.
The full-screen
(still) image
provides a
wider
contextual
shot to locate
and frame
the monologue
shown in
close-up
(video).
(Chameleons 1)

Figure 6.
The full-screen
image here is
a blow-up of
a frozen
moment from
the inset
video footage.
As the video
plays, an
interesting
visual tension
and sense of
anticipation
is established
which is
released and
resolved when
the two
images
synchronise.
(Chameleons 1)

form that points towards its regression to its literary genesis: 'read' by one person from a two-dimensional flat plane.

4. Theatre > screen remediation

The interactive nature of theatre is often cited as its essential live element. Thus, there is a genuine, though often highly subtle, stimulus-response interchange between actors and audience that constantly affects the live event. Though the notion of interactivity is equally fundamental to hypermedia, theatre's remediation into digital data within the computer completely disengages live theatre's intrinsic interactivity, although different interactive paradigms may be programmed in its place. The theatre piece is recorded and therefore 'dead'. Worse still for the theatre purist, by nature of its new 4:3 ratio screen domain, the performance is transposed to something closer to television.

It is widely acknowledged that theatre does not transpose well to television. The two media have broadly opposite conventions in audience point-of-view (long distance versus close-up), mise-en-scene (representational versus realistic) and acting technique (externalised versus internalised). Actors particularly dislike theatre-to-video remediation as it highlights the technical aspects of stagecraft such as the use of gestures and projected vocal techniques, which can appear melodramatic or 'false' when reproduced on video. However, the same piece of apparently exaggerated performance when witnessed in theatrical space may have genuine power and sincerity. As Stanislavski once noted, "scenic truth is different from truth in real life".

Video recordings distort the actuality of theatrical events. Theatre is conceived for theatrical space and as a live event, and critics rightly note video's flattening of three-dimensional perspective; the medium's inability to convey mood and presence; and its inadequacy in encapsulating the subtle interplay between audiences and actors. The intimacy of a live event is stripped of its atmosphere and 'magic'. Docu-

menting theatre on video can be compared to the story of The Emperor's New Clothes; once the complicity of the audience to use its imagination and willingly suspend disbelief is no longer present, the entire artifice and sense of illusion can completely collapse.

5. The paradox of scale

If full-screen video recordings of theatre performances are therefore unsatisfactory due to the incompatible scales and conventions of the two media, then it should follow that video recordings when further remediated into digital multimedia environments should be equally distorting and unacceptable. More so, perhaps, since the relatively minute scale of the standard digital movie, filling only a small proportion of the screen, could be viewed as reducing the grand scale of theatre to laughably bathetic proportions.

But this is not the case. On the contrary, I would argue that, like a homeopathic dosage, the tiny QuickTime movie format remediates theatre more acceptably and accurately than a conventional video recording on a TV monitor. The very limitations (small window size, choppy movement, pixelated resolution) of the default domestic QuickTime/ MoviePlayer video software of recent years actually serve to distance and differentiate the remediation from its televisual antecedent. Paradoxically, this renders the digital multimedia reproduction more successful, engaging and theatrical.

I suggest a number of reasons for this:
1. When sitting in front of a computer screen, the size of the QuickTime movie stage corresponds to a comparable area and angle of view of a proscenium arch stage as viewed from the most expensive seats (rear stalls) of a large theatre auditorium. Where screen interface design also utilises an austere (and currently fashionable) black background, this particularly highlights the effect, recreating the illusion of a darkened auditorium with a brightly-lit stage in the distance.

2. Where full-screen video and television conventions generally tend towards a closure of illusion, the low-resolution digital window inherently acknowledges and admits its own technical inadequacies. There is an implicit honesty about what it actually is — a remediation (digitally compressed copy) of a remediation (a video record of a live event) struggling within embryonic software. Brecht's alienation effect is intrinsic to its very form since the medium is foregrounded and draws attention to itself. This encourages users to view the material from a more objective perspective, rather than trying to immerse themselves in a subjective experience which would ultimately disappoint since it would fail to adequately simulate the experience of the live theatre audience.

3. Just as the stuttering jerks and poor resolution of CCTV footage gives a gritty realism and sense of 'truth' to views of streets and shops, so too does the computer's flickering QuickTime proscenium. The remediated theatre event becomes documentary actuality, and is viewed as such. We are witnesses after the fact.

4. There is a particular aesthetic quality to the flickering low-resolution footage of QuickTime movies. Like audiences watching the first What the Butler Saw nickelodeons in the early days of film, we too are witnessing the pioneering stages of a new technological medium. There is a strange, evocative, nostalgic quality to the image, like we are watching something that, like the technology itself, is at once revolutionary, but also antique.

6. Conclusion

In the early days of film, cinema technology rapidly developed to overcome the quaint, flickering effect in the projector gate. High picture resolution and realism became the goals. Likewise, with recent developments such as DVD-ROM drives, home computers have already advanced to the point where the flickering QuickTime qualities I am praising will very soon become a thing of the past. However, theatrical archivists and remediators could do well to remember the particular virtues of the smaller window format for theatrical footage, rather than embracing full-screen video as it inexorably becomes the new gold standard. Full-screen digital video is not computational multimedia; it is just television, and television remediates theatre badly, as I have sought to demonstrate.

By contrast, the dual proscenium of small-window digital movie placed within a wider frame where other elements, codes and images co-exist and interact with the footage creates a new and poetic form of digital theatre. The theatre movie file becomes a play within a play. The remediated performance footage is ritualised within the wider computer proscenium as a totem, a fetishised object. Though small and flickering, it is nonetheless powerful, evanescent and inherently theatrical.

Reference

Laurel, B. (1991) *Computers as Theater*. Addison-Wesley, Reading, MA.

Steve Dixon is Senior Lecturer at the School of Media, Music and Performance at the University of Salford, UK and co-director of the Digital Performance Archive, which records and analyses developments in virtual-theatre and cyber-performance (see http://art.ntu.ac.uk/dpa). He has published internationally on a range of subjects including performance studies, virtual theatre, hypermedia theory, and film hermeneutics. Steve is also director of the multimedia theatre company *The Chameleons Group*. He is currently completing a book and accompanying DVD with Barry Smith entitled *Digital performance: new technologies in theatre, dance and performance art*.

This article first appeared in *Digital Creativity* 10(3) 135–142 (1999).

Drama in the digital domain: Commedia dell'Arte, characterisation, collaboration and computers

Mika Tuomola

Helsinki University of Art and Design, Finland

Abstract

The article discusses how Commedia dell'Arte (CdA) may be used as a design metaphor for Multi-user Virtual World (MVW). The introduction gives an overview of the beginning ideas and the general findings of the research, as well as connects CdA and MVW with other forms of improvisational and masked performance. An explanatory introduction to CdA is followed by examples on the possibilities of transforming practices and ideas from CdA characters, properties, staging, scenarios, themes and improvisations to MVW.

Keywords: avatar, Commedia dell'Arte, multi-user virtual world

1. Introduction

The primitive notion, usually developed among normative circles, of some linear development forward will be done away with. It will be found out that any truly relevant step forward is always accompanied with returning to primeval beginning, or more correctly, with renewal of the beginning. It is possible to move forward only by recollection, not by oblivion. (Baktin 1979)

Working for the digital media concept development and production-company Coronet Interactive, I did the research for this article during 1998 as a consultation for ICL Finland. Following my suggestion, ICL wished to use Commedia dell'Arte (CdA) — a five hundred-year-old improvisational form of street theatre, the origins of which date back to primitive cultures — as a beginning approach for designing an avatar world[1] on Internet. The Multi-user Virtual World (MVW) was to be created using Fujitsu's *WorldsAway* technology <http://www.worldsaway.com/>[2].

This article takes a general look at CdA for designing MVWs, which I believe to be among the most promising applications of networked computers with respect to the future of story-telling as a real-time "negotiated narrative"[3] based upon community intelligence as a source of information, knowledge and wisdom.

My first intuition to look into CdA as a design metaphor for MVW was inspired by the dramaturge Esko Salervo. Salervo concludes his research paper on CdA (Salervo 1984) with three aspects of "this farting adult play requiring high professional skills" that challenge current linear media.

Ho quanteal guadagnar son reti teſe
ma piu deſtro non ue dl' ceratano
coghor per frappe a danar freſchi m mano

(1568)

- CdA was theatre in open interaction with its environment. It didn't try to regulate the environment from above, but rather developed according to its audience. The movement was from bottom to top: everyday human life and absurd accidents had more actuality than ceremonies given from above.
- CdA showed that there can be theatre without the domination of prewritten text. CdA developed an alternative of its own that used well-functional elements many times (*chiusetti*) and poorly functional elements only by accident.
- CdA's history reminds us that a form of representation that does not maintain a relationship with the surrounding reality and cultural circumstances, will die.

All three aspects are apt in the case of MVWs. MVW develops in interaction with an inhabiting community, it produces its text in real-time improvisations and it will die if it loses a meaningful relationship with the surrounding reality.

The final point is essential. Theatre, film, MVW and other media are never separate from what virtual inhabitants call the Real World (RW) or Real Life (RL). In order to remain attractive to its audience, media must always maintain a living relationship with existing cultural reality. The reality consists of a variety of thoughts, activities and incidents that change constantly on the scales of private/public, family/society, practical/theoretical, current/historic, mundane/spiritual, philosophical/political and so on. A person must be offered the possibility to place her/himself on all these changing scales, unless we want to create something that will reach audiences only for a short period of time.

Studying CdA's historic background and currently-known practices led me to psychological and neurological studies of human perception, as well as to anthropological and sociological perspectives. They all provided tools for understanding CdA's development as a theatrical form and why it still has a strong relevance to the way modern media communicate. The tools connected European CdA with the Noh theatre of Japan, the Topeng theatre of Bali, the Hindu iconography and performance of India, film imagery in common use, post-modern theatre and more.

CdA seems to provide tools for a universal way to communicate with people through masked performances, what MVWs are really all about. Even during the last century of 'passive' television and theatre — which I believe to have been merely an interim period between interactive theatre and interactive mass medium (Beardon and Tuomola 1998 19) — CdA's representational solutions have been used by Molière, Shakespeare, Chaplin and today's soap operas and comedies (Green and Swan 1986). How is this possible from an old form of theatre born among the riffraff of the Italian market squares? Because CdA was born from people to people. In order to entertain the international audiences of Venice, Rome and Bologna, it had to find a universal language familiar to people already from their birth and even from the animal origins of human culture. During CdA's centuries-long practice of success and failure with various audiences, it was forced to dig into the place where the very notion of playful communication is first born in the human mind. The notion seems to be astoundingly similar all over the globe, as far as the similarities between independently born forms of masked performance indicate (Emigh 1996).

In the market places of the past centuries — and of today — CdA and its different forms had to capture and maintain audience attention in the middle of a lot of other information provided by salesmen, charlatans, beggars, public speakers, other entertainers and all sorts of people (Figure 1). Today's web art, entertainment, information and commerce, trying to attract and keep an audience during the 24 hour rush hour of the 'information superhighway', is much in the same position as CdA was on the market squares. In order to survive, a CdA group had to be able to address all the social classes present on the market square and, in time, it actually evolved into a small community in itself. The CdA stock of characters, their desires and relationships, as well as the plot lines, etc. started to reflect the society as a whole. Expectedly, Internet has started to do the same in the form of MVWs. To me, the old recipes of CdA proved themselves handy in this situation.

NOTE: Each time I write about the CdA elements on the left hand side of the following list, I strongly suggest the reader to reflect on replacing them with the MVW terms on the right hand side of the same list.

character, actor	avatar, player, virtual actor/ human, icon
movement, mimicry, choreography	(avatar) animation, gestures, expressions
mask	(avatar) head, avatar
property, prop	object, tool
stage, staging	locale, world/environment
scene, scenario	event, incident

2. Commedia dell'Arte

Around 1500–1600, CdA had the greatest influence in Italy and France, but disseminated all over Europe as far as Great Britain, Russia, Czechoslovakia and Scandinavia. It adjusted to local circumstances without compromising in essentials, and the national variations contributed to its universality (Rudlin 1994).

The essentials of CdA can be found in almost any form of ritual and entertainment rising from people themselves, whether we refer to the masked celebration of the communal past of the *Mudmen* of Makehuku (Emigh 1996 7–14), to the rules of costume and behaviour in funerals and weddings, or to the *nethics* and the masked identities of virtual community events. Mihail Baktin would say that this is the case because all these events originate from the same source of human folklore, play and carnival.

> *The essentials of Commedia dell'Arte can be found in almost any form of ritual and entertainment rising from people themselves ...*

> *...there's no division between performers and observers... At the time of carnival one can live only according to its own rules.*

> *In this sense, carnival wasn't a form of artistic*

Figure 2. Zanni's and Pantalone's poses communicate clearly their social standing. This gives us an idea how CdA gestures may have related to each other on stage and how avatar types may become clearly identifiable by their animation and poses in MVW.

theatre, but like life's own real (but temporary) form. It wasn't only acted out, but actually almost lived out (during the carnival).

So, in carnival the play itself becomes life for a while.

(Baktin 1995 9–10)

The popular essentials of CdA included the set of predefined rules for improvisation (*Commedia all Improvisa*) and the use of the same masked characters (see Figures 6–9) whatever the plot (*Commedia delle Maschere*). CdA scenario only included the list of roles and properties, as well as a summary of entrances, actions and exits. A CdA actor then improvised according to the general rules, his mask and the summary. In improvisation, an actor also used parts of performance often inherited from older actors of his character. The parts consisted, for example, of *lazzi*, astonishing sight-gags such as acrobatics, and of *battute* and *concetti*, eloquent phrases and longer speeches that were used when confessing one's love, giving a mock

speech on philosophy and so on[4].

A small number of actors (usually no more than seven) were able to perform a large repertoire of plays, ranging from farces to heavy melodramas, even though none of the plays had a written script. They did so by developing predictable formulas of interaction that gave shape to their improvisations.

(Murray 1997 235)

CdA stage scenery (*canavaccio*) was simple and put emphasis on characters and their relationships. The stage was usually a platform with a painted canvas behind. The canvas most commonly presented a city landscape with houses, thus easily merging with the market square scenery, but it could also present completely imaginary landscapes for the purposes of a fantasy play.

Entertaining music played an essential part in CdA performances. A performance often started with music, had love serenades and comic dances in the middle, and ended up with an easy-to-catch tune that would remain in the audience's mind even after their departure. The music lured people to see the performance in a market square, kept their attention by focusing on the themes of the performance and sent them home happily recollecting what had happened.

CdA was much like a chess game. It created interesting, dramatic situations not because the 'game' was written beforehand but because the rules of representation were predefined and clear. Each character, like each chess piece, could only do certain things. They could only use certain masks, mimics, passages and properties.

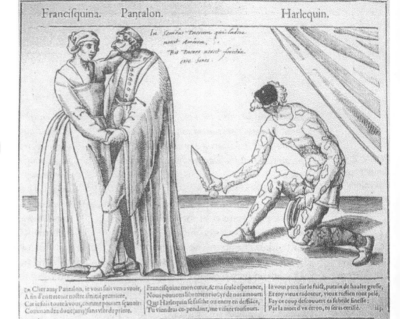

Francifquina. Pantalon. Harlequin.

3. Examples of Commedia dell'Arte in multi-user virtual world design and social maintenance

Is it possible? Can a Drama which holds the stage for two centuries be created without the assistance of the literary man? It can. Then if it can be created once it can be created twice? It can.
(Edward Gordon Craig quoted in Rudlin 1994 3)

According to Sherry Turkle, a role-playing character serves the psychological needs man has. As the needs change, characters change[5]. Constructing a virtual being to represent oneself is work in constant progress. Trusting Turkle, a good variety of MVW avatara is a necessity, if we want to serve the varying needs that participators have. CdA can provide us with a formula for sets of varieties that have the potential to create dramatic action in MVW for the pleasure of participators and observers.

I find correct, in fact, the idea proposed by some scholars, of calling this genre, instead of Commedia dell'Arte, more specifically 'comedy of comedians' or 'of actors'. The entire theatrical transaction rests on their shoulders: the actor as historian and author, stage manager, storyteller, director...
(Dario Fo quoted in Rudlin 1994 15)
Like CdA, MVW always ends up to be the work of its actors, virtual world inhabitants. Thus the most important single design issue is a user's representation in the virtual world. A participator's ambitions are mediated via her/his avatar to drive action in the world.

3.1 First example: focused avatara
In a rehearsal of Luciano Brogi's CdA group, as a young actor rehearsed Il Capitano with maestro Luciano[6], I truly realised the meaning of

focusing body gestures in order to carry avatar emotions clearly. The young actor, Luka, having his learning mainly in the mainstream of psychological, reality-imitating acting, would not comprehend nor accept the way of CdA's simple and powerful character presentation. On video, as Luciano and Luka rehearse Il Capitano side by side, one can clearly see that Luka's way of increasing inner emotion is not the key for communicating the character. As one looks at Luciano beside him, one sees that the physical gestures of focusing attention first on one step, then on another, then on hands, audience, the right leg, etc. really convey the character's emotions more powerfully. Well-considered focus of movement has much stronger impact than merely increasing gestural nuances with emotion.

In CdA mask acting, this ability to create a character by focusing visibly on the points of attention is referred to as the *stare* of mask. The mask must stare at whatever is in focus: audience in theatre or by screen, fellow actor or avatar, theatrical property or generally usable object. In order to achieve this, CdA actors and MVW participants must *live up* to the mask, realise its limited focus points and make the best out of them. The stare must naturally be created already in the design phase, or it cannot

Figure 3. The pose of lower social status does not prevent the servant Harlequin from ridiculing the master Pantalone. Wooden blades, like the one Harlequin is holding, were commonly used as phallic symbols in CdA performances (see Section 3.2).

Harlequin.   Zany Corneto.   Il Segnor Pantalon.

*Figure 4.
At the end
of a CdA
performance,
the character-
related
status poses
were put
aside as the
concluding
song began.
After ridicul-
ing the false
hierarchies of
the real world,
all actors were
presented as
equals, in the
true state of
all people.*

become animated and lived up to.

A CdA actor imagines that his mask has only one eye situated at the end of the nose in order to achieve the stare. An avatar animator working with CdA principles thinks the same and pulls the animated avatar from its nose in order to achieve the most powerful focusing ability.

The neck has to become alive in a manner that is rarely demanded of it in the three-dimensional world... In Commedia mask work the body is often required to be doing something different, working contrapuntally or even paradoxically.

The shoulders are part of the trunk, of the body and its intentions, not of the neck and the gaze of the mask.
(Rudlin 1994 40–41)

Focus points as emotion carriers may be made even more powerful by using effect sounds and music in order to create a stronger sense of presence. Indeed, nearly in all forms of body movement oriented representation — like CdA, Topeng, Noh, Hindu performance and dance — movement and gestures are given further emphasis by music and sound[7].

The choreographic simplicity of CdA's dramatic impact is very encouraging for designing avatar gestures and movements for MVW.

We can breathe life into an avatar without attempting fashionable naturalism lent from film imagery and reality. The Balinese Topeng performers do the same as their CdA colleagues: simple character movements and their relationships towards each other communicate character emotions (Figures 2–4). *Topeng is not 'like life' either; but watching a Topeng performance is a great deal 'like living,' and living very well, with all senses alert, an awakened sense of humour, an appreciation of those who have gone before, and a heightened sense of the consequences and potential of human actions.* (Emigh 1996 191)

It is possible — and currently necessary — for technology-restricted MVWs to focus on simple, yet powerful, avatar gesture and movement design rather than attempt complex and bandwidth-consuming reality imitation.

3.2 Second example: symbolic objects

CdA employed strong symbolism in its use of properties. The wooden blades used by Arlecchino, Il Capitano, Pantalone and others were often used to show their level of erection. Franceschina could talk and demonstrate how she stirs — stirs, stirs, stirs — the soup when cooking, while actually telling to adult audiences about her ways of love making[8]. Similar symbolism can also be found from the drawings that have described CdA performances (Figure 5). This was, of course, necessary at a time of severe censorship practised by the Catholic Church. In order to deepen the meaning of actions taking place in MVW, symbolic significance for objects should certainly be implied — also for purposes other than the use of ambiguous humour.

3.3 Third example: staging avatara

According to Reid Hoffman, a former director of Fujitsu's *WorldsAway* technology, the two most important evolutions and capacities of virtual communities are their casual environments and visual overlay (Damer 1998 448-449). For CdA staging these were also important elements. The stage had to be easy to put up by the performance group and easy to approach by audience. Thus visual overlay usually was a square platform with a familiar background painting of a city house that could be inhabited by a multitude of CdA characters. Similarly, MVW locales need to be easy to put up by world maintainers in order to serve quickly the unpredictable needs of a community. And maybe the set-up of a whole world should merge to the surrounding 'Real World' as the CdA stages did to familiar market squares.

When locating characters on the square platform with classical CdA manner, maestro Luciano Brogi crosses the stage with two diagonals for each character, creating a kind of chess board for CdA characters.

one character   two characters   three characters

Characters are located at the meeting points of the diagonals. Centre place is given to the character that is to have the strongest influence on the audience.

I don't know why, but when there's more than one centre on the entire stage, the right side makes a character stronger,

says Brogi as he refers to a scene with, for example, two or four actors.

On the narrow platform spaces of CdA performed on market squares, there really wasn't any depth, just as there isn't on a computer screen. The most important matter was the visibility of characters and their two-dimensional location in relationship to each other on the platform. The situation is similar on a computer screen as the medium of MVW. If an avatar is at great distance (in a three-dimensional world) from the viewer, it really disappears from the 'stage' and may not serve the needs that participators have for proper communication.

Learning from CdA, MVW maintainers and event designers should pay attention to their and their colleague's locations in the spaces they appear in. Do they want to give attention to other community members or is it necessary to draw attention to themselves? Also, the co-ordinates into which avatara are designed to move to when entering a locale in MVW becomes important when considering the psychological influence Brogi talks about. Do we want avatara to become centres of attention as they enter space (visible on the screens of other participators) or should they just sneak in relatively unnoticed? The first alternative would provide support for constantly changing situations in the world, while the latter would enhance the continuity of ongoing activity as a newcomer enters the space. With the means of technology in hand, can we locate avatara automatically, as Brogi does, according to their number in space, so attention would be directed as desired by MVW designers?

CdA character staging, which varies from scene to scene in order to keep performance constantly interesting, suggests that there should be differently automated ways of entering different spaces for different avatara. As CdA changes character staging by time, so MVW can do it by space[9].

For the sake of casual environments, we must build up MVW stages that are easy to approach and that call for participation with the kind of means described above. They also should be visually attractive and interesting, offering 'additional value' to what reality offers — as do the exaggerated features of CdA masks. This calls for fantastic design that is, however, familiar to people from their everyday life or from the media they are following.

3.4 Fourth example: structured world events

Though CdA was improvised on the basis of its representational rules, one should not underestimate underlying work usually done by the maestro, leading actor, who designed scenarios that were acted out. World maintainers and active avatara are much in the same position as CdA maestri. They need to design suggested activities well in order to carry them through successfully in a virtual community.

In CdA, each scenario included always, 1) a proposition, 2) development and 3) a solution. The practice was the same in the Japanese Noh theatre that used the principles of *Jo* (introduction), *Ha* (breaking; exposition) and *Kyu* (rapid; denouement) (Rudlin 1994 54). The smallest actions (like *lazzi* and *concetti*) were designed in the same manner in order to provide constant possibilities for other characters to enter without spoiling the drama: each solution provided a place for entrance, a new proposition (Rudlin 1994 51–55).

Verbal repetitions of previous scenarios were often practised between acts (also divided in three) to inform newcomers in the audience. Also each act began with a musical piece or something entertaining and capturing in order to bring new people into watching the performance. MVW maintainer may use similar repetitions and attractions as more avatara enter to listen to her/his scenario proposition.

The three-part scenario may further be used in MVW, for example, by providing a participator with a tempting proposition on the very first step upon entering a world. The task would be designed to teach about the world and how to function in it and to put the participator in contact with other avatara. After these developments, a participator should be offered a clear reward on learning, like additional abilities or object(s). The challenge of the scenario would be making the process of learning the world, its interface, rules and customs entertaining. Learning these limits by fun will attract participators to stay, at the same time leading them to the sources for having an even better time than learning about the possibilities and necessities provided by design limitations.

> *People have ceremonies of joining societies, they get married, change apartments, possessions and their virtual identities …*
>
> *Virtual life in itself is transitional by nature, a shift from one reality to another*

3.5 Fifth example: dynamic themes

The basic plot lines and scenarios of CdA really turned around three or four goals: love, money, vengeance and food (Rudlin 1994 53). Eight to nine characters portrayed nearly the entire society. There was *Pantalone* representing the power of money, *Il Capitano* the military and *Il Dottore* law and the academic world. Nobility presented chased-after love and revenge, while servants and charlatans were usually after money and food. Only the church and religion as social factors were lacking.

Today's soap operas and other entertainment turn around the same themes and, not surprisingly, usually do not engage in discussion over people's belief systems. Perhaps that's why American soap culture can be popular even in India and Africa.

CdA usually presented the same universal battle again and again. The conflict was always between the old and the new, very often between young lovers (nobility, or servants like Arlecchino and Colombina) and the old forces of society (Pantalone, Il Dottore, Il Capitano). The same battle and the change from old to new we witness constantly in all forms of drama and ritual, as well as in our own lives.

Love, business and change have also become central in social avatar worlds. Moving to new phases in virtual life is constant in them. People have ceremonies of joining societies, they get married, change apartments, possessions and their virtual identities. Events born from a virtual community are those familiar to us already from the beginning of human ceremonies acted out during transitional events such as birth, death, initiation, marriage, and seasonal change (Emigh 1996). Virtual life in itself is transitional by nature, a shift from one reality to another.

The celebration of change is at the very core of community. As developing further overall themes of the transitional world of virtual community, it should be noted, however, that

...rest or a break in work cannot become a celebration in itself merely. In order to be celebrations, they must be connected with something from another sphere of existence, from a spiritual-ideological sphere. They need a sanction that does not come from the world of facilities and necessities, but from the world of higher aims of human existence, in other words, from the world of ideals. Without it there can be no celebration.
(Baktin 1995 10)

3.6 Sixth example: tools for improvisation

Anything is permitted: the customary hierarchies vanish, along with all social, sex, caste, and trade distinctions. Men disguise themselves as women, gentlemen as slaves, the poor as rich.
(Octavio Paz in Rudlin 1994 13)

When rules for improvisation were clear and the basic premises accepted, it was time for the CdA group to pay attention to the subject (*Andare a soggetto*). All material — masks, costumes, properties, etc. — had to be at arm's length (*Commedia a braccia*), so actors could concentrate on the spontaneous flow of improvisation rather than on looking for necessary objects. It was time for *Commedia all'improvvisa*. Anything was allowed to happen inside premises.

Improvisation was made more fluent by a few practices, which may be used to enrich communication in MVW as well. In addition to ready rehearsed *lazzi* (sight gags), there were also memorised passages like *battute* (stock repartees) and *concetti* (stock speeches). Monologues were also stock, taken from *repertorio* or *zibaldone* (gag-book) kept by actor.

As *lazzi* can be implemented into MVW character animations, a management system for stock speeches and gags can also be provided to a participator. The *WorldsAway* worlds have shown that this sort of system would be highly appreciated, as participators themselves have started to create the kind of programs that insert text files (jokes, poems, etc.) into their avatar speech bars. For MVW designers and maintainers such a tool can be efficient as well, as they can drive action in an avatar world also by providing participators with ready-made passages according to the themes of MVW or some event. Text-based world design and management tools allow much faster execution of new ideas at the level of writing.

For MVW maintainers involved with CdA-based organisation of the chaos of MVW improvisations, as they lead the participators according to the themes of world, the thoughts of Maurice Sand on what can go wrong with improvisation may prove useful:

The strange thing is that, when you begin to improvise, far from having nothing to say, you find yourself overflowing with dialogue and make scenes last too long as a result. The hidden

Figure 5. Pantalone holds a flower in his waist as the symbol of a penis and the nature of his passions towards Cornelia. She, however, is flirting with Arlecchino, while at the same time offering her branch clustered with nuts' to Zanni! Yet Zanni obviously cares more about the wine the tavern keeper is offering. The consequences are symbolised by the rabbit. Symbolism can also bring complex layers of meaning

danger in this genre is to sacrifice the development of the basic idea to incidents which stem from it. You must also be very alert... to the possibility of having to sacrifice what you were going to say as a result of something your partner has said, and also to revitalise the action when you sense him flagging; to bring the scene back to its objective when the others are wandering off the point and stick to it yourself when your imagination is trying to persuade you to go off into dreamland.
(Rudlin 1994)

4. Conclusion

People always comes up with an explanation, a theory or a world of ideas that justifies what she/he has done and does in life. By nature, we aim towards unity between our actions and thinking of the world. Thus our actions and activities in the worlds — whether real or virtual — formulate the worlds to us, change constantly our vision of them. As building up MVW, it is imperative to recognise this and understand that whatever an avatar world encourages/discourages its inhabitants to do or from doing, it will formulate the final idea of community. It becomes a necessity to provide an MVW with a limited, carefully designed set of possible and necessary actions. Action formulates the world, as it formulates drama (Aristotle 1999).

Interaction between virtual and real worlds is constant. A virtual community's actions also influence the real world and the running of the MVW service. The community will express its feelings and requirements and is thus an essential part of developing an avatar world. For example, the US Fujitsu flat-rate payment decision for current *WorldsAway* customers originated from its virtual communities. On the other hand, the decision also reflected the general drive of telecommunications services in the real world.

As MVW design and its set of possible actions given to participators influence the way they concretely want to change the nature of the service, service providers need to think about future change and development in their MVW when the world is under design. For example, avatar world participators may soon enter MVW not only through wired computer terminals. They will enter through mobile phone-computers even for just a five-minute chat. This brings a challenge to today's MVW service designers also wanting to address future target groups.

CdA and communal performance all over the world show us that it is possible to unite a multitude of human activities within MVWs (Emigh 1996). Spectators of CdA did their shopping, played cards and listened to public announcements at the same time and in the same place as a CdA performance took place. This suggests that MVW can be a social world as well as a gaming world at the same time — and much more.

CdA offers us a set of rules for MVW participator representation and action. The past success of the rules was due to their capability of providing a form that attracted a multitude of different audiences — from the riffraff of the streets to the highest courts in Europe. Demand for the interactive form was great and thus performance groups could make a very nice living with it. CdA spread all over Europe not because it was established art, but because it was a good production concept for a multitude of contents that varied depending on culture and

Figures 6–9 show the development of the Commedia dell'Arte character Arrlechino. The costume, the name and even the gender of Arrlechino changed, but the character type remained clearly recognisable. By the 18th century, actors revealed their face behind masks (Figures 8–9) at the end of the performance in order to receive recognition for their mastery in acting a character. The artist and the individual behind the mask had become important, as they have become in Internet. An avatar's unmasking in a virtual community usually occurs by revealing the owner's homepage for other community members to investigate.

country. It is my belief that the same concept can be revitalised in the development of MVWs.

In the research, I aimed to take my first steps in continuing the interrupted development of Commedia dell'Arte and applying it to the current places of interactive performance, Multi-user Virtual Worlds. There is a lot of catching up to do, but let us not despair.

> ...*any truly relevant step forward is always accompanied with returning to primeval beginning, or more correctly, with renewal of the beginning. It is possible to move forward only by recollection, not by oblivion.*
> (Baktin 1979)

Acknowledgement

All the images in the article are from the collections of SIAE Biblioteca del Burcardo, photographed by Luciano Brogi and digitally edited by Mika Tuomola.

Notes

[1] In Sanskrit and Indian mythology, avatar means a Hindu deity's incarnation. The deities took various avatara in order to accomplish different worldly tasks. The seduction of a princess required an attractive youth avatar, while fighting a demon needed a lion or another beast-like incarnation. Currently, avatara (or avatars, the English plural in common use) refer to people's incarnations or representations in virtual worlds. Like the avatara of Hindu deities, the avatara of people should also, naturally, be designed to be useful to whatever task they are needed for. An avatar world thus means a virtual world, which can be inhabited by user/ participator representations.

[2] Due to various corporate policy decisions, the *WorldsAway* production never took place. However, Coronet Interactive is still planning an avatar world production based on the research. The interested reader may obtain more specific and applicable information on the research, the workshops based on it and the future production by contacting the author. See also the Helsinki University of Art and Design workshop results at http://www.mlab.uiah.fi/echora/. Other workshops have included 'Design of

Dramatic Action for Avatar Worlds' at the Art and Communication Department of Malmö University <http://www.kk.mah.se> and 'Commedia dell'Arte in Virtual Community Design' at Satama Interactive Ltd.

[3] Ylva Gislèn at the Narrativity and Communication Studio of the Swedish Interactive Institute <http://www.interactiveinstitute.se/> has introduced the term *negotiated narrative*. In her ongoing PhD thesis, she replaces *interactive* with *negotiated*, and is looking for the live role-playing games as a narrative approach for digital media.

[4] In MVW, an actor can be considered as a user/ participator. MVW designers provide her/him with the set of masks (avatara), properties (objects, spaces to use) and rules (gesture language, terms of service, etc.), as MVW maintainers bring in scenarios, the day-to-day vision, theme and activities. Each user learns from old community members additional tricks (like shorthand phrases of communication and how to make better use of the world and its elements).

[5] Windows, which access different personalities and realities, keep on multiplying on our computer screens. One of Turkle's research subjects describes: "I split my mind. I'm getting better at it. I can see myself as being two or three or more. RL is just one more window." (Turkle 1997 13).

[6] Tuomola, a video clip from the first attended rehearsal.

[7] The *Natyasastra*, a Sanskrit manual of acting written and compiled between 450 BC and 200 AD, outlines two approaches to performance. One is *lokadharmi* (the path of nature/the world) and the other *natyadharmi* (the path of art/dance). *Lokadharmi* stresses conversational dialogue and familiar movement, as *natyadharmi* stresses music, dance, poetry and song (Emigh 1996 pp. 27-28). As it is impossible with current web technology to replicate the reality of daily life, I believe our way with MVWs must be that of *natyadharmi*. Having chosen the way, let us use all its potential including sound and music.

[8] A video clip from the rehearsal of Luciano Brogi's CdA group (Tuomola 1998a).

[9] Making the space to convey rhythm usually conveyed by changes in time in linear media was also used in our *Daisy* production (Tuomola 1998b).

References

Aristotle (1999) *Poetics*. University of Chicago Press, Illinois.

Baktin, M. (1979) *Kirjallisuuden ja estetiikan ongelmia* [Problems of literature and aesthetics]. In Salervo (1984).

Baktin, M. (1995) *Francois Rabelais: Keskiajan ja renessanssin nauru* [Francois Rabelais: the laughter of Medieaval and Renaissance]. Kustannus Oy Taifuuni, Helsinki.

Beardon, C. and Tuomola, M. (1998) Multimedia learning for the theatre. *InterELIA* **3** 17–22.

Brogi, L. (1978) Video recording of his students' Commedia dell'Arte performance in the Central Park of New York.

Damer, B. (1998) *Avatara! Exploring and building virtual worlds on the Internet*. Peachpitt Press, Berkeley, CA.

Emigh, J. (1996) *Masked performance: the play of self and other in ritual and theatre*. University of Pennsylvania Press, Philadelphia.

Green, M. and Swan, J. (1986). *The triumph of Pierrot: the Commedia dell'Arte and the modern imagination*. Macmillan Publishing Company, London.

Murray, J. H. (1997) *Hamlet on the holodeck: the future of narrative in cyberspace*. The MIT Press, Cambridge, MA.

Rudlin, J. (1994) *Commedia dell'Arte: an actor's handbook*. Routledge, London.

Salervo, E. (1984) *Commedia dell'Arte*. Unpublished, available from the Finnish Central Library of Theatre and Dance.

Tuomola, M. (1998a). Digital video recordings of the rehearsals of Luciano Brogi's Commedia dell'Arte group at IALS, Istituto Addestramento Lavoratori dello Spettacolo, Rome, July 26-31.

Tuomola, M. (1998b) Daisy's amazing discoveries: Part II - learning from interactive drama. *Digital Creativity* 9(3)137–152.

Turkle, S. (1997) *Life On the screen: identity in the age of the Internet*. Touchstone, New York.

Mika Tuomola is an award-winning dramaturge and director for interactive digital media. His productions include the world's first audio-visual and spatially navigable web drama *Daisy's Amazing Discoveries* (http://daisy.uiah.fi/, Coronet Interactive Ltd. 1996) and the philosophical strategy game *Socrates* (Werner Söderström Publishing Ltd. 1998). The production awards include the first prize in the EuroPrix Knowledge and Discovery competition 1998 and the second prize in the International Computer Art Competition in Beijing 1997. Mika is currently the Visiting Artist of the Media Lab of Helsinki University of Art and Design (http://mlab.uiah.fi/), where he teaches regularly. His and his students' latest research productions can be found at: http://ml-project.uiah.fi/myth/ and http://mlab.uiah.fi/insideout/.

This article first appeared in
Digital Creativity **10**(3) 167–179 (1999).

Interactive dance-making: online creative collaborations

Sita Popat

University of Leeds, UK

Abstract

This article presents the author's interactive dance composition projects, the Hands-On Dance Project and the TRIAD Project. It examines the potential for computer technology to enhance the interactive art-making process, enabling participation in choreography via Internet communications. By facilitating human-to-human communication, interactive creative environments can be created for participants with a variety of levels of previous dance experience. Participation in these projects is shown to have the capacity to provide a learning environment for all participants.

Keywords: creative process, dance, interactive, Internet, participation

1. Introduction

The advent of computer technology transports interactivity in the arts into realms that it has never before been able to achieve. Interactive art-making exposes the creative process to the audience asking them to become active participants, and the Internet provides interaction on a different scale from previous approaches of this type. This paper examines the author's online dance composition research projects: the *Hands-On Dance Project* and the *TRIAD Project*. These projects bring an outward focus to creativity via the Internet, facilitating an interactive choreographic process for participants all over the world. The emphasis of the *Hands-On Dance Project* research was on the use of basic software and equipment to implement a complex interactive creative process with a single group of dancers via the Internet. The *TRIAD Project* employed a more sophisticated environment to facilitate an innovative method of choreographing with dancers in three different countries[1].

2. Interactive theatre and computer technology

Interactive CD-ROM artist, Elizabeth Hinkle-Turner, states,

> *Interactive artwork by its very nature suspends the 'space-time' continuum that is often the enemy of audience enlightenment.*
> (Hinkle-Turner 1999 52)

The interactive situation allows the participant to 'play' within the artwork, trying out options and possibilities. In doing this, he or she can perceive in detail what is happening as a result of the playing, and how the artwork is (re-)constructed through that play. Where the interactive creative situation is established and the participant is involved in the making of the artwork, he or she has the potential to perceive and understand the creative process and its resolution to the art product. Yet this situation seems to be an ideal that has not been readily achieved. Graham quotes interactive novelist Thomas Disch describing his experience of hypertext:

As long as readers cannot add new words to the story and change it, … the creativity of interactivity fiction lies solely with the author. (Disch, cited in Graham 1996 159)

Many CD-ROMs are marketed as being interactive, and so they are in the sense that the user controls the CD-ROM by navigating its contents, and the CD-ROM provides information in response to the input of the user's control. However, the CD-ROM itself is a 'write-only' environment, so that the viewer cannot make any alterations to the material presented on it. Smith (1997) writes of his CD-ROM for creating dance interactively, *Natural Trips (And Some Not Quite So)*, that he enabled more than twenty-five million unique combinations from which the user could choose to construct the dance. He then offered another range of options that multiplied this by over a million[2]. This apparently vast range of possibilities stems from certain variables and tasks that are offered to the user. The user has a remarkably rich number of choices within the variables, but he or she cannot create anything outside of these very specific boundaries. In spite of so many possible experiences, all are predetermined.

This does not seem to be a truly interactive creative experience, as inter-action implies that the communication is two-way, with the parties concerned having a mutual affect upon each other (Berlo 1960 131, Dix et al. 1998 551). Perhaps it is necessary to return to the theatre setting to clarify how interactivity functions in the artistic creative process.

Interactivity in art, and particularly performance, is not so innovative as it might seem. As early as the Dionysian theatre of the Greeks, theatre performers and audiences engaged in interaction, bridging the gap between observed and observer. This approach has continued to emerge, to a greater or lesser extent, throughout the development of theatre, enjoying a particularly strong revival in the twentieth century (Bennett 1990 3). Such performances are 'interactive' in the sense that they are concerned with the communication between the audience and the artist affecting the outcome of the performance. In a truly interactive work nobody, not even the designer or the performer, can predict the outcome that is the product of this communication (Graham 1997, Izzo 1997).

So how can computer technology contribute to the interactive performance arts, when we are already so beautifully adapted to interact as humans? The answer lies in the fact that the theatre situation also has its faults. The nature of working within the theatre, where the audience sits in a defined area separated from the performers, is that it is difficult for the individual to make a perceptible difference to the performance, even when invited to do so. Should the individual be isolated, only the bravest are prepared to make such input in front of the rest of the audience. Also, because the performance must take place over a limited period of time, audience members' responses tend to be 'reactive', born of a reaction to the moment, rather than 'reflective', stemming from a considered evaluation of the situation. By contrast, communication via new technologies allows the individual inter-actors to send and receive words, images, sounds and movies at the touch of a button. It enables them to speak to and see one or more people anywhere in the world in real-time. It allows participants to view repeatedly and consider the movement material and ideas presented on a Web site. In short, it permits both reactive and reflective interaction, where the humans involved in the art-making process can communicate using multimedia on an individual basis and see the results of that communication in the developing artwork.

3. The Hands-On Dance Project

The *Hands-On Dance Project* combines the individuality of interaction via the computer, with the flexible inter-action of human-to-human communication. It uses the unique communications facilities available on the Internet to enable the project director, dancers and participants to view, discuss and make decisions on the movement material as it develops. Ideas, suggestions, questions and feedback can be exchanged on a personal level, so that all participants can be equally involved, and the process is flexible enough to take account of all input. The combination of both synchronous and asynchronous communications encourages the blend of 'reactive' and 'reflective' responses that support the creative process. The aim is not to design a guided 'creative' experience, where the choreographer leads the participant by the hand through a predefined maze of possibilities, as in Smith's CD-ROM. Instead the creative process becomes a collaborative venture with participants, dancers and project director working together towards a creative outcome.

The author directed three *Hands-On Dance Projects* over the period of 1999 to 2000, working with undergraduate dance students at University of Leeds, and thirty-six participants on the Internet. Each project took place over a period of several weeks, and was open to participants from anywhere in the world, with

> *In a truly interactive work nobody, not even the designer or the performer, can predict the outcome that is the product of this communication*

no previous dance experience necessary. The project aimed to create an environment in which participants with little previous dance experience could take part and feel involved in the creative dance-making activity alongside those with higher levels of dance experience.

Through email discussion, Internet videoconference rehearsals[3], and an interactive Web site, participants could choose the level of involvement that they had in the project.

Each project began with a group discussion via email or the Web site, to determine the theme for the dance. Participants were requested to submit images, text, movies or sound files as inspiration for the dancers. All input was displayed on the Web site. The dancers then created short phrases of movement inspired by the submissions. These were made into movies for the Web site, and feedback was requested from participants. As more phrases were created, participants were asked to consider and make suggestions, via email or tasks on the Web site, concerning the forming of the material into the dance. Participants were also invited to join the dancers in videoconference rehearsals in order to be able to supply synchronous input, where ideas can be tested and evaluated quickly and easily. The feedback 'loop' of discussion and presentation of results on the Web site progressed to the formation of the dance product, and culminated in a performance via videoconferencing and on the Web site, with free CD-ROMs of the performance sent to participants.

The *Hands-On Dance Project* required a

high level of commitment from both project team and participants. All emails submitted to the director during the projects received replies as quickly as possible to maintain a sense of involvement, and the attempt was made to respond to all suggestions and ideas. For a positive experience, it was necessary for participants to return that commitment. Interaction is a two-way process, whether it is face to face, or mediated via Internet communications. Unless both interactors are equally involved, the interaction breaks down (Wellman and Gulia 1999 181). However, where the interaction was successful, participants became closely involved in the choreographic process and stated that they felt a strong connection with the final dance product.

4. Applying dance knowledge in the Hands-On Dance Project

The choreographic process that is reproduced in the *Hands-On Dance Project* is based on the devising method, in which the choreographer gives the dancers stimuli to inspire movement material, and then selects, shapes and forms that material into the dance. This process does not require the choreographer to be able to dance, as the initial movement is created by the dancers. Instead, it requires the visual and imaginative ability to arrange that movement. While for most choreographers these abilities will come from experience and knowledge of dance, it is also possible for skills associated with the visual arts or other sources to be applied to the dance context.

Participant A was the only participant to take part in all three projects. She stated that she had experience of visual arts and drama but very little knowledge of dance prior to her association with the project. In project 1, she selected with care the inspiration that she submitted, in order to communicate a particular 'feeling'. The dancers created a phrase from the inspiration but participant A was not satisfied with it, stating that it did not convey the feelings that

she wished to communicate, and she 'knew' how the movement should look. Her intuitive knowledge, together with encouragement from the project director, led her to give precise instructions to the dancers via video-conferencing, to mould the phrase that they created to be as she 'felt' it should be. In doing so, she used a variety of dance-based skills, yet when asked to comment on other dance phrases, she stated that she did not have enough dance knowledge to do so. With regard to what she perceived as 'her' phrase, her desire to communicate through the dancers enabled her to overcome her perception of her own lack of specific dance knowledge, and to apply intuitive knowledge based on experiences gathered from other sources.

In project 2, only invited participants could take part, and more emphasis was placed on group discussion. Participant A did not seem comfortable in this situation and chose to participate very little. In project 3, where she could communicate on a one-to-one basis with

Figure 1. Image from the movement phrase created by participant A and the dancers from 'Hands-On Dance Project 1 (Dancers: Natashja Botham, Jez Gregg). Image taken from movie on Hands-On Dance Project web site, November 1999.

the project director again, she seemed willing to renew her commitment. Table 1 shows the different types of dance-based skills that she applied. By the third project, she was still unwilling to comment on movement phrases inspired by other people's submissions. However, within the context of the phrases inspired by her own submissions, she seemed able to select movement and suggest developments more easily that she had previously done. She was also able to supply suggestions on the forming of the final dance performance, which none of the other participants with little previous dance experience did in any of the projects. She had apparently acquired some new understandings of the choreographic process during her participation in the three projects.

However, while some of the participants with little dance knowledge became highly engaged with the creative process in the *Hands-On Dance Project*, those participants with higher levels of dance knowledge became frustrated by the lack of physical access to the dance. The small movie windows, low frame rates and poor quality image in videoconferencing meant that they felt isolated from the dancers and the choreographic process, particularly in view of their previous experiences of the 'normal' studio-based creative process. The *Hands-On Dance*

	Project 1	Project 2	Project 3
Interpretation	*	*	*
Applying personal experience	*	*	*
Evaluation	*	*	*
Movement memory	*		*
Perception of form			*
Movement selection	*		*
Elaboration	*		*
Refinement			
Spatial awareness			*

Table 1. Dance-based skills shown by participant A. (An asterisk indicates that this type of knowledge or skill was evident in the participant 3's responses.)

Figure 2. UK performer (left) demonstrates the movement phrase, and Portuguese performers (right) show their duet developed from the phrase. Images taken from movies on TRIAD web site, March 2001.

Project did not permit them direct contact with the dancers, and so a new model was conceived to allow for this.

5. The TRIAD Project

The new model was called the *TRIAD Project*, and it used the Internet to link three groups of young people aged between 9 and 20 from Portugal, UK and USA. They and their group leaders became both choreographers and dancers in this new Internet-based creative process. The project ran from January to April 2001 and involved more than forty dancers. Using the web site builder environment, *Think.com*, the dancers and their group leaders each had an email address and personal web space within the password-protected project web site. They could also leave 'stickies' for each other on the pages, for quick notes. *Think.com* is a complex piece of software, but it is designed to facilitate Internet-based communication with the minimum of technical knowledge, thus maintaining the focus on the dance-making process. It was intended that the young people would learn from sharing their ideas about dance and trying out different styles and approaches to the dance-making process. It was also hoped that their shared interest in dance would help the dancers to forge individual friendships and group links.

6. The TRIAD process

It was recognised that choreographic direction was required in order to achieve a cohesive dance performance at the end of the project. As all the group leaders were competent choreographers it was agreed that each group would lead one 5-minute section within the 15-minute dance. Thus for the 5-minute section directed by Portugal, the Portuguese dancers began rehearsals, putting up movies and giving instructions for how they wanted the UK and USA groups to work on complementary dance material. The Portuguese group structured the

section, making a storyboard from which the UK and USA groups worked to construct their parts of the dance. This produced a 5-minute dance in each of the three countries, directed by the Portuguese group. The UK and USA groups also directed sections in the same manner. Each country finished the process with three 5-minute dance sections: one directed by themselves, and the other two directed by the other groups. Although the collaboration took place on the Internet, all participants worked in the studio situation where they had direct access to the physical process of choreographing the dance.

The project began with an online meeting to decide on the theme of the dance. Representatives from the three countries met via *iVisit* Internet videoconferencing to discuss ideas. The three groups chose the theme 'who we are and what we dream of'. An article was constructed on the web site for each country entitled *Meet the dancers*. An image and a small amount of text about each dancer were included in their country's page as an introduction. This quick-reference guide was popular among the participants, and was supplemented by personal web pages.

Each of the three groups began rehearsals based on the theme, and constructed rehearsal records on Think.com. Each rehearsal record consisted of an article containing a movie of dance made in the rehearsal, with notes from the dancers or their group leaders. The notes explained how the movement was made, and how it might develop. Where appropriate, notes included information about how the directing group would like the other two groups to use the movement in their work. For example, in one rehearsal, the UK group filmed a short dance sequence, asking the USA and Portuguese groups to learn it and make slow duets based on it. The Portuguese group responded with five slow duets, which were used in the section directed by the UK group. On another occasion the Portuguese group made some short solos

Figure 3. The dancers from the TRIAD Project chatting about their experiences (from top to bottom: Portugal, UK, USA) Images taken from movies on TRIAD Web site, March 2001.

7. TRIAD outcomes

The project was challenging for the dancers for a number of reasons. The three groups came from different dance backgrounds, and therefore they were all required to work in styles with which they were unfamiliar. The UK group had a streetdance background, while the Portuguese group were trained in contemporary dance, and the USA group were from ballet and jazz backgrounds. This was highly successful for the Portuguese and UK groups. The UK dancers had previously expressed some dislike of contemporary dance, and were unwilling to try it. However, when they saw their Portuguese peer group working in that style, they were willing to attempt it. At the end of the project, the UK dancers agreed that trying out new styles had been one of the most rewarding aspects of the project:

It's been really great trying out new styles, because sometimes it gets boring always doing the same style - so thanks!
(Quote from Richard, in the UK group)

The Portuguese dancers also expressed admiration for the UK group's streetdance style, and they enjoyed experimenting with it, although they joked that it bruised their knees. The Portuguese and UK dancers agreed that a key aspect of the project had been getting to know people in other countries:

My favourite thing is listening to the people from the other countries talking, finding out what they think is interesting.
(Quote from Georgina in the UK group)

using a chair, and the UK group responded with a series of duets in which the chair was replaced by another dancer. Stickies and emails were used to give feedback on the movement in the rehearsal records.

The performances in each country consisted of a live dance by the host group, with video from the other two countries. The host group performed on the stage, with the videos from the other countries projected behind them, so that the dance was effectively performed in each venue by all three groups. There were live online discussions afterwards with the other groups and their audiences to explain the collaborative process and celebrate the performance.

It's interesting because you get to know new people...

(Quote from Francine in the Portuguese group)

The social element was important, bringing together young people who would probably never be able to work together in any other way, and enabling them to share a multicultural connection. This mutual peer group inspiration was an essential element in the creative process.

Both the UK and Portuguese groups became closely involved in the collaborative choreographic process. The UK group became more adept at creating movement as a direct result of the project, since before this they had usually had movement imposed upon them. During the project, they experimented with making their own dance movement in response to their Portuguese and USA peers. The process itself as mediated via the technology carried inherent learning properties, since it made the dancers constantly examine the choreographic process and their roles within it. The Portuguese and UK dancers agreed that it was challenging to make choices at every rehearsal about what to film for rehearsal records, and then to write notes explaining what they had done. This made them more aware of the continuing creative process and helped them to understand what was happening in detail, both in terms of their own processes and the ongoing collaboration.

Although the process was highly successful for the UK and Portuguese groups, problems were experienced in working with the USA group. Schedules were regularly sent to group leaders in all three countries and the process was explained numerous times, yet there still appeared to be considerable misunderstandings regarding both process and performance on the part of the USA group. They put up fewer rehearsals records than the UK and Portuguese groups, and did not become involved in the sharing of the choreographic process. They communicated very little in comparison to the interactions in progress between the UK and Portuguese groups. It seems that there are inherent difficulties in collaborating online where communication is asynchronous or via text-chat, and when communication breakdown does occur, it may go undetected for some time. The interaction between the USA and the other two countries did not become a two-way channel on a human-to-human level, and thus no amount of technology could support the process.

8. Conclusions

Internet technology supplies a platform where artists and participant can meet and create art together. It facilitates interaction on an individual basis, both synchronously and asynchronously to allow for reactive play and reflective consideration. The *Hands-On Dance Project* illustrates the fact that the technology to implement a project does not have to be complex for a highly interactive situation to be established, if the project team and participants are prepared to make a commitment to communicate. This leads to the ideal human-to-human form of interaction, where the project can be flexible enough to accommodate all ideas and suggestions.

The potential, illustrated by participant A's experience, for knowledge from a variety of sources to be applied in an arts context with support from practising artists, indicates that the *Hands-On Dance Project* could have ramifications for other art forms. The *TRIAD Project* shows that the creative process may be extended via Internet technology, with the potential for collaborative projects between artists all over the world. Both projects show that participation in the online interactive creative process requires a high level of commitment that is rewarded by a deeper understanding and clarification of personal and group processes, since those processes must be represented for other participants to view. The two-way interaction means that other participants may then respond and ask questions or give comments on the developing process. The medium for these projects is the Internet, but their focus is the human-human interaction and the creative process.

Acknowledgements

Thanks to Oracle Corporation for funding the *TRIAD Project* and providing use of the *Think.com* web site builder environment. Thanks to Kris Popat and ULTRALAB, Anglia Polytechnic University, for supporting both projects.
Group leaders for the *TRIAD Project* were: Eddie Copp and Claire Nicholson (Momentum Youth Dance Company), Stephan Jürgens and Darren Scully, Jeffrey Gray Miller and Kristi Miller.

Notes

[1] The *Hands-On Dance Project* was designed and implemented using off-the-shelf software, *Netscape Communicator*, *Adobe Premiere* and *Adobe Photoshop*, and free downloadable software, *iVisit*, *QuickTime 4*, and *Fetch FTP* software. A G3 Apple Macintosh laptop computer, a small, analogue video-camera and an ISDN connection were also used. The intention was to create a framework that could be replicated by other choreographers or within other art forms, without requiring large amounts of technical knowledge or financial investment.

The *TRIAD Project* took place using the *Think.com* web site builder designed by ULTRALAB and implemented by the Oracle Corporation. This was a password-protected Web site where all participants had access to simple tools to construct articles and other page-types within the environment.

Hands-On Dance Project web site is at: http://www.satorimedia.com/hands_on/
TRIAD Project web site is at: http://www.triadance.com

[2] See (Smith 1997). Smith calculates the initial figure at around 25,794,969,600.

[3] *iVisit* Internet videoconferencing software was used for videoconference rehearsals, as it is free to download and use. The frame rate and picture quality tends to be poor, but the lack of cost and ease of access to the software were essential to the project. The synchronous communication, allowing informal chat, also seemed to be intrinsic to the rehearsal experience for participants.

References

Bennett, S. (1990) *Theatre audiences: a theory of production and reception*. Routledge, London.

Berlo, D. (1960) *The process of communication: an introduction to theory and practice*. Holt, Rinehart and Winston, Inc.

Dix, A., Finlay, J., Abowd, G. and Beale, R. (1998) *Human computer interaction*. 2nd Edition. Prentice Hall Europe, UK.

Graham, B. (1996) Playing with yourself: pleasure and interactive art. In Dovey, J. (ed.) *Fractal dreams: new media in social context*. Lawrence and Wishart Ltd, London, pp. 154–177.

Graham, B. (1997) *A study of audience relationships with interactive computer-based visual artworks in gallery settings, through observation, art practice, and curation*. PhD thesis available in PDF format at http://www.sunderland.ac.uk/~as0bgr/thesisintro.html

Hinkle-Turner, E. (1999) Coming full circle: composing a cathartic experience with CD-ROM technology. *Leonardo* 32 49–52.

Izzo, G. (1997) *The art of play: the new genre of interactive theatre*. Heinemann, Portsmouth, NH.

Smith, A. W. (1997) Interactive multimedia-dance: individual freedom to control one's own aesthetic. *Proceedings of Dance On '97 Conference*. Hong Kong, pp. 198–213.

Wellman, B. and Gulia, M. (1999) Virtual communities as communities: net surfers don't ride alone. In Smith, M. and Kollock, P. (eds.) *Communities in cyberspace*. Routledge, London, pp. 167–194.

Sita Popat (PhD) is a lecturer in dance at University of Leeds, Bretton Hall Campus. Her research area is choreography with Internet communities. Current research projects include the Eurodans Project, which uses the Internet to link dance students in higher education institutions across Europe. She is also the Curriculum Expert for dance and drama on the DfES/ULTRALAB research project Notschool.net.

This article first appeared in *Digital Creativity* 12(4) 205–214 (2001).

Loa and behold: voice ghosts in the new technoculture

Jools Gilson-Ellis

University College Cork, Ireland

Abstract

This article suggests that the use of femininity and voice in digital art practice has a powerful potential to conjure provocative spaces in the new technoculture. Using a range of theoretical writers including Margaret Morse, Nell Tenhaaf, Simon Penny, Brenda Laurel and Sue-Ellen Case, the article traces contemporary thought on femininity, technology and voice. Gilson-Ellis uses her own choreographic / poetic practice as examples in these discussions. Through an adaptation of Sue-Ellen Case's proposal of the voudou vever and the loa, the article suggests that the voice in relation to writing and new technologies has a radical potential to open up alternative kinds of spaces in digital art practice.

Keywords: choreography, digital art practice, feminism, poetry, voice

Telephone call from RTE
(Radio Telefís Éireann - Irish National Television)

RTE: We're doing a millennium special, and we heard that you work with dance and technology. Do you have something that you're working on at the moment?

JGE: Yes, we've just finished making The Secret Project.

RTE: Right. And is it about the future, you know, space?

JGE: Well, no. It uses poetic text and choreography to explore the idea of the secret. It's quite tender.

RTE: Right.

ৡ

This article attempts the unlikely wrestle between femininity and the promises of the new technoculture. It takes as its focus the meanderings of orality and textuality. It sees promise in the fallen moment between listening and looking; in the ravishing drench of voice.

One of the main theoretical and practical innovations of my thesis is the proposal of the 'os-text'. The os-text describes practices in which the same individual is the writer and the speaker of a text. Incorporating the meanings of orality, oscillation and kissing (osculation), this term describes a shimmering relation of text to orality. The os-text is a text which is neither written nor spoken, neither is it both written and spoken. This is a text which survives in oscillation not between but because of the mouth and the text. Its place is on the side of the feminine. It has no secure place in the oral or in the written, but flies instead in the face of

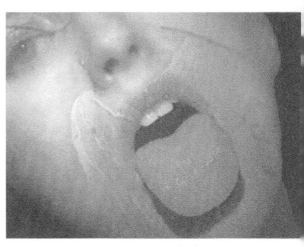

both. This is a text which refuses stillness. A text marked by the grain of the voice. A text written in the mouths of writers. In this article I focus on locating such a practice in relation to contemporary thought and art practice on new technologies and the feminine. I use my own practice as material example in the weaving of this argument.

ঽ

Margaret Morse in her essay *What do cyborgs eat?* (1994) examines contemporary negotiations of the machine / human relation[1]. Morse follows the thread of a contemporary desire to be done with the 'meat' of corporeality in the thrall of immersive technologies. Morse's analysis of 'oral logic' examines the structural dynamics of this relation between humanity and technology. She links the zeitgeist passion for immersion in a digital sea to the psychoanalytic category of the oral phase. The combination of a feminised space of submersion and a rejection of the corporeal (also a feminised cultural space) suggests trouble indeed for a feminist politics of performance technology. Dangers abound in attempting to wrestle with these categories, since arguing either for the body as an especial feminine space, or for the logics of engulfment reify existing gendered tropes. The refusal / rejection of the body in cyberculture wreaks of rejection of aspects of the feminine, whilst at the same time the logic of submersion is a fantasy of feminine engulfment.[2]

Nell Tenhaaf negotiates similar ground in her essay *Mysteries of the bioapparatus* (1996) when she draws parallels between femininity's relationship to the corporeal and new technologies:

The familiar feminine condition of being too close to and too distant from the body, constrained by its material reality yet psychically open to penetration, could be said to characterise the experience of being in cyberspace.
(Tenhaaf 1996 52)

For Tenhaaf, femininity's symbolic gymnastics are also those of cyberspace. She goes on to suggest that cyberspace
implies a feminisation of the symbolic order and of subjectivity.
(Tenhaaf 1996 52)
If this is the case, then what has such a feminisation got to do with femininity itself?

Sadie Plant picks up this troubled relationship of femininity and technology in her book *Zeros and ones* (1997). Plant undermines the traditional dramaturgy of femininity and technological change. Instead of seeing women as victims of technology or its symbolic other, she details their historical intimacy. She argues that they have tended machines for generations, the operators of looms, typewriters, computers and switchboards. The suggestion that the rhythms of femininities worked out over centuries are the rhythms of the new technoculture, also implies that testosterone-laden strength and singular knowledge is a fast waning commodity in the dissipative, associative, fragmentary, hypertextual structures of cyberculture.[3]

In these scenarios femininity is figured symbolically as the realm of the rejected and the desired, as well as materially lacking at the traditional centres of new technologies — not directors of companies or managers, but typists and telephonists, in which their prevailing peripherality over decades and centuries ironically trains them comprehensively for the new cyberculture. Such positionality is characterised by plurality, by an ability to be literally and symbolically in two places at once.

Figure 1. Image from 'Mouthplace' (1997) © half/angel.

Sue-Ellen Case has a sense of this positionality when she brings in a discussion of voudou practice and the vever into her analysis of spatial relations (Case 1996 51–56). Conceptions of femininity within the new technoculture are contradictory in relation to space, (just as they are in relation to the corporeal[4]); the feminine comprises virtual space itself and what must be disavowed in order to accede to such a realm. The analogy between voudou and virtual systems is that both access other kinds of space. Case proposes such an analogy as counter to what she sees as the retrograde logic of Euclidean space.

Case summarises Euclid in relation to the 'point' in her discussion of bodies, technology and space; the point

> performs its Euclidean distribution of space across the body and through the body into surrounding space.
> (Case 1996 50)

It does so by creating what Allucquère Rosanne Stone perceives as

> relentlessly monistic articulations of physical and virtual space that law and science favour.
> (Stone 1995 42, cited by Case 1995 50)

This singular negotiation of literal and virtual worlds functions only for a body configured as masculine. The feminine operates obliquely to such a paradigm, since it clearly exceeds the singular Euclidean point of negotiation between virtual and corporeal worlds. In Case's argument, it is precisely this oblique relation to space that suggests femininity might be re-thought progressively in these realms.

Case is not the first to engage Afro-centric practices in relation to new technologies.[5] She contextualises her gesture within what Mark Dery terms 'Afrofuturism' (Dery 1993). Case is drawn to the voudou vever because it practices a "complex signification of space" (Case 1996 52) which pre-dates Eurocentric scientific rational conceptions. The vever is

> a figure drawn to chart the particular course through space that the need of the moment would employ to evoke the appropriate spirit.
> (Case 1996 54)

Case reads such figures as sophisticated contingent spatial negotiations that challenge the kinds of space organised by current software. The vever accesses these windows of space (the loas[6]) through the dancing body. These vevers are;

> . . . figures for the communal dance to work with, producing "possession" by the loa — a term that signifies the way the body opens as a window into the virtual space. The practice of "dancing space" plants flesh at the root of spatial relations.
> (Case 1996 55)

Case suggests that the voudou vever resists both the seductions of immersion (no bodily boundaries) and the easy dismissal of the 'meat' of corporeality (entirely bodily bound) through the multiple dancing body. The vever in Case's argument, is a cipher for spatial relations in the new technoculture. The configuration of the body and virtual space as integrated plural motifs, suggests a way of thinking about space and technology able to engage progressively with femininity. Case proposes the voudou vever as a talisman

Such nomadic text-telling is structurally similar to the texts of the typing pool, produced by women moved around an organisation to listen to telling in order to produce text

to be held in the techno-imaginary to ward off
the piercing Euclidean point.
(Case 1996 56)

Case's 'talisman' is intended to operate for queer (lesbian) cultures as a mobilising image; a provocation for a more complex, body-acknowl-edged engagement with the new technoculture.[7] But I want to do a different thing. I want to propose the voudou vever as more than just an amulet for the techno-imaginary; I want it as practical spur in the actual doing of plural dancing as it grazes and produces provocative space. Like the best arguments, I want to forge a practice which resists the easy difference between material and symbolic realms. I want to extend the talisman for dancing bodies into one for dancing uttering bodies (she cries and shouts as she dances, she whispers, gasps, stuns you with her composure,[8] gnawing narrative she swings away from you). I want to propose utterance and movement as a single thing that sweat-sound provocative space into being in one gesture. I want to cry out that the voice operates in such a context as the 'loa' itself. It does this by weaving a connection between the antitheses of flesh (Gibson's 'meat') and the bathing pleasure of voice. In a subversive conjuring trick, the voice as loa asserts the possibility of a progressive space for femininity in the new technoculture.

I would like fables of the unbounded body to
abound in cyberspace.
(Tenhaaf 1996 68)

We[9] whisk such tales into being; corpo-real and temporal boundaries shimmer in our breath. This is enchantment. Here, between seeing and hearing slips a curving navigational wisdom. Listen. If we see this body before us, what could unbind its boundaries? (voice, in playful engagement with new technologies). If we hear this body before us, what could unbind its univocality? (games with time and space wrought with BIG EYES). She speaks in blood and tongue, weaving gesture and breath and utterance into a single thing. Winding time along veins, she plays with present speech and

the speech of another time. And in this flurried turn the body opens as a window into virtual space, through the loa of voice.

Loa and behold.

I'm forging fables. Believe me.

ঽ

Derry derry ding dason, My name is John Cheston
We wedon, we woden, we wedon, we woden
Bim boom, bim boom, bim boom, bim boom [10]

What has a woman's voice got to do with the tending of machines? *Derry derry ding dason* is a round sung in twelve parts. Its sound mimics the rhythm of the moving loom around which it was composed and performed as a work song. Here is a nineteenth century loa — a communal singing and moving (weaving) in relation to new technologies. Its interlocking rhythm in twelve movements conjures the heft and pulse of interlacing threads, and the interlacing women who wrought cloth and song from community; met the space of work with an invigorated feminine space of embodied voice.

This musicality of the interaction of woman and machine arose again in the training of secretaries where women were taught to type in rhythmic patterns,

Words per minute, beats per minute, the clatter
of the typist's strokes, the striking of the keys,
thump of carriage return marked by the ringing
of a bell at the end of every line.
(Plant 1997 118–119)

And then the rhythms of the switchboard operator; constant greeting and plugging in, listening to conversations and chatting between calls — the electronic negotiation of speaking voices. She has always been accused of talking too much, of being a nag, of going on. She has his voice in her ear dictating letters, translating utterance to the pressing of keys. Dictaphone. Her skills are unimportant, apparently. Supportive, but not at the hub. She doesn't speak into his ear, and send his fingers flurrying over lettered buttons. Henry Sayre in his analysis of Laurie Anderson's *United States* (Sayre 1989) suggests something of the typist's lack of agency when he says of her work

> ... *the peculiar lack of an organizing conscious-ness, of an inner essence, in her narratives . . . is the most destabilizing element in her work.*
> *(Sayre 1989 148)*

Such nomadic text-telling is structurally similar to the texts of the typing pool, produced by women moved around an organisation to listen to telling in order to produce text.

I want to suggest that such moving telling (this is meaning on the move) is a characteristic of art practice which engages with technology and the feminine through the use of the voice as loa. Such shifting embodied utterance provokes the production of different kinds of space. The writing of texts in relation to the pang of telling is a characteristic of these voices. Such a pang is often *os-textual* (the writer is also the one who utters the text in perform-ance); the drench of voice is capable of different poetries in the breath of writing. This winding of voice/writing/body nudges odd geographies out of the new technoculture, resisting and redoubling its symbolic logic.

Case's discussion of the operations of the voudou vever focuses not on performance in particular, but on the new technoculture in general. This article's focus is technology and performance; this could include the use of technology in live performance, in installation spaces, or digital platforms such as CD-ROM. It

is my proposal that whatever the different formats for performance, the operations of femininity in relation to the space of new technologies are progressively engaged through the model of the voudou vever, and specifically the voice as loa. Within live performance, the *os-text* is able to operate in an oscillatory economy between writing and the voicing of that writing. In performances, or media which involve recorded written/voices, the same oscillatory prowess is not able to operate in the same way. But in progressive play with new technologies, other kinds of oscillation might be negotiated between writing, the byte and the tongue.

Case's argument emphasises the commu-nal nature of the dancing figures operating through the cipher of the vever. Since my analysis is focused on performance, the nature of plurality is different. In such contexts, multiplic-ity might operate through the many 'users' of installations composed from intelligent environ-ments, or through the 'driving' of CD-ROM art works. Within live performance, plurality is often engaged within the dynamics of the practice itself, both in terms of multiple per-forming bodies, and through the weaving operations of femininity, technology and voice. Such 'community' also operates across the dynamic of audience and performers. Case's 'case' operates compellingly in such contexts; this is a plurality which grazes voices and flesh to trouble conceptions of space as well as feminin-ity in the new technoculture.

ৰ

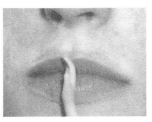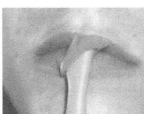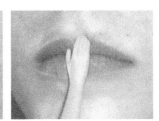

Figure 2.
Image from
'Mouthplace'
(1997)
© half/angel.

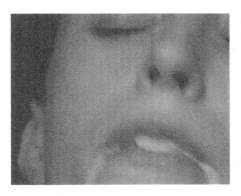

Figure 3.
Image from
'Mouthplace'
(1997)
© *half/angel.*

What is particular about the operations of voice in performance in relation to technology? Frances Dyson in her essay on sound and cyberculture *When is the ear pierced?* (Dyson 1996) suggests that radio produced intimate voices through the use of microphones at close proximity. Such voices "gave the listening experience a particular authenticity" (Dyson 1996 78). Dyson goes on to analyse the difference between such live uses of microphones, and the operations of recorded sound:

> *Recorded sound cannot claim the so-called authenticity of direct, live transmission, since the recording is tied to neither the here nor the now of the sonic event but rather to a system of representation guided by technology.*
> *(Dyson 1996 87)*

I want to use Dyson's comments to analyse the operations of recorded and live voice in our dance theatre production *The Secret Project*. Sections of *The Secret Project* intonate space through the textures of live voice (amplified through a headset microphone) and recorded voice (sampled and triggered by motion). Such a spatial intonation resists the distinction between live and recorded media; the voice speaking live before you, and the voice sampled and triggered by motion, is the same voice. Because the live voice is amplified, it sounds qualitatively the same as the recorded voice. Both 'tongues of text' operate together through a choreographic practice of moving / speaking. In this practice it isn't always clear when I utter text, and when I trigger a pre-recorded sample. The apprehension of such a process is troubled by the knowledge that there are too many voices for this one performer to be articulating them all 'live'. Yet they 'fit' with her body — pulses of movement are accompanied by flurries of text. Such a practice fables the unbound body into being through the loa of voice. It disturbs the distinction between live and recorded media by asserting the presentness of utterance in mouth and flesh, as well as preserving a sense of another temporal operation within the sound world.

When we were at an early stage of research for *The Secret Project*, we developed our use of the motion-sensing software *BigEye* using colour as a trigger. This meant that we told the camera to 'see' the movement of a particular colour. The colour we chose needed to contrast strongly to other colours in the visual field. This involved us in experiments with brightly coloured gloves, scarlet lipstick and orange vests. On the computer screen, we drew boxes for our trigger to 'hit'. We played with various operations of trigger-text relation. I moved from performance space to the computer screen and back again checking 'where' the triggers were. My choreography was beleagured by these attempts to 'hit' triggers. Sampled texts blurted their voices into awkward space. This failure is a failure which Case traces in her discussion of Euclidean space. Our triggers, like the Euclidean point, were only able to articulate a monistic relationship to space. Voices were either triggered or not triggered; boundaries of screenic boxes entered or not entered. Such spatial and performic negotiations are unable to vever provocative space because they cannot engage with the grain of utterance and physicality. When we shifted to using motion as a trigger, we began to develop a practice which could engage in the internal ache of movement and utterance; a practice which could operate like the voudou vever and allow the body to open into different kinds of space; a practice where she could use both her tongues to engage the voice as loa.

one tongue for tasting
and another for speaking
there's no fork here
just two
I know you'd like a tale of natural and synthetic
or a tale of splitting and engorging
but I've only something more confusing
there are two tongues here
one for tasting
and one for speaking
it's true there are tiny
thread wires
spun throughout
and speaking has a greater range
and tasting too
but I could not tell you which was first
which she was made with
which she made herself
the design is creative
and intelligent
each will move up or down and lie still
If the other is on high
but there are other times
when silicon muscle webs
work on oral opera
she has two tongues
and sometimes uses both
to her advantage
somehow her widened
taste buds shot with pixels
improve her speaking tongue
and the two articulate their differences
with skilled co-ordination
to see her speaking with her mouth full
is a fine thing -
(little iridescences here and there
light the half-light in murmurs)

ॐ

As discussed earlier, Case proposes the voudou vever as a 'map' for sophisticated contingent spatial negotiations that challenge the kinds of space organised by current software. My own argument extends Case's point to assert voice as the loa in these relations (i.e. voice as 'cipher' for the way the body opens as a window onto virtual space). As we shift here from the realm of live performance to that of recorded perform-

ance, and from stage space to cyberspace, my thesis of the voice as loa operates directly in a context of digitally organised space. Such spaces often struggle to meet the grain of voice. The proposal of the body and virtual space as 'integrated plural motifs' falters when such visual space stumbles at plurality itself. If the voice operates as a loa in these contexts to produce different kinds of space, they do so in a way that reinforces the particular failures of visual over vocal worlds. Her textual tongue, woven through these spaces, weaves a connection between flesh and utterance. Her lick makes space for the feminine, but what 'she' tastes is often no space at all.

fluidly then
(look down)
I moisten the space
between your
small fingers
and that
plate of buttons
south of you

corpuscle
to pixel

Simon Penny in an essay called *Virtual reality as the completion of the Enlightenment project* (Penny 1994) argues that the space of virtual reality largely lags behind the imagination of its attendant cultural thrall. This essay was written in 1994; six years ago (I write this in 2000). In the world of new technologies six years is equivalent to many decades prior to the digital revolution. Nonetheless, Penny's essay remains relevant in many aspects. Penny's thesis is that the revolutionary rhetoric around the advent of virtual reality largely conceals traditional conceptions of space and identity.[11]

Penny makes the same point as Case in relation to the limitations of the kinds of space organised by current software. Even more interestingly, his argument uses an example of dancing bodies as a way to imagine a contrary conception of space:

But what if VR had developed in a culture with a different attitude to the body? Take for example, this discussion of Indian dance: 'The sense of space was wholly different . . . no long runs or soaring leaps or efforts to transform the stage into a boundless arena, a kind of metaphysical everywhere . . . but content with the realm of the body, comfortable with dimension and gravity, all ease, all centred.'
The teacher of this dance technique described the attitude to the body thus:
'no sense of elevation or extension . . . body self-contained . . . inwardness, inwardness . . . In Hinduism, there is no beyond.'
(Penny 1994 239 quoting Wetzsteon 1992)

It is compelling that Penny and Case independently express their sense of the limitations of digital space, through a proposal of the transgressive possibilities of non-Western dance forms (Case through the African cultural practice of voudou, Penny through Indian dance).[12] Whilst Case uses the voudou vever to propose a mobilising image for engagement with new technologies, Penny leaves his own question ("what if VR had developed in a culture with a different attitude to the body?") largely unanswered beyond his provocative example of the Indian dancer.

Earlier in the same essay, Penny describes digital space in a context of classical mechanics:
On a technical level, the grid (and polygonal construction within the grid) radically limits the possibility of constructing organic, amorphous forms. It privileges clean, crystalline, coherent, independent forms. . . this space is the space of classical mechanics (which) resolve the messy, complex, and overlapping world into clean, self-contained mathematical objects, like the polygonal bodies floating in virtual space.
(Penny 1994 233)

Let's compare this description with a footnote from Brenda Laurel's book Computers as theatre (1993).
Using computers to store recipes is one of the oldest jokes in the personal computer business -

in the early days, that's what all marketing executives thought women would do with them. The obvious drawback is that cookie dough, pasta sauce, and other goo-based substances will get all over the keys when you try to retrieve a recipe file. A speech interface is the obvious solution, but it would seem that the marketing executives haven't thought of that one yet.
(Laurel 1993 174)

Penny and Laurel's descriptions seem to me to sum up much about the contemporary wranglings of femininity and technology. If femininity is caricatured as approaching the terminal covered in 'goo-based substances' how might 'she' engage in 'polygonal construction within the grid'? Indeed.

Jeanne Randolph in her essay A city for bachelors (Randolph 1996) analyses the virtual reality project Archaeology of a mother tongue by Toni Dove and Michael Mckenzie (1993). This is a piece made in the early years of VR, and certainly the dissonance described here is partly consequent to this, but I would argue that the points made here to do with the contrast in visual and sound worlds are too frequent an observation to be only the result of an emergent technology.
throughout the piece there is a contradiction between the purity of the image world and the organic disintegration expressed in the aural world . . .
(Randolph 1996 223)
. . . in the visual field, the skeleton of the virtual city remains fleshless and unredeemed, a dreamlike condensation in an aural envelope of voices.
(Randolph 1996 225)

I want to suggest a connection between Penny's crystalline spaces, Laurel's joke about a 'speech interface' and these comments on Dove and Mckenzie's VR project. Whilst it is clear that Randolph's description of the "purity of the image" accords directly with Penny's "crystalline spaces", what is less clear is how Missy cooking disaster might connect with "an aural envelope

Figure 4.
Image from
'Mouthplace'
(1997)
© *half/angel.*

of voices". It seems to me that the messy dynamics of cookie dough and pasta sauce on keyboards is an unwitting depiction of a fable of the unbound body (slipping from literal to symbolic realms). Its drowning of technology with the dynamic of 'goo' has everything to do with the operations of voice as loa. Laurel suggests (for different reasons) a 'speech inter-face' in this context of viscous disaster. This makes every kind of symbolic sense — since voice, like cookie dough, gets 'all over the keys'.

… cyberspace beyond its business uses, can invoke a parallel and sometimes a transcendent or spiritual world that revives the dead or the spirits of things in the limbo of the possible.
(Morse 1996 206)

One of the characteristics of emerging technologies is the elimination of duration and the collapse of time into real time.[13] I want to end this chapter by asking what such digital prowess might weave with us, out of the box again, and into spaces which an audience can inhabit directly. Can such cartographies, as Margaret Morse suggests, 'revive the spirits of things'?

At the article's end, I want to tell you a ghost story.

In the middle of our dance theatre production *The Secret Project*, there is a story called *Snow Ghosts*. This is a story about falling. In writing this text, I was interested in the moment of slipping as a provocative place for femininity. I wrote this narrative in the first few days of arriving in the Canadian Rockies. Its turns are redolent of the place of writing — snow, pine, valleys, coffee in diners. In the curve of such geography I wanted to conjure a magical space for the sideways energies of language and the feminine. This is *Snow Ghosts*. When Richard[14] arrived, and we began to work in the studio, one of the first things we did was record this story. This was Easter 1998. The recording

session was one of those odd times when we 'got it' in one take.

Eighteen months later we are back in Banff[15] on our final production residency for *The Secret Project*. Richard and I know that we will use 'snow ghosts' in the piece, but we are not sure exactly how. I thought I would perform the piece live. But Richard has a strange sugges-tion; that we should simply play the recording. I am hesitant — the story is seven minutes long; I worry that we'll lose our audience. Richard persuades me. He writes a musical score that opens and closes the work and erupts in the middle. I suggest darkness, and tiny glimpses of falling caught in the light at brief moments. We try it. It's a risk — making our audience sit in the dark for seven minutes listening to a story. But we go with it.

(Sit in the dark and listen to 'snow ghosts' now. If there's no darkness, you could make some under your closed eyelids)

In the performance of *The Secret Project*, this story forged a fable of unbound bodies in a context of multi-tongued dancing women. It allowed our audience the pleasures of cyberspace in literal space, by being engulfed in the dark-ness by sound. We make a space for the femininity of hearing in a context of the seeing / hearing of our moving bodies and technology. The "source beyond the field of inscription" (Dyson 1996 87) of recording, is for me, a memory of my first few days in Canada, of a text that fell out of me like a tripped-up thing. (And I hear this in the taste of the particular recording). For the audience, amplified voice has been woven in the textures of live and recorded tenors throughout the piece, so that time here is both undone and reinforced of the charge of presentness. Whether this voice is 'beyond the field of inscription' or not, is secondary to the communal listening in the dark that attends its apprehension. I bathe you in my vowels. What kind of haunting is this?

In *The Domain Matrix*, Sue-Ellen Case quotes Verena Andermatt Conley on the space of narrative in a context of new technologies;

> By way of feminists such as Hélène Cixous, through geographers, philosophers and culture critics, time and again we hear the need for becoming in cultural contexts of resingularisation through storytelling, narrative or poetry.
> Through voice, storytelling brings the body, or one's story into History. . . it reopens onto space in time, away from technological reduction into grids . . .
> (Conley 1993 88, cited by Case 1996 108)

Snow Ghosts attempts a strange spell. It tries to conjure utterance as a "limbo of the possible" (Morse 1996 206). It uses text as a cipher to produce 'other spaces' through the loa of voice. Its storytelling

> brings the body . . . into History . . . it reopens onto space in time, away from technological reduction into grids . . .
> (Morse 1996 206)

વ

Alongside the performance of *The Secret Project* there is an installation version of the work. This is composed of a series of apparently empty boxes, which contain adapted motion-sensing systems, similar to the ones used in the dance theatre production. 'Users' are invited to explore the interior of these boxes with their hands. As they do so, they trigger little sound worlds — a box of gasps, fragments of a story, poetry. These

are empty boxes which contain textual ghosts; ghosts you can find if you touch them, weaving words from air. Such spaces revive the 'spirits of things' through text, voice and touch. We bring ghosts to your fingertips by connecting their gesture to the pang of utterance. These are spaces that unsettle the difference between listening and moving; spaces which trouble voices out of 'empty' space. Spaces made strange through voice, femininities and new technologies - the loa of voice.

વ

The provocative possibilities of voice / writing (the *os-text*) woven in relation to new (and old) technologies suggests a transgressive potential and actuality in contemporary digital art practice. This is often exemplified as a desire for content, for emotion, for stories and spaces that compel us to different spaces and original practice. These ghosts speak out loud. Listen.

I'm forging fables. Believe me.

Notes

1 Johannes Birringer introduced me to this essay during our performance project *Lively Bodies - Lively Machines* at Chichester in 1996. See Birringer (1998 105–44) for an analysis of this project.

2 William Gibson's description of the body as 'meat' (1984) and the heralding of VR (virtual reality) as the loss of the body, is accompanied by the characterisation of cyberspace as a "female realm of pure body" (Morse 1994 163). Morse suggests that "cyberspace is a largely male domain where gender constructs under critique in other spheres of contemporary society return with a vengeance" (Morse 1994 168).

3 This is the same point as Tenhaaf makes in her earlier article (Tenhaaf 1996 52). The

difference between the two arguments is that Plant focuses on material historical processes and Tenhaaf on symbolic. This is a difference between women and femininity. The fact that the two accord in their conclusions, seems to me to make both more compelling.

4 This is because space and the body in these relations are both characterised as feminine.

5 Case borrows the terms 'voudou vever' and 'loa' from African cultural practices with an acknowledgement of the colonial dynamic of such a gesture. She does so with the aim of 'queering' the discourse around 'performing lesbian at the end of print culture' (Case 1996 51–56). Whether such borrowing is legitimate is a complex question. Using non-Western tropes to progress thinking around Western technoculture, could be said to be a revolutionary gesture, it could also be said to reinforce the dynamics of colonialism. I would argue that prohibiting areas of thinking / practice from discourse is more disturbing than making intelligent contextual use of such material.

6 William Gibson uses the voudou term 'loa' in *Count Zero* (Gibson 1986). Stone summarises Gibson's use of the term usefully; "... certain emergent phenomena in the Net - sentient beings which are unwarrantable to human or machine agency — are in fact loas. This raises the question of whether the loas invaded the net, or originated there, or manifested as a consequence of distributed human expectation" (Stone 1995 188). Case extends this fictional use of the term in her proposal of the voudou vever as a 'talisman' for engaging with the space of new technologies.

7 Case's connection between the operations of the voudou vever and queer culture seems to me to be the weakest part of what is a compelling argument. It isn't clear to me how the operations of 'queer' are specifically configured in relation to a plural, fleshly dancing.

8 *The stunning composure of Hand Fall . . . the work of Jools Gilson-Ellis. . . For something so*

intimate to become so declamatory on stage takes the dancer into a new relationship with her body and her audience, and for this vision alone Solo Independents would have to be welcomed.
Mary Leland, Review of *Hand Fall*, solo choreography. *The Irish Times* 7th March 1998.

9 *halfangel*, a performance production company founded in 1995, based in Ireland and England, directed by Jools Gilson-Ellis and Richard Povall. www.halfangel.org.uk

10 This song was taught to me by a group of women in Totnes, Devon who were part of a choir called Global Harmony. These women told me that *Derry derry ding dason* originated in nineteenth century weaving mills tended by women. This round is sung in twelve parts and mimics the rhythms of loom and shuttle. My citation for this song, like my learning of it, is a heard thing; understood through the sharing of rhythms and stories. I place it here as example in content and transmission.

11 Penny quotes Nell Tenhaaf on this:
The philosophy of technology ... has been articulated from a masculinist perspective in terms that metaphorise and marginalise the feminine. In real social discourse, this claiming of technology has been reinforced by, and has probably encouraged, a male monopoly on technical expertise, diminishing or excluding the historical contributions of women to technological developments.

She goes on to assert that this invisibility of the feminine calls for 'a radical reconstitution of technology', but we must ask ourselves whether the architecture of the machine and the premises of software engineering themselves are not so encumbered with old philosophical ideas that any such 'reconstitution' would amount only to 'surface decoration'.
(Penny 1994 238 quoting Tenhaaf 1992)

12 Case does not mention Penny's essay in *The Domain Matrix* (which predates it) (Case 1996).

[13] See Mary Anne Moser's introduction to *Immersed in technology: art and virtual environments* (Moser 1996).

[14] Richard Povall — co-artistic director with myself of *halflangel*, our performance production company.

[15] This is the Banff Centre for the Arts, Department of Media & Visual Arts, who were co-producers of *The Secret Project*. We did a series of pre-production residencies at Banff during 1998 / 9 before our final production residency in August / September 1999. The work premiered at The Eric Harvey Theatre in early October 1999.

References

Birringer, J. (1998) *Media and performance: along the border*. John Hopkins University Press, Baltimore.

Case, S-E. (1996) *The Domain-Matrix: performing lesbian at the end of print culture*. Indiana University Press, Bloomington.

Conley, V. A. (1993) Eco subjects. In Conley, V. A. (ed. on behalf of the Miami Theory Collective) *Rethinking technologies*. University of Minnesota Press, Minneapolis, pp. 77–91.

Dery, M. (1993) Black to the future: interviews with Samuel R. Delaney, Greg Tate, and Tricia Rose. Flame wars: the discourse of cyberculture. *South Atlantic Quarterly* 92(4) 735–778.

Dyson, F. (1996) When is the ear pierced? The clashes of sound, technology, and cyberculture. In Moser, M. A. (ed.) *Immersed in technology: art and virtual environments*. MIT Press, Cambridge, pp. 73–101.

Gibson, W. (1984) *Neuromancer*. Ace Books, New York.

Gibson, W. (1986) *Count Zero*. Ace Books, New York.

Laurel, B. (1993) *Computers as theatre*. Addison-Wesley, Reading, Massachusetts.

Morse, M. (1994) What do cyborgs eat? Oral logic in an information society. In Bender, G. and Druckrey, T. (eds.) *Culture on the brink: ideologies of technology*. Bay Press, Seattle, pp.157–89.

Moser, M. A. (ed.) (1996) *Immersed in technology: art and virtual environments*. MIT Press, Cambridge.

Penny, S. (1994) Virtual reality as the completion of the Enlightenment project. In Bender, G. and Druckrey, T. (eds.) *Culture on the brink: ideologies of technology*. Bay Press, Seattle, pp. 231–48.

Plant, S. (1997) *Zeros and ones: digital women and the new technoculture*. Fourth Estate, London.

Randolph, J. (1996) A city for bachelors. In Moser, M. A. (ed.) *Immersed in technology: art and virtual environments*. MIT Press, Cambridge, pp.151–78.

Sayre, H. M. (1989) *The object of performance: the American avant-garde since 1970*. The University of Chicago Press, Chicago.

Stone, A. R. (1995) *The war of desire and technology at the close of the mechanical age*. MIT Press, Cambridge.

Tenhaaf, N.(1992) Technology and the feminine. *Parallelogram* 18(3).

Tenhaaf, N. (1996) Mysteries of the bioapparatus. In Moser, M. A. (ed.) *Immersed in technology: art and virtual environments*. MIT Press, Cambridge, pp. 51–71.

Wetzsteon, R. (1992) The cosmic dance. *Village Voice* 11 Feb 1992.

Jools Gilson-Ellis received her PhD in Theatre and Performance Studies from the University of Surrey in November 2000. This was a practice-based doctorate which explored the connections between voice, writing and performance in relation to new technologies. Jools is co-artistic director of the performance production company *halflangel* (along with Richard Povall). *halfl angel* makes work in a range of disciplines including CD-ROM, installation and performance. All their work involves voice, writing and new technologies. Jools Gilson-Ellis is a writer / choreographer and teaches performance practice, new technologies and theatre at University College Cork in Ireland. *The Secret Project* (dance theatre) has been performed in Canada, Ireland and The Netherlands, and will tour Argentina in 2001.

This article first appeared in *Digital Creativity* 12(2) 77–88 (2001).

Playing on a holo-stage: towards the interaction between real and virtual performers

Kia Ng[1], Vítor Sequeira[2], Emanuele Bovisio[2], Neil Johnson[1], David Cooper[1], João G.M. Gonçalves[2] and David Hogg[1]

[1] University of Leeds, UK

[2] European Commission - Joint Research Centre, Italy

Abstract

This paper presents a number of ongoing projects that will be valuable to the development of technologies for digital theatre and performance. This paper describes an EU ACTS project called RESOLV which develops an integrated system to capture real 3D environments using laser and video. Current research on motion tracking, statistical behaviour modelling and simulation is presented, and possible applications, both for visual augmentation and audio generation, are discussed. The projects presented were not originally designed in the domain of theatre and performance, however their results and output seem to be well suited to be applied in this area.

Keywords: behaviour modelling, computer music, model-based tracking, robotics, 3D model, virtual reality

1. Introduction

For many years the cinema has offered the possibility of creating illusory spaces and fantastic interactions between characters. Modern digital techniques have rendered such interactions almost seamless, though at the expense of considerable time, effort and computation. Over the last decade, developers such as Mark Reaney at the Department of Theatre and Film of the University of Kansas have shown how the advances offered by high performance computing can be employed in theatre and live performance (Reaney 1996). Such implementations involve the development of three-dimensional (3D) models of virtual environments which may be viewed using devices such as head-mounted displays or shutter glasses. This application of 3D modelling involves heavy manual design work, usually using some kind of 3D modelling software or editor.

Our research extends this work into the automatic reconstruction or capture, and subsequent manipulation, of any physical space, and the automatic sensing and tracking of the performance (the performers' positions, movements and physical and acoustic gestures) within the real space. While the former aspect of this work may be useful in the archival of existing spaces (and the fire in the La Fenice Opera

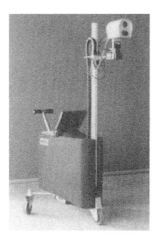 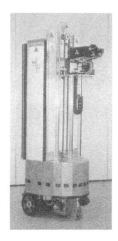

Figure 1. (left) shows the manual version of the prototype called the EST (Environmental Sensor for Telepresence), and (right) shows the autonomous version (AEST).

Figure 2. Several screen snapshots from a textured 3D model of a living room.

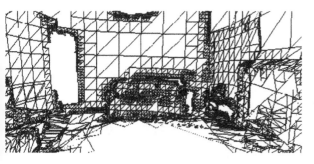

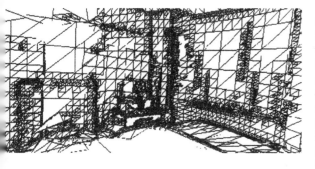

Figure 3. A wire-frame view of the textured model as shown in Figure 2.

Originally the project started with the intention of reconstructing only the interiors of buildings, however, with the advances of the laser technology, we can now capture both interiors and exteriors (for example, the Vienna State Opera House as shown in Figure 4), and we are working on a portable system that can be transported and set up more easily. More details of the hardware and software design of the EST can be found in Ng et al (1998), Sequeira et al (1999a) and Sequeira et al (1999b).

Figure 2 shows screen snapshots from a reconstructed model of a living room with textures and Figure 3 illustrates the underlying wire-frame of the model. The model is acquired in eight capture positions and is automatically reconstructed and triangulated. After that, colour texture images are used to texture-map the model, and finally output in VRML (Virtual Reality Modelling Language) file format which can be viewed over the Web. Details on the texture mapping process can be found in Ng et al (1998) and Sequeira et al (1999a).

Since the whole scene is represented by graphical primitives (i.e. triangles), the surfaces can be modified and edited with commercially available 3D modelling software. Operations such as transformation, translation, and many other functions are possible. Surfaces can be removed and new surfaces or objects can be added (for example, the carpet at the centre of the room was interactively added to enhance the visual appearance), or physically demanding scenarios can be created (for example the joining of two models that are geographically remote from each other as illustrated in Figure 5) so that the visitor can move from one space to the other.

Current research is focused on improving the visual quality of the model. From the example reconstruction, this technology is capable of capturing accurate and realistic 3D models of real environments. With the appropriate equipment and settings, it would be

House in Venice shows just how important it is to retain a record of the cultural heritage), the latter aspect, sensing and tracking of live performers, offers opportunities for an even greater degree of interactivity between them and the performance space. Some of the enabling technologies under development by the authors and their collaborators are considered below.

2. 3D reconstruction of real environments

The RESOLV project has developed an integrated system for the reconstruction of realistic 3D environments using video and laser sensors. Currently we have a prototype in a manual form and also a fully autonomous robot (see Figure 1), both carrying all software and hardware needed to perform the data acquisition (3D distances and video images) and all the processing to reconstruct real environments, such as the model of a living room as shown in Figure 2.

Figure 4. 3D model of the Vienna State Opera House.

possible to virtually teleport one environment (both interior and exterior) to another, for example, to perform (or to see a performance) in a virtual Vienna Opera House in a local theatre, or to perform *Aida* beside a virtual pyramid in a virtual Egypt! While such an application of the technology may seem prosaic, the opportunities exist for the creative development of novel environments from the combination or digital manipulation (for example, morphing) of existing spaces.

All 3D models presented in this paper are available online via the RESOLV web-site at http://www.scs.leeds.ac.uk/resolv/.

3. Tracking performers and modelling their behaviour

The automated observation of humans by a machine requires their accurate identification and tracking over long video sequences. Our tracker (Baumberg and Hogg 1994) uses a 'deformable contour' model, constructed from automatically acquired training data, to represent the variation in shape of the walking human. This system provides efficient real-time tracking of a number of people and copes with moderate levels of occlusion (where they are partly hidden by other people or objects), and

Figure 5. A combined model.

has been demonstrated on a variety of outdoor pedestrian scenes. The ability to handle such occlusions will be of particular interest for theatrical performance where the paths of actors cross each other.

The human visual system is capable of interpreting a remarkable variety of often subtle, learnt, characteristic behaviours. For instance we can determine the gender of a distant walking figure from their gait, interpret a facial expression, such as that of surprise, or identify suspicious behaviour in the movements of an individual within a car park. Our research (Johnson and Hogg 1996, Johnson 1998) aims to provide the computer with the ability to learn and use detailed statistical models of characteristic behaviours from the extended observation of humans. Experimental results from this research suggest a variety of possible applications, including: automated visual surveillance; object tracking; gesture recognition; and the automatic generation of realistic object behaviours within animations, virtual worlds and computer generated film sequences.

In addition, we have investigated the provision of more natural user-machine interaction, allowing the computer to acquire models of behaviour from the observation of interactions between humans, and using these acquired models, to equip a virtual human with the ability to interact in a natural way (Johnson et al 1998, Johnson 1998). Figure 6 shows a selection of frames from an experiment demonstrating the simulation of a plausible (if rather spectral) interactive partner using a learnt model of human handshaking.

In the future, it is possible to envisage the use of more detailed models of individuals and their behaviours, capable of much richer kinds of interaction — a kind of 'virtual immortality'?

4. Virtual reality and real virtuality

The research on tracking and behaviour modelling described in the previous section has been used to demonstrate the statistically accurate simulation of human behaviour within RESOLV models. In addition to the generation of a physical environment model, video footage of people moving within a site may be captured and used to automatically generate detailed statistical models of typical trajectories. Having acquired such models, realistic behaviours can be randomly generated and applied to VRML manikins for animation within VRML models. Figure 7 illustrates the principal stages in this process — tracking, behaviour modelling, and animation.

Although a simple VRML manikin has been used in these demonstrations, the technique could clearly be extended to control autonomous '3D virtual humans' for the simulation of actors and performers (see, for example, Volino and Magnenat-Thalmann 1999, Badler et al 1999). With the addition of interactive capabilities and the use of more detailed models, it is possible to envisage the user entering the virtual world and

...we can determine the gender of a distant walking figure from their gait, interpret a facial expression, such as that of surprise, or identify suspicious behaviour in the movements of an individual within a car park

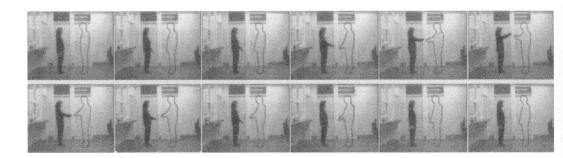

Figure 6.
Virtual
interaction
results.

interacting naturally with its occupants.

It is also possible for live performers and actors to perform inside a reconstructed 3D model. To demonstrate this concept, a trial has been set up to insert live video of actors into the reconstructed 3D environment (see Figure 8). The 3D model of the living room model as shown in Figure 2 was used to create the artificial stage. In reality, the living room model was captured in the UK and the virtual visitors sequence was performed in Italy. Figure 8 shows some frames illustrating the interaction of real actors with the environment (e.g. the woman sitting on a virtual sofa). Since the virtual stage is created by a 3D model, the position of the video camera that is capturing the live performance is tracked continuously and used to control the viewpoint of the final mixed output. The sequence was produced in near real time.

The actors performed against a blue background and set so that they could be segmented out using chroma-keying technique (see Figure 9). The video camera capturing the live sequence is fixed to a Faro arm which provides information about the 3D position and orientation of the camera, which in turn, controls the VRML viewpoints. There was some delay between the real performance and the reconstruction when the set-up was tested using a Silicon Graphics O2 workstation. However this delay is expected to decrease as the available computing power increases.

As our area of research is mainly in the fields of music and dance, we are particularly interested in the possibility of enhancing the performer's control of the sonic and visual environments. Trivial examples of manipulations which might be mapped to performer's gestures, positions or movement include: changing the model (for example from exterior to interior); modifying aspects of the model's appearance (e.g. hue, saturation and zoom); and movement of the models with respect to the performers (e.g. panning, tilting, rotating and zooming). This is analogous to our work in musical pitch tracking where live performers' gestures have been used to trigger musical events (Cooper and Ng 1996).

In reality, the living room model was captured in the UK and the virtual visitors sequence was performed in Italy

*Figure 7. Simulation of human behaviours
within RESOLV models.*

*Figure 8. Virtual actors in an omni-directional
virtual studio using a RESOLV model as shown
in Figure 2.*

*Figure 9. The same sequence as in Figure 8
with overlaid window showing the real
environment where the actors performed.*

5. Conclusion

We have described a number of current projects which we could contribute to the development of an interactive virtual-reality environment for performance art bringing together aspects of live and simulated performance. We hope to develop a hybrid approach using vision-based tracking enhanced by small and non-intrusive sensors to track the movement of the performers and create autonomous 3D avatars in response. We also intend to provide controlling or mapping functions to generate or 'conduct' music, and to integrate different sensors and tracking systems for both visual and audio sensing (Cooper and Ng 1996, Cooper and Ng 1998). As suggested by this article's title, our idealistic aim is to develop 3D computer models of artificial environments with virtual performers that can mimic, interact with and react to live performers. With a suitably equipped stage, such as a CAVE (Cruz-Neira 1993), the real and virtual performers can occupy the same time and space and perform live, together, in a digital theatre, a holo-stage.

Acknowledgement

The authors would like to thanks all partners of the RESOLV consortium for their support and co-operation, Dr. Johannes Riegl for providing the data captured with the latest RIEGL GmbH laser-range-finder (Riegl LMS GmbH 1998), for the outdoor experiments and his kind permission to allow us the use of the data in this paper, the two anonymous referees, and Prof. David Hogg for allowing us to advertise his living room.

References

Badler, N.I., Bindiganavale, R., Rourne, J., Allbeck, J., Shi, J., and Palmer, M. (1999) Real time virtual humans. *Proceedings of the 4th International Conference on Digital Media Futures*. National Museum of Photography, Film & Television, Bradford, UK, 13-15 April 1999.

Baumberg, A. and Hogg, D. (1994) An efficient method for contour tracking using active shape models. *Proceedings IEEE Workshop on Motion of Non-Rigid and Articulated Objects*. IEEE Computer Society Press, Texas, pp. 194–199.

Cooper, D. and Ng, K.C. (1996) A monophonic pitch-tracking algorithm based on waveform periodicity determinations using landmark points. *Computer Music Journal* 20(3) 70–78.

Cooper, D. and Ng, K.C. (1998) Studio report of the Leeds University Electronic Studio. *International Computer Music Conference (ICMC'98)*. University of Michigan, Ann Arbor, USA, pp. 304–307.

Cruz-Neira, C., Sandin, D.J. and DeFanti, T.A. (1993) Surround-screen projection-based virtual reality: the design and implementation of the CAVE. *Proceedings of ACM SIGGRAPH '93*. Anaheim, CA, pp. 135–142.

Johnson, N. (1998) *Learning object behaviour models*. PhD thesis, School of Computer Studies, The University of Leeds, UK.

Johnson, N., Galata, A. and Hogg, D. (1998) The acquisition and use of interaction behaviour models. *Proceedings IEEE Computer Society Conference on Computer Vision and Pattern Recognition*, IEEE Computer Society Press, Santa Barbara, CA, pp. 866–871.

Johnson, N. and Hogg, D. (1996) Learning the distribution of object trajectories for event recognition. *Image and Vision Computing* 14(8) 609–615.

Ng, K.C., Sequeira, V., Butterfield, S., Hogg, D.C. and Gonçalves, J.G.M. (1998) An integrated multi-sensory system for photo-realistic 3D scene reconstruction. *Proc. of ISPRS International Symposium on Real-Time Imaging and Dynamic Analysis*. Hakodate, Japan, pp. 356–363.

Reaney, M. (1996) Virtual scenography: the actor, audience, computer interface. *Theatre Design and Technology* 32(1) 36–43.

Riegl LMS GmbH (1998) 3D Imaging Sensor LMS-Z210 data sheet. Riegl Laser Measurement Systems GmbH, September 1998.

Sequeira, V., Ng, K.C., Wolfart, E., Gonçalves, J.G.M. and Hogg, D.C. (1999a) Automated reconstruction of 3D models from real environment. *ISPRS Journal of Photogrammetry and Remote Sensing* 54(1) 1–22.

Sequeira, V., Ng, K.C., Wolfart, E., Gonçalves, J.G.M. and Hogg, D.C. (1999b) Automated 3D reconstruction of interiors with multiple scan-views. *Proceedings of SPIE, Electronic Imaging '99.* IS&T/SPIE's 11th Annual Symposium, San Jose Convention Center, San Jose, California, USA, pp. 106–117.

Volino, P. and Magnenat-Thalmann, N. (1999) 3D fashion design and the virtual catwalk. *Proceedings of the 4th International Conference on Digital Media Futures.* National Museum of Photography, Film & Television, Bradford, UK, 13-15 April 1999.

Kia Ng is Director of the Interdisciplinary Centre for Scientific Research in Music (ICSRiM) of the University of Leeds. His research interests include computer vision, computer music and digital media. He is an Editorial Consultant of the Computer Music Journal, MIT Press, and Chairman of the Music Imaging Ltd., UK. Web: www.kcng.org

Vítor Sequeira is a Scientific Officer of the EU Joint Research Centre in Ispra, Italy. His research interests are 3D Reconstruction of Real Scenes 'as-built' including the design information verification and surveillance of safeguards relevant plants, Internet based control of remote devices, Mobile Information Systems, Augmented Reality and Tele/Virtual Presence applications.

Emanuele Bovisio is with the EU Joint Research Centre in Ispra, Italy. Current research focuses on identification and authentication of fuel elements for nuclear safeguards and non-proliferation.

Neil Johnson is Chief Software Scientist at InfraRed Integrated Systems Limited (IRISYS), U.K. His research interests lie within the fields of computer vision and pattern recognition, with particular interest in the learning and analysis of behaviour.

David Cooper is Head of the School of Music of the University of Leeds and Founding Director of ICSRiM. He has recently completed a book on Bernard Herrmann's score for the film *Vertigo* and a new edition of George Petrie's *The Petrie collection of the ancient music of Ireland.*

João G.M. Gonçalves is with the Joint Research Centre of the European Union in Ispra, Italy. His main research interests are 3D reconstruction, augmented reality and tele-presence. His current research objective is to develop remote verification instrumentation in the field of nuclear safeguards and non-proliferation.

David Hogg has been Professor of Artificial Intelligence at the University of Leeds since 1990 and Pro-Vice-Chancellor since 2000. His research is in computer vision with special interest in learning and the analysis of behaviour..

This article first appeared in
Digital Creativity 11(2) 109–117 (2000).

Printed and bound by CPI Group (UK) Ltd, Croydon, CR0 4YY

23/10/2024

01777679-0003